TRAVELLERS' TALES
FROM 'BLACKWOOD'

TRAVELLERS' TALES

from

' BLACKWOOD '

WILLIAM BLACKWOOD

EDINBURGH AND LONDON

1969

WILLIAM BLACKWOOD & SONS LTD
45 GEORGE STREET
EDINBURGH EH2 2JA

PRINTED AT THE PRESS OF THE PUBLISHER
WILLIAM BLACKWOOD & SONS LTD, EDINBURGH

SBN 85158 096 3

CONTENTS

Continued overleaf

These stories first appeared in *Blackwood's Magazine*
on the dates indicated

1

ZANZIBAR

Sir Richard Burton

In 1856, Sir Richard Burton formed an expedition
to cross equatorial Africa. Accompanied by John
Speke, who discovered Lake Victoria (his story is
told in ' Discovery of the Victoria Nyanza '), his
aim was to investigate the true source of the Nile.
The following extract is taken from his journal
' Zanzibar; and two months in East Africa ',
which appeared serially in *Blackwood's Magazine*
in 1858.

African travel in the heroic ages of Bruce, Mungo Park,
and Clapperton, had a prestige which lived through two
generations; and, as is the fate of things sublunary, came to
an untimely end. The public, satiated with adventure and
invention, suffers in these days of ' damnable license of
printing ' from the humours of severe surfeit. It nauseates
the monotonous recital of rapine, treachery, and murder;
of ugly savages—the *mala gens*, as was said anent Kentish
men, of a *bona terra*—of bleared misery by day, and animated filth by night, and of hunting adventures and
hairbreadth escapes, lacking the interest of catastrophe.
It laments the absence of tradition and monuments of the
olden time, the dearth of variety, of beauty, of romance.
Yet the theme still continues to fulfil all the conditions of
attractiveness set forth by Leigh Hunt. It has remoteness

and obscurity of place, difference of custom, marvellousness of hearsay. Events surpassing, yet credible; sometimes barbaric splendour—at least luxuriance of nature; savage contentment, personal danger and suffering, with a moral enthusiasm. And to the writer, no hours are more fraught with smiling recollections—nothing can be more charming than the contrast between his vantage-ground at present ease and that past perspective of wants, hardships, and accidents, upon which he gazes through the softening medium of time.

We arose early in the morning after arrival at Pangany, and repaired to the terrace for the better enjoyment of the view. The vista of the river—with low coco-groves to the north, tall yellow cliffs on the southern side, a distance of blue hill, the broad stream bounded by walls of verdure, and the azure sea, dotted with diobolites, or little black rocks—wanted nothing but the finish and polish of art to bring out the infinitude and rude magnificence of nature. A few donjon-ruins upon the hills would enable it to compare with the most admired prospects of the Rhine, and with half a dozen white kiosks, minarets, and latticed summer-houses, it would almost rival that gem of creation, the Bosporus.

Pangany 'in the hole', and its smaller neighbour Kumba, hug the left bank of the river, upon a strip of shore bounded by the sea, and a hill-range ten or eleven miles distant. Opposite are Bueny and Mzimo Pia, villages built under yellow sandstone bluffs, impenetrably covered with wild trees. The river, which separates these rival couples, may be two hundred yards broad. The mouth has a bar and a wash at low tide, except at the south, where there is a narrow channel, now seven or eight—in Captain Owen's time, twelve—feet deep. The entrance

2

for vessels—they lie snugly opposite the town—is difficult and dangerous : even Hamid, most niggardly of niggard Suris, expended a dollar upon a pilot. At low water the bed of this tidal stream shrinks. During the rains, swelling with hill-freshes, it is almost potable; and when the sea flows, it is briny as the main. The wells produce heavy and brackish drink; but who, as the people say, will take the trouble to fetch sweeter? The climate is said to be healthy in the dry season, but the long and severe rains are rich in fatal bilious remittents.

Pangany boasts of nineteen or twenty stone houses. The remainder is a mass of cadjan huts, each with its wide mat-encircled yard, wherein all the business of life is transacted. The settlement is surrounded by a thorny jungle, which at times harbours a host of leopards. One of these beasts lately scaled the high terrace of our house, and seized upon a slave-girl. Her master, the burly backwali, who was sleeping by her side, gallantly caught up his sword, ran into the house, and bolted the door, heedless of the miserable cry, " Bwana, help me ! " The wretch was carried to the jungle and devoured. The river is equally full of alligators, and whilst we were at Pangany a boy disappeared. When asked by strangers why they do not shoot their alligators, and burn their wood, the people reply that the former bring good luck, and the latter is a fort to which they can fly in need. Cocos, arecas, and plantains grow about the town. Around are gardens of papaws, betel, and jamlis; and somewhat farther, lie extensive plantations of holcus and maize, of sesamum, and other grains. The clove flourishes; and, as elsewhere upon the coast, a little cotton is cultivated for domestic use. Beasts are rare. Cows die after eating the grass; goats give no milk; and sheep are hardly procurable. But fish abounds. Poultry thrives, as it does all over Africa; and before the late feuds, clarified cow-butter, that ' one sauce ' of the outer East, was cheap and well-flavoured.

Pangany, with the three other villages, may contain a total of four thousand inhabitants—Arabs, Moslem Swahili, and heathens. Of these, female slaves form a large proportion. Twenty Banyans manage the lucrative ivory trade of the Nguru, Masai, and Chhaga countries. These merchants complain loudly of their *pagazi*, or porters, who receive ten dollars for the journey, half paid down, the remainder upon return; and the proprietor congratulates himself if, after payment, only fifteen per cent run away. The Hindus' profits, however, must be enormous. I saw one man to whom twenty-six thousand dollars were owed by the people. What part must interest and compound-interest have played in making up such sum, where even Europeans demand forty per cent for monies lent on safe mortgage and bottomry! Their only drawback is the inveterate beggary of the people. Here the very princes are mendicants; and the Banyan dare not refuse the seventy or eighty savages who every evening besiege his door with cries for grain, butter, or a little oil. Besides Zanzibar rafters, which are cut in the river, holcus, maize, and ghee, Pangany, I am told, exports annually 35,000 lb. of ivory, 1,750 lb. of black rhinoceros' horn, and sixteen of hippopotamus' teeth.

After the dancing ceremony arose a variety of difficulties, resulting from the African travellers' twin banes, the dollar and the blood-feud. Pangany and Bueny, like all settlements upon this coast, belong, by a right of succession, to the Sazzid, or Prince-Regnant of Zanzibar, who confirms and invests the governors and diwans. At Pangany, however, these officials are *par congé d'élire* selected by

Kimwere, Sultan of Usembara, whose ancestors received tribute and allegiance from Para to the seaboard. On the other hand, Bueny is in the territory of the Wazegura, a violent and turbulent heathen race, inveterate slave-dealers, and thoughtlessly allowed by the Arabs to lay up goodly stores of muskets, powder, and ball. Of course the two tribes, Wasumbara and Wazegura, are deadly foes. Moreover, about a year ago, a violent intestine feud broke out amongst the Wazegura, who, at the time of our visit, were burning and murdering, kidnapping and slave-selling in all directions. The citizens of Pangany, therefore, hearing that we were bearers of a letter from the Sazzid of Zanzibar to Sultan Kimwere, marked out for us the circuitous route via Tangate, where no Wazegura could try their valour. We, on the other hand, wishing to inspect the Pangany River, determined upon proceeding by the directest line along its left or northern bank. The timid townsmen had also circulated a report that we were bound for Chhaga and Kilimanjaro; the Masai were ' out ', the rains were setting in, and they saw with us no armed escort. They resolved, therefore, not to accompany us; but not the less did each man expect as usual his gift of dollars and bribe of inducement.

The expense of the journey was even a more serious consideration. In these lands the dollar is almighty. If deficient, you must travel alone, unaccompanied at least by any but blacks without other instrument but a notebook, and with few arms; you must conform to every nauseous custom; you will be subjected, at the most interesting points, to perpetual stoppages; your remarks will be well-nigh worthless; and you may make up your mind that, unless one in a million, want and hardship will conduct you to sickness and death. This is one extreme, and from it to the other there is no golden mean. With abundance of money—certainly not less than £5,000 per annum—an exploring party can trace its own line, paying off all opposers; it can study whatever is requisite; handle sextants in presence of Negroes, who would cut every throat for one inch of brass; and by travelling in comfort, can secure a fair chance of return. Either from Mombasa or from Pangany, with an escort of one hundred matchlockmen, we might have marched through the Masai plunderers to Chhaga and Kilimanjaro. But pay, porterage, and provisions for such a party would have amounted to at least £100 per week : a month and a half would have absorbed our means. Thus it was, gentle reader, that we were compelled to rest contented with a visit to Fuga.

Presently the plot thickened. Muigni Khatib, son of Sultan Kimwere, a black of most unprepossessing physiognomy, with a ' villainous trick of the eye, and a foolish hanging of the nether lip ', a prognathous jaw, garnished with cat-like moustaches and cobweb beard, a sour frown, and abundant surliness by way of dignity, dressed like an Arab, and raised by El Islam above his fellows, sent a message directing us to place in his hands what we intended for his father. This chief was travelling to Zanzibar in fear and trembling. He had tried to establish at his village, Kirore, a Romulian asylum for runaway slaves, and, having partially succeeded, he dreaded the consequences. The Beloch jemadar strongly urged us privily to cause his detention at the islands; a precaution somewhat too oriental for our tastes. We refused, however, the Muigni's demand in his own tone. Following their prince, the dancing diwans claimed a fee for permission to reside; as they worded it, *el adah*—the habit; based it upon an ancient present from Colonel Hamerton; and were in manifest process of establishing a local custom which, in Africa, becomes law to remotest posterity. We flatly objected, showed our letters, and, in the angriest of moods, threatened reference to Zanzibar. Briefly all began to beg baksheesh; but I cannot remember anyone obtaining it.

Weary of these importunities, we resolved to visit Chogway, a Beloch outpost, and thence, aided by the jemadar who had preceded us from Pangany, to push for the capital-village of Usumbara. We made preparations secretly, dismissed the ' Riami ', rejected the diwans who wished to accompany us as spies, left Said bin Salim and one Portuguese to watch our property in the house of Meriko, the governor, who had accompanied his Muigni to Zanzibar, and, under pretext of a short shooting excursion, hired a long canoe with four men, loaded it with the luggage required for a fortnight, and started with the tide at eleven a.m. on the 6th of January 1857.

First we grounded; then we were taken back; then a puff of wind drove us forward with railway speed; then we grounded again. At last we were successful in turning the first dangerous angle of the river. Here, when seabreeze and tide meet the ' buffing stream '—as usual at the mouths of African rivers the wind is high and fair from the interior—navigation is perilous to small craft. Many have filled and sunk beneath the ridge of short chopping waves. After five miles, during which the stream, streaked with lines of froth, gradually narrowed, we found it barely brackish; and somewhat farther, sweet as the celebrated creek-water of Guiana.

And now, while writing amid the soughing blasts, the rain and the darkened air of a south-west monsoon, I remember with yearning the bright and beautiful spectacle of those African rivers, whose loveliness, like that of the dead, seems enhanced by proximity to decay. We had changed the amene and graceful sandstone scenery, on the seaboard, for a view novel and most characteristic. The hippopotamus now raised his head from the waters, snorted, gazed upon us, and sank into his native depths. Alligators, terrified by the splash of oars, waddled down with their horrid claws, dinting the slimy bank, and lay like yellow logs, measuring us with small, malignant, green eyes, deep set under warty brows. Monkeys rustled the tall trees. Below, jungle-men and women—

> ' So withered, and so wild in their attire,
> That look not like th' inhabitants o' the earth,
> And yet are on't '—

planted their shoulder-cloths, their rude crates, and coarse weirs, upon the mud inlets where fish abounded. The sky was sparkling blue, the water bluer, and over both spread the thinnest haze, tempering raw tones of colour to absolute beauty. On both sides of the shrinking stream a dense curtain of many-tinted vegetation, shadowed swirling pools, where the current swept upon the growth of intertwisted fibres. The Nakhl el Shaytan, or Devil's Date, eccentric in foliage and frondage, projected gracefully curved arms, sometimes thirty and forty feet long, over the wave. This dwarf-giant of palms has no trunk, but the mid-rib of each branch is thick as a man's thigh. Upon the watery margin large lilies of snowy brightness, some sealed by day, others, wide expanded, gleamed beautifully against the dark verdure and the russet-brown of the bank-stream. In scattered spots were interwoven traces of human presence; tall arecas and cocos waving over a now

8

impenetrable jungle; plantains, sugar-cane and bitter oranges, choked with wild growth, still lingered about the homestead, blackened by the murderer's fire. And all around reigned the eternal African silence, deep and saddening, broken only by the curlew's scream, or by the breeze rustling the tree-tops, whispering among the matted foliage, and swooning upon the tepid bosom of the wave.

Amid such scenes we rowed and poled till the setting sun spread its cloak of purple over a low white cliff, at whose base the wave breaks, and on whose hoary head linger venerable trees, contrasting with the underwood of the other bank. Here lies the Pir of Wasin, a saint described by our Beloch guide as a " very angry holy man ". A Sherif of pure blood, he gallantly headed, in centuries gone by, his Moslem followers, flying from Pangany when it was attacked by a ravenous pack of Infidels. The latter seem to have had the advantage in running. They caught the Faithful at these cliffs, and were proceeding to exterminate them, when Mother Earth, at the Sherif's prayer, opening wide, received them in her bosom. This Pir will not allow the trees to be cut down, or the inundation to rise above his tomb. Moreover, if the devotee, after cooking food at the grave in honour of its tenant, ventures to lick fingers— napkins are not used in East Africa—he is at once delivered over to haunting jinns. The Belochies never pass the place without casting a handful of leaves, a bullet, or a few grains of powder, into the stream. The guide once told, in a voice of awe, how a Suri Arab, doubtless tainted with Wallali heresy, had expressed an opinion that this Pir had been a mere mortal, but little better than himself; how the scoffer's ship was wrecked within the year; and how he passed through water into jehannumfire. *Probatum est.* Defend us, Allah, from the Sins of Reason!

The tide, running like a mill-race, compelled our crew to turn into a little inlet near Pombui, a stockaded village on the river's left bank. The people, who are subject to Zanzibar, flocked out to welcome their strangers, laid down a bridge of coco-ribs, brought chairs, and offered a dish of small green mangos, here a great luxury. We sat under a tree till midnight, unsatiated with the charm of the hour. The moon rained molten silver over the dark foliage of the wild palms, the stars were as golden lamps suspended in the limpid air, and Venus glittered diamond-like upon the front of the firmament. The fire-flies now sparkled simultaneously over the earth; then, as if by concerted impulse, their glow vanished in the glooms of the ground. At our feet lay the black creek; in the jungle beasts roared fitfully; and the night wind mingled melancholy sounds with the swelling murmuring of the stream.

The tide flowing about midnight, we resumed our way. The river then became a sable streak between lofty rows of trees. The hippopotamus snorted close to our stern, and the crew begged me to fire, for the purpose of frightening Sultan Momba—a pernicious rogue. At times we heard the splashing of the beasts as they scrambled over the shoals; at others, they struggled with loud grunts up the miry banks. Then again all was quiet. After a protracted interval of silence, the near voice of a man startled us in the deep drear stillness of night, as though it had been some ghostly sound. At two a.m., reaching a clear tract on the river-side—the Ghaut or landing-place of Chogway—we made fast the canoe, looked to our weapons, and, covering our faces against the heavy clammy dew, lay down to snatch an hour's sleep. The total distance rowed was about thirteen and a half miles.

We began the next morning with an inspection of Chogway, the Bazar, to which we were escorted by the jemadar with sundry discharges of matchlocks. It was first occupied about five years ago, when Sultan Kimwere offered Tongway or Meringa—a lofty peak in the continuous range to the north-west—with cheap generosity, as a mission-station to Dr Krapf. The position is badly chosen, water is distant, the rugged soil produces nothing but vetches and manive, and it is exposed to miasma when the inundation subsides upon the black alluvial plain below the hillock. Commanding, however, the Southern Usumbara road, it affords opportunity for something in the looting line. The garrison ever suffers from sickness; and the men, dull as a whaler's crew, abhor the melancholy desolate situation. The frequent creeks around are crossed by tree-bridges. The walk to Pangany, over a rugged road, occupies from five to six hours, yet few but the slaves avail themselves of the proximity. A stout snake-fence surrounds the hill-top, crested by the cadjan penthouses of these Bashi Buzuks: its fortifications are two platforms for matchlockmen planted on high poles, like the Indian ' Maychan '. The Washenzy savages sometimes creep up at night to the huts, shoot a few arrows, set fire to the matting, and hurriedly levant. When we visited Chogway, the Wazegura were fighting with one another, but they did not molest the Belochies. South of the river rises a detached hill, ' Tongway Muanapiro ', called in our charts ' Gendagenda ', which may be seen from Zanzibar. Here rules one Mwere, a chief hostile to the Bashi Buzuks, who, not caring to soil their hands with Negro blood, make their slaves fight his men, even as the ingenuous youth of Eton sent their scouts to contend at

11

cricket with the ambitious youth of Rugby. Fifty stout fellows, with an ambitious leader and a little money, might soon conquer the whole country, and establish there an absolute monarchy.

These Beloch mercenaries merit some notice. They were preferred, as being somewhat disciplinable, by the late Sazzid Said, to his futile blacks and his unruly and self-willed Oman Arabs. He entertained from one thousand to one thousand five hundred men, and scattered them over the country in charge of the forts. The others hate them—divisions even amongst his own children was the ruler's policy—and nickname them 'Kurara Kurara'. The jemadar and the governor are rarely on speaking terms. Calling themselves Belochies, they are mostly from the regions about Kech and Bampur. They are mixed up with a rabble-rout of Affghans and Arabs, Indians and Sudies, and they speak half-a-dozen different languages. Many of these gentry have left their country for their country's weal. A body of convicts, however, fights well. The Mekrani are first-rate behind walls; and if paid, drilled, and officered, they would make as 'varmint' light-bobs as Arnauts. They have a knightly fondness for arms. A 'young barrel and an old blade' are their delight. All use the matchlock, and many are skilful with sword and shield. Their pay is from two to three dollars a month, out of which they find food and clothes. They never see money from the year's one end to the other, and are as ragged a crew as ever left the barren hills of the north to seek fortune in Africa. They live in tattered hovels, with one meal of grain a day for themselves and slave-girls. To the greediness of mountaineers, the poor devils add the insatiable desires of beggars. The Banyans have a proverb that ' a Beloch, a Brahmin, and a buck-goat eat the trees to which they are tied '. Like schoolboys, they think nought so fine as the noise of a gun, consequently ammunition is served out to them by the jemadar only before a fight. Sudden and sharp in quarrel, they draw their daggers upon the least provocation, have no ' mitigation or remorse of voice ', and pray in the proportion of one to a dozen. All look forward to ' *Hindustan, bagh o bustan* '—India, the garden; but the Arabs have a canny proverb importing that ' the fool who falleth into the fire rarely falleth out of it '.

' *Fraudare stipendio,*' saith ancient Justin, was the practice of the great king's satraps: the modern East has strictly preserved the custom. Each station is commanded by a jemadar upon four or five dollars a month, and full licence to peculate. The class is at once under-paid and over-trusted. The jemadar advances money upon usury to his men, and keeps them six months in arrears; he exacts perquisites from all who fear his hate and need his aid; and he falsifies the muster-rolls most impudently, giving twenty-five names to perhaps four men. Thus the jemadar supports a wife and a dozen slaves; sports a fine scarlet coat, a grand dagger, and a silver-hilted sword; keeps flocks of sheep and goats, and trades with the interior for ivory and captives, whilst his company has not a sandal amongst them. Such has been, is, and ever will be the result of that false economy which, in the East, from Stamboul to Japan, grudges the penny and flings away the pound.

Having communicated our project to the jemadar of Chogway, he promised, for a consideration, all aid; told us that we should start the next day; and, curious to relate, kept his word. The little settlement, however, affording but five matchlockmen as a guard, and four slave-boys as porters, the C.O. engaged for us a guide and his attendant

13

—nominally paying ten dollars, and doubtless retaining one-half.

After a night spent in the Magchan, where wind, dust, and ants conspired to make us miserable, we arose early to prepare for marching. About midday, issuing from our shed, we placed the kit—now reduced to a somewhat *stricte necessaire*—in the sun; thus mutely appealing to the 'sharm' or shame of our Beloch comrades. A start was effected at five p.m., every slave complaining of his load, snatching up the lightest, and hurrying on regardless of what was left behind. This nuisance endured till summarily stopped by an outward application easily divined. At length, escorted in token of honour by the consumptive jemadar and most of his company, we departed in a straggling Indian file towards Tongway.

The path wound over stony ridges. After an hour it plunged into a dense and thorny thicket, which, during the rains, must be impassable. The evening belling of deer, and the 'clock-clock' of partridge, struck our ears. In the open places were the *lesses* of elephants, and footprints retained by the last year's mud. These animals descend to the plains during the monsoon, and in summer retire to the cool hills. The Belochies shoot, the wild people kill them with poisoned arrows. More than once during our wanderings, we found the grave-like trap-pits, called in India 'ogi'. These are artfully dug in little rises, to fit exactly the elephant, who easily extricates himself from one too large or too small. We did not meet a single specimen; but, judging from the prints—three to three and a half circumferences showing the shoulder height—they are not remarkable for size. The farther interior, however, exports the finest, whitest, largest, heaviest, and softest ivory in the world. Tusks weighing 100 lb. each are common, those of 175 lb. are not rare, and I have heard of a pair whose joint weight was 560 lb. It was a severe disappointment to us that we could not revisit this country during the rains. Colonel Hamerton strongly dissuaded us from again risking jungle-fever, and we had a duty to perform in Inner Africa. Sporting, indeed, is a labour which occupies the whole man: to shoot for specimens, between work, is to waste time in two ways. Game was rare throughout our march. None lives where the land is peopled. In the deserts it is persecuted by the Belochies; and the wild Jägers slay and eat even rats. We heard, however, of mabogo or buffalo antelope, and a hog— probably the masked boar—lions, leopards in plenty; the nilghae, and an elk, resembling the Indian sambar.

Another hour's marching brought us to the Makam Sazzid Sulayman, a half-cleared ring in the bush, bounded on one side by a rocky and tree-fringed ravine, where water stagnates in pools during the dry season. The pedometer showed six miles. Then we passed the night in a small babel of Belochies. One recited his Koran; another prayed; a third told funny stories; whilst a fourth trolled lays of love and war, long ago made familiar to my ear upon the rugged Asian hills. This was varied by slapping lank mosquitoes that flocked to the camp-fires; by rising to get rid of huge black pismires, whose bite burned like a red-hot needle; and by challenging two parties of savages, who, armed with bows and arrows, passed amongst us, carrying maize to Pangany. The Belochies kept a truly Oriental watch. They sang and shouted during early night, when there is no danger; but they all slept like the dead through the ' small hours ', the time always chosen by the African freebooter to make his cowardly onslaught.

At daybreak on the 9th of February, accompanied by a small detachment, we resumed our march. The *poitrinaire* jemadar, who was crippled by the moonlight and the cold dew, resolved to return, when thawed, with the rest of his company to Chogway. An hour's hard walking brought us to the foot of rugged Tongway, the 'great hill'. Ascending the flank of the north-eastern spur, we found ourselves, at eight a.m., after five bad miles, upon the chine of a lower ridge—with summer towards the sea—and landward, a wind of winter. Thence pursuing the rugged incline, in another half-hour we entered the Fort, a small, square, crenellated, flat-roofed, and white-washed room, tenanted by two Belochies, who appeared in the muster-rolls as twenty men. They complained of loneliness and the horrors. Though several goats had been sacrificed, a fearsome demon still haunted the hill, and the weeping and wailing of distressed spirits made their thin blood run chill.

Tongway is the first off-set of the mountain-terrace composing the land of Usumbara. It rises abruptly from the plain; lies north-west of, and nine miles, as the crow flies, distant from Chogway. The summit, about two-thousand feet above the sea-level, is clothed with jungle, through which, seeking compass sights, we cut a way with our swords. The deserted ground showed signs of former culture, and our Negro guide sighed as he said that his kinsmen had been driven from their ancient seats into the far inner wastes. Tongway projects long spurs into the plain, where the Pangany river flows noisily through a rocky trough. The mountain surface is a reddish agrillaceous and vegetable soil, overlying grey and ruddy granites and schist. These stones bear the 'gold and silver complexion' which was fatal to the chivalrous

Shepherd of the Ocean, and the glistening mica still feeds the fancy of the Beloch mercenary. The thickness of the jungle—which contains stunted cocos and bitter oranges, the castor, the wild egg-plant, and bird-pepper— renders the mountain inaccessible from any but the eastern and northern flanks. Around the Fort are slender plantations of maize and manive. Below, a deep hole supplies the sweetest rock-water; and upon the plain a boulder of well-weathered granite, striped with snowy quartz, and about twenty feet high, contains two crevices ever filled by the purest springs. The climate appeared delicious— temperate in the full blaze of an African and tropical summer; and whilst the hill was green, the land around was baked like bread crust.

We had work to do before leaving Tongway. The jemadar ordered an escort for us; but amongst these people, obedience to orders is somewhat optional. Moreover, the Belochies, enervated by climate and want of exercise, looked forward to a mountain march with displeasure. Shoeless, bedless, and wellnigh clotheless, even the hope of dollars could scarcely induce them to leave for a week their lazy huts, their piccaninnies, and their black Venuses. They felt happy at Tongway, twice a day devouring our rice—an unknown luxury; and they were at infinite pains to defer the evil hour. One man declared it impossible to travel without salt, and proposed sending back a slave to Chogway. This involved the loss of at least three days, and was at once rejected.

By hard talking we managed to secure a small party, which demands a few words of introduction to the reader. We have four slave-boys, idle, worthless dogs, who never work save under the rod, think solely of their stomachs, and are addicted to running away. Petty pilferers to the

17

backbone, they steal, like magpies, by instinct. On the march they lag behind, and, not being professional porters, they are restive as camels when receiving their load. One of these youths, happening to be brother-in-law—after a fashion—to the jemadar, requires incessant supervision to prevent him burdening the others with his own share. The guide, Muigni Wazira, is a huge broad-shouldered Swahili, with a coal-black skin: his high, massive, and regular features look as if carved in ebony, and he frowns like a demon in the *Arabian Nights*. He is purblind, a defect which does not, however, prevent his leading us into every village, that we may be mulcted in sprig-muslin. Wazira is our rogue, rich in all the peculiarities of African cunning. A prayerless Sherif, he thoroughly despises the *Makapry* or Infidels; he has a hot temper, and, when provoked, roars like a wild beast. He began by refusing his load, but yielded when it was gently placed upon his heavy shoulder, with a significant gesture in case of recusance. He does not, however, neglect occasionally to pass it to his slave, who, poor wretch, is almost broken down by the double burden.

Rahewat, the Mekrani, calls himself a Beloch, and wears the title of Shah-Sawar, or the Rider-king. He is the ' Chelebi ', the dandy and tiger of our party. A ' good-looking brown man ', about twenty-five years old, with a certain girlishness and affectation of *tournure* and manner, which bode no good, the Rider-king deals in the externals of respectability; he washes and prays with pompous regularity, combs his long hair and beard, trains his busy moustaches to touch his eyes, and binds a huge turban. He affects the jemadar. He would have taken charge, had we permitted, of the general store of gunpowder—a small leather bottle wrung from the commandant of Chogway; and having somewhat high ideas of discipline, he began with stabbing a slave-boy by way of lesson. He talks loud in his native Mekrani and base Persian; moreover, his opinion is ever to the fore. The Rider-king, pleading soldier, positively refuses to carry anything but his matchlock, and a private stock of dates which he keeps ungenerously to himself. He boasts of prowess in vert and venison: we never saw him hit the mark, but we missed some powder and ball, with which he may be more fortunate.

Hamdan, a Maskat Arab, has 'seen better days'. Melancholia and strong waters have removed all traces of them, except a tincture of letters. Our Mullah, or learned man, is small, thin, brown, long-nosed, and green-eyed, with little spirit and less muscularity. A crafty old traveller, he has a store of comforts for the way; he carries, with his childish matchlock, a drinking-gourd and a ghee-pot, and he sits apart from the crowd for more reasons than one. Strongly contrasting with him is the ancient Mekrani, Shaaban, a hideous decrepit giant, with the Negroid type of countenance. He is of the pig-headed, opposed to the soft-headed, order of old man; hard and opinionated, selfish and unmanageable. He smokes, and must drink water all day. He dispenses the wisdom of a Dogberry, much to his hearers' disgust, and he coughs through the hours of night. This senior will carry nothing but his gun, pipe, and gourd, and, despite his grey beard, he is the drone of the party.

Jemal and Murad Ali are our working-men, excellent specimens of the true Beloch—*vieux grognards*—with a grim, sour humour, especially when the fair sex is concerned. They have black frowning faces, wrinkled and rugged as their natal hills, with pads of muscle upon their short forearms, and high, sinewy, angular calves, remarkable in this land of 'sheep-shanks'. Sparing of words, when addressed, they merely grunt; but when they speak, it is in a scream. They are angry men, and uncommonly handy with their greasy daggers. With the promise of an extra dollar, they walk off under heavy loads, besides their guns and necessaries.

The gem of the party is Sudy Mubarak, who has taken to himself the cognomen of 'Bombay'. His sooty skin, and teeth pointed like those of the reptilia, denote his Mhiav origin. He is one of those real Sudies that delight the passengers in Indian steamers. Bombay, sold in early youth, carried to Cutch by some Banyan, and there emancipated, looks fondly back upon the home of his adoption, and sighs for the day when a few dollars will enable him to return. He has ineffable contempt for all 'jungly niggers'. His head is a triumph to phrenology; a high narrow cranium, flat-fronted, denoting, by arched and rounded crown, full development of the moral region, with deficiency of the perceptives and reflectives. He works on principle, and works like a horse, openly declaring, that not love of us, but attachment to his stomach, makes him industrious. With a sprained ankle, and a load quite disproportioned to his *chétif* body, he insists upon carrying two guns. He attends us everywhere, manages our purchases, is trusted with all messages, and, when otherwise disengaged, is at every man's beck and call. He had enlisted under the jemadar of Chogway. We thought, however, so highly of his qualifications, that persuasion and paying his debts induced him, after a little coquetting, to take leave of soldiering and follow our fortunes. Sudy Bombay will be our head gun-carrier, if he survives his present fever, and, I doubt not, will prove himself a rascal in the end.

A machine so formed could hardly be expected to move without some creaking. The Belochies were not entirely under us, and in the East no man will serve two masters. For the first few days, many a loud wrangling and muttered cursing showed signs of a dissolution. One would not proceed because the Rider-king monopolised the powder; another started on his way home because he was refused some dates; and during the first night all Bombay's efforts were required to prevent a *sauve qui peut*. But by degrees the component parts fitted smoothly and worked steadily: at last we had little to complain of, and the men volunteered to follow wherever we might lead.

[March 1858

2

DISCOVERY OF THE VICTORIA NYANZA

J. H. Speke

This day's march, 1st August, 1858, commenced at six a.m., differs but little from the last. Following down the creek which, gradually increasing in breadth as it extended northwards, was here of very considerable dimensions, we saw many little islands, well-wooded elevations, standing boldly out of its waters, which, together with the hill-dotted country around, afforded a most agreeable prospect. Would that my eyes had been strong enough to dwell, unshaded, upon such scenery! But my French grey spectacles so excited the crowds of sable gentry who followed the caravan, and they were so boisterously rude, stooping and peering underneath my wide-awake to gain a better sight of my double eyes, as they chose to term them, that it became impossible for me to wear them. I therefore pocketed the instrument, closed my eyes, and allowed the donkey I was riding to be quietly pulled along. The evil effects of granting an indulgence to those who cannot appreciate it was more obvious every day. To secure speed and contentment, I had indulged the Pagazis by hiring double numbers, and giving each only half a recognised burden; but what has been the return?

Yesterday the Pagazis stopped at the eighth mile, because they said that so large a jungle was in our front that we could not cross it during daylight. I disbelieved their story, and gave them to understand, on submitting to their request, that I was sure their trick for stopping me would turn to their own disadvantage; for if my surmise proved true, as the morrow would show, I should give them no more indulgence, and especially no more meat.

On our arrival today there was a great hubbub amongst them, because I ordered the jemadar and kirangozi, with many of their principal men, to sit in state before me; when I gave a cloth to the soldiers to buy a goat with, and, turning to the kirangozi, told him I was sorry I was obliged to keep my word of yesterday, and, their story having proved false, I must depart from the principle I had commenced upon, of feeding both parties alike, and now they might feel assured that I would do nothing further for their comfort until I could see in them some desire to please me. The screw was on the tenderest part: a black man's belly is his god; and they no sooner found themselves deprived of their wonted feast, than they clamorously declared they would be my devoted servants; that they had come expressly to serve me, and were willing to do anything I wished. The village chief offered me a goat; but as it came at the last moment before starting, I declined it.

Today's track lay for the first half of the way over a jungly depression, where we saw ostriches, flonikans, and the small Saltiana antelopes; but as their shyness did not allow of an open approach, I amused myself by shooting partridges. During the remainder of the way, the caravan threaded between villages and cultivation lying in small valleys, or crossed over low hills, accomplishing a total distance of twelve miles. Here we put up at a village called Ukumbi, occupied by the Walaswanda tribe.

We set out at six a.m., and travelled thirteen miles by a tortuous route, sometimes close by the creek, at other times winding between small hills, the valleys of which were thickly inhabited by both agricultural and pastoral people. Here some small perennial streams, exuding from springs by the base of these hills, meander through the valleys, and keep all vegetable life in a constant state of verdant freshness. The creek still increases in width as it extends northward, and is studded with numerous small rocky island hills, covered with brushwood, which, standing out from the bosom of the deep-blue waters, reminded me of a voyage I once had in the Grecian archipelago. The route also being so diversified with hills, afforded fresh objects of attraction at every turn, and today, by good fortune, the usually troublesome people have attended more to their harvest-making, and left me to the enjoyment of the scenery. My trusty Blissett made a flonikan pay the penalty of death for his temerity in attempting a flight across the track. The day's journey lasted thirteen miles, and brought us into a village called Isamiro.

The caravan, after quitting Isamiro, began winding up a long but gradually inclined hill—which, as it bears no native name, I will call Somerset—until it reached its summit, when the vast expanse of the pale-blue waters of the Nyanza burst suddenly upon my gaze. It was early morning. The distant sea-line of the north horizon was defined in the calm atmosphere between the north and west points of the compass; but even this did not afford me any idea of the breadth of the lake, as an archipelago of islands, each consisting of a single hill, rising to a height of two hundred or three hundred feet above the water, intersected the line of vision to the left; while on the right the western horn of the Ukerewé Island cut off any further view of its distant waters to the eastward of north. A sheet of water—an elbow of the sea, however, at the base of the low range on which I stood—extended far away to the eastward, to where, in the dim distance, a hummock-like elevation of the mainland marked what I understood to be the south and east angle of the lake. The large and important islands of Ukerewé and Mzita, distant about twenty or thirty miles, formed the visible north shore of this firth. The name of the former of these islands was familiar to us as that by which this long-desired lake was usually known. It is reported by the natives to be of no great extent; and though of no considerable elevation, I could discover several spurs stretching down to the water's edge from its central ridge of hills. The other island, Mzita, is of greater elevation, of a hog-backed shape, but being more distant, its physical features were not so distinctly visible. In consequence of the northern islands of the archipelago before mentioned obstructing the view, the western shore of the lake could not be defined: a series of low hill-tops extended in this direction as far as the eye could reach; while below me, at no great distance, was the debouchure of the creek, which enters the lake from the south, and along the banks of which my last three days' journey had led me.

This view was one which, even in a well-known and explored country, would have arrested the traveller by its peaceful beauty. The islands, each swelling in a gentle slope to a rounded summit, clothed with wood between the rugged angular closely-cropping rocks of granite, seemed mirrored in the calm surface of the lake; on which I here and there detected a small black speck, the tiny canoe of some Muanza fisherman. On the gently shelving plain below me, blue smoke curled above the trees, which here and there partially concealed villages and hamlets, their brown thatched roofs contrasting with the emerald green of the beautiful milk-bush, the coral branches of which cluster in such profusion round the cottages, and form alleys and hedgerows about the villages as ornamental as any garden shrub in England. But the pleasure of the mere view vanished in the presence of those more intense and exciting emotions which are called up by the consideration of the commercial and geographical importance of the prospect before me. I no longer felt any doubt that the lake at my feet gave birth to that interesting river, the source of which has been the subject of so much speculation, and the object of so many explorers. This is a far more extensive lake than the Tanganyika; 'so broad you could not see across it, and so long that nobody knew its length'. *

I had now the pleasure of perceiving that a map I had constructed on Arab testimony, and sent home to the Royal Geographical Society before leaving Unyanyembé, was so substantially correct that in its general outlines I had nothing whatever to alter. Further, as I drew that map after proving their first statements about the Tanganyika, which were made before my going there, I have every reason to feel confident of their veracity relative to their travels north through Karagwah, and to Kibuga in Uganda. When Shaykh Snay told us of the Ukerewé, as he called the Nyanza, on our first arrival at Kazeh, proceeding westward from Zanzibar, he said, " If you have come only to see a large bit of water, you had better go northwards and see the Ukerewé; for it is much greater in every respect than the Tanganyika." And so, as far as I can ascertain, it is.

* This magnificent sheet of water I have ventured to name VICTORIA, after our gracious Sovereign.

Muanza, our journey's end, now lay at our feet. It is an open, well-cultivated plain on the southern end, and lies almost flush with the lake; a happy, secluded-looking corner, containing every natural facility to make life pleasant. After descending the hill, we followed along the borders of the lake, and at first entered the settlement, when the absence of boats arousing my suspicions, made me inquire where the Arabs, on coming to Muanza, and wishing to visit Ukerewé, usually resided. This, I heard, was some way farther on; so with great difficulty I persuaded the porters to come away and proceed at once to where they said an Arab was actually living. It was a singular coincidence that, after Shaykh Snay's caution as to my avoiding Sultan Mahaya's village, by inquiring diligently about him yesterday, and finding no one who knew his name, the first person I should have encountered was himself, and that, too, in his own village. The reason of this was, that big men in this country, to keep up their dignity, have several names, and thus mystify the traveller.

I then proceeded along the shore of the lake in an easterly direction, and on the way shot a number of red Egyptian geese, which were very numerous; they are the same sort here as I once saw in the Somali country. Another goose, which unfortunately I could not kill, is very different from any I ever saw or heard of: it stands as high as the Canadian bird, or higher, and is black all over, saving one little white patch beneath the lower mandible. It was fortunate that I came on here, for the Arab in question, called Mansur bin Salim, treated me very kindly, and he had retainers belonging to the country, who knew as much about the lake as anybody, and were of very great assistance. I also found a good station for making observations on the lake. It was Mansur who first informed me of my mistake of the morning, but said that the evil report spread at Unyany-embé about Mahaya had no foundation; on the contrary, he had found him a very excellent and obliging person.

Today we marched eight miles, and have concluded our journey northwards, a total distance of 226 miles from Kazeh, which, occupying twenty-five days, is at the rate of nine miles *per diem*, halts inclusive.

Early in the morning I took a walk of three miles easterly along the shore of the lake, and ascending a small hill (which, to distinguish it, I have called Observatory Hill), took compass-bearings of all the principal features of the lake. Mansur and a native, the greatest traveller of the place, kindly accompanied and gave me every obtainable information. This man had traversed the island, as he called it, of Ukerewé from north to south. But by his rough mode of describing it, I am rather inclined to think that instead of its being an actual island, it is a connected tongue of land, stretching southwards from a promontory lying at right angles to the eastern shore of the lake, which, being a wash, affords a passage to the mainland during the fine season, but during the wet becomes submerged, and thus makes Ukerewé temporarily an island. If this conjecture be true, Mzita must be similarly circumstanced. Cattle, he says, can cross over from the mainland at all seasons of the year, by swimming from one elevation of the promontory to another; but the Warudi, who live upon the eastern shore of the lake, and bring their ivory for sale to Ukerewé, usually employ boats for the transit. A sultan called Machunda lives at the southern extremity of the Ukerewé, and has dealings in ivory with all the Arabs who go there. One Arab at this time was stopping there, and had sent his men coasting along this said promontory to deal with the natives on the mainland, as he could not obtain enough ivory on the island itself. Considering how near the eastern shore of the lake is to Zanzibar, it appears surprising that it can pay men to carry ivory all the way round by Unyanyembé. But the Masai, and especially those tribes who live near to the lake, are so hostile to travellers, that the risk of going there is considered too great to be profitable, though all Arabs concur in stating that a surprising quantity of ivory is to be obtained there at a very cheap rate.

The little hill alluded to as marking the south-east angle of the lake, I again saw; but so indistinctly, though the atmosphere was very clear, that I imagined it to be at least forty miles distant. It is due east of my station on Observatory Hill. I further draw my conclusions from the fact that all the hills in the country are much about the same height—two or three hundred feet above the basial surface of the land; and I could only see the top of the hill like a hazy brown spot, contrasted in relief against the clear blue sky. Indeed, had my attention not been drawn to it, I probably should have overlooked it, and have thought there was only a sea horizon before me. On facing to the W.N.W., I could only see a sea horizon; and on inquiring how far back the land lay, was assured that, beyond the island of Ukerewé, there was an equal expanse of it east and west, and that it would be more than double the distance of the little hill before alluded to, or from eighty to one hundred miles in breadth. On my inquiring about the lake's length, the man faced to the north, and began nodding his head to it; at the same time he kept throwing forward his right hand, and, making repeated snaps of his fingers, endeavoured to indicate something immeasurable; and added, that nobody knew, but he thought it probably extended to the end of the world. To the east of the Observatory, a six hours' journey, probably fourteen or fifteen miles, the village of Sukuma is situated, and there canoes are obtainable for crossing to Ukerewé, which island being six hours' paddling, and lying due north of it, must give the firth a breadth of about fifteen miles. Whilst walking back to camp, I shot two red geese and a horikan, like those I once shot in the Somali country. This must have been a dainty dish for my half-starved Arab companion, who had lost all his property on first arriving here, and was now living on Mahaya's generosity. It appears that nine months ago he was enabled, by the assistance of Mahaya, to hire some boats and men at Sukuma, and had sent his property, consisting of fifteen loads of cloth and 250 jembis or hoes by them to Ukerewé, to exchange for ivory. But by the advice of Mahaya, and fearing to trust himself as a stranger amongst the islanders, he did not accompany his merchandise. Sultan Machunda, a man of the highest character by Unyanyembé report, on seeing such a prize enter his port, gave orders for its seizure, and will now give no redress to the unfortunate Mansur. All Mahaya's exertions to recover it have proved abortive: and Mansur has therefore been desirous of taking his revenge by making an attack in person on Ukerewé, but the ' generous ' Mahaya said, " No, your life is yet safe, do not risk it; but let my men do what they can, and in the meanwhile, as I have been a party to your losses, I will feed you and your people; and if I do not succeed in the end, you shall be my guest until I can amass sufficient property to reimburse your losses." Mansur has all this time been living, like the slaves of the country, on jowari porridge, which is made by grinding the seed into flour and boiling it in water until it forms a good thick paste, when master and man sit round the earthen pot it is boiled in, pick out lumps, and suck it off their fingers.

It was a delicious sight yesterday, on coming through Muanza, to see the great deference paid to Sich Belooch, Shadad, mistaken for the great Arab merchant (or Mundewa), my humble self, in consequence of his riding the donkey, and to perceive the stoical manner in which he treated their attentions; but, more fortunate than I usually have been, he escaped the rude peeping and peering of the crowd, for he did not, like his employer, wear ' double eyes '. During the last five or six marches, the word Marabu, for Arab, instead of Mzungu, European, has usually been applied to me; and no one, I am sure, would have discovered the difference, were it not that the tiresome Pagazis, to increase their own dignity and importance generally, gave the clue by singing the song of ' the White Man '. The Arabs at Unyanyembé had advised my donning their habit for the trip, in order to attract less attention: a vain precaution, which I believe they suggested more to gratify their own vanity in seeing an Englishman lower himself to their position, than for any benefit that I might receive by doing so. At any rate, I was more comfortable and better off in my flannel shirt, long togs, and wide-awake, than I should have been, both mentally and physically, had I degraded myself, and adopted their hot, long, and particularly uncomfortable gown.

Sultan Mahaya sent a messenger to say that he was hurt at the cavalier manner in which I treated him yesterday, and, to show his wounded feelings, gave an order to his subjects that no man should supply me with provisions, or render me any assistance during my sojourn at Muanza. Luckily my larder was well supplied with game, or I should have had to go supperless to bed, for no inducement would prevail on the people to sell anything to me after the mandate had been proclaimed. This morning, however, we

settled the difference in the most amicable manner, thus:
previously to my departure for Observatory Hill, I sent the
jemadar, the kirangozi, and a large deputation of the
Belooches and Pagazis, to explain away the reason of my
having left his house so rudely, and to tender apologies,
which were accompanied, as an earnest of good-will, with a
large kahongo, consisting of one barsati, one dhoti Ameri-
kan, and one gora kiniki, as also an intimation that I would
pay him a visit the next day. This pleased him excessively;
it was considered a visit of itself; and he returned the usual
bullock, with a notification that I must remain where I was,
to enable him to return the compliment I had paid him, for
he intended walking out to see me on the morrow.

As my time was getting short, I forestalled Mahaya in
his intentions, and changed ground to the Sultanat, a rural-
looking little place, perched on a small rocky promontory,
shrouded by green trees, facing the N.W. side of the lake.
Mahaya received me with great courtesy, arranged a hut
comfortably, and presented a number of eggs and fresh
milk, as he had heard that I was partial to such fare. He is a
man of more than ordinary stature, a giant in miniature,
with massive and muscular but well-proportioned limbs: he
must number fifty years or more. His dress was the
ordinary barsati; his arms were set off by heavy brass and
copper ornaments encircling the wrists, and by numberless
sambo, or thin circles made from the twisted fibres of an
aloetic plant, on each of which a single infi, or white
porcelain bead resembling a little piece of tobacco-pipe, was
strung; these ranged in massive rows down the whole of
his upper arm. Just above his elbow-joints sat a pair of
large ivory rings. On his forehead two small goat or deer
horns were fastened by thin talismanic ornaments of thong
for keeping off the evil eye; and, finally, his neck was

adorned with two strings of very coarse blue beads. Mahaya has the fame of being the best and most just sultan in these quarters, and his benign square countenance, lit up with a pleasing expression when in conversation, confirms this opinion, though a casual observer passing by that dark, broad massive face, still more darkened by a matting of short, close, and tightly curled-up ringlets, would be apt to carry away a contrary impression.

Before leaving Kazeh, I notified my intention of visiting Ukerewé, supposing I could do so in three or four days, and explained to my men my wishes on this point. Hearing this, they told both Mahaya and Mansur, in direct terms, that I was going, and so needlessly set them to work finessing to show how much they were in earnest in their consideration of me. However, they have both been very warm in dissuading me from visiting Ukerewé, apparently quite in a parental way, for each seems to think himself in a measure my guardian. Mahaya thinks it his duty to caution those who visit him from running into danger, which a journey to Ukerewé, he considers, would be. Mansur, on the other hand, says, as I have come from his Sultan Majid, he also is bound to render me any assistance in his power; but strongly advises my giving up the notion of going across the water. I could get boats from Usukuma, he said, but there would be great delay in the business, as I should have first to send over and ask permission from Machunda to land, and then the collecting men and boats would occupy a long time. As regards the collection of boats taking a long time, these arguments are very fair, as I know from experience; but the only danger would consist in the circumstance of the two sultans being at enmity with each other, as in this land anyone coming direct from an enemy's country is suspected and treated as an enemy. This difficulty I should have avoided by going straight to Sukuma (where the boats, I am inclined to think, usually do start from, though all concur in stating that this is their point of departure), and there obtaining boats direct. However, I told them that I should have gone if I had found boats ready at once to take me across; but now I saw the probability of so much delay, that I could not afford to waste time in trying to obtain boats, which, had I succeeded in getting, I should have employed my time not in going to Ukerewé, but to the more elevated and friendly island of Mzita, this being a more suitable observatory than the former.

These Negroes' manœuvres are quite incomprehensible. If Mahaya had desired to fleece me—and one can hardly give a despotic Negro credit for anything short of that—he surely would have tried to detain me under false hopes, and have thus necessitated my spending cloths in his village, while, on the contrary, he lost all chance of gaining anything by giving advice, which induced me to leave him at once, never to return again to see him.

[October 1859

3

A WINTER JOURNEY

Margaret Oliphant

When one thinks of a road along the coast, one imagines a placid level road in sight of the sea, with no great difference of altitude from one point to another. That is to say, I thought so, thinking of the road to Nice, which I promised myself wound snugly along the coast, finding out bays and headlands, under the sunshine, in a reasonable and moderate way. This, of course, only shows my ignorance; but I am thankful to believe that at home there are people of my standing who do not know everything. Of course, the young generation are all perfectly aware that one has to wind up and down among the Maritime Alps when one travels along the coast of the Mediterranean; but, for my own part, I did not anticipate this mountainous road. Here we go up, up—horses (six of them) labouring on in a toilsome walk—*conducteur* arching with shouts of encouragement, now on this side, now on the other— great shoulders of hills folding us in on all sides, with here and there a line of wall visible upon the heights above, which surely cannot mean the road which we have yet to reach? High cones and hill-tops overhead, of which, straining from the windows of the diligence, one can scarcely see the summit; and deep precipitous descents below, to which the rash vehicle approaches close enough to give one many a shudder. All green, green, and still more green, as one ascends higher, with the grey foliage of those trees through which the sun broke this morning, and which are olive trees—with the vegetation fresher and more verdant, of groves of cork—and greenest of all, with pine trees, fresh and luxuriant, which make a summer on the hills. Up, and still up, till on the landward side these vast green slopes open wide towards the more majestic hills, and show us, far away, the white peaks dipping into the clouds, the heights from which ' Jura answers in her misty shroud ', and higher still, till we have gained the topmost ribbon of road which circles the highest head of all these leafy hills.

To this ledge—which is a good road when one reaches it, though it looks from below like a morsel of grey wall built into the face of the hill—comes up with flying leaps the telegraph which has travelled in our sight all the way— in our sight, but not beside us; striding, like some wonderful giant, over the precipices, drawing its daring bridge, like a spider's thread, from mount to mount, striking straight, as the crow flies, with an arbitrary directness which impresses the imagination most strangely, and with a total disregard of all obstacles, to the topmost height, towards which we, who are not giants and magi, but only some twenty helpless human creatures in a diligence, have been creeping and winding for an hour or two in a hopeless roundabout. Of course I have heard a great deal about the electric telegraph, like everybody else, and, heaven help us, like most other people, have heard news by it in my day sufficiently startling, sudden, and terrible; but I never before saw this big Ethiopian mute, and voiceless confidant of nations, show himself so like a weird spirit and jinn of

Arabian tales. He is a very humdrum person when he draws those big lines of his like a bit of manuscript prepared for a musician, though they are lines that thrill with many a dirge, and echo many a triumph, alongside of our peaceable railways; but when one sees those fairy threads scaling hills and crossing precipices, one gets startled into wonder and admiration. I confess, however, that after the first moment my thoughts were not sentimental ones, touching the private joys and calamities which could thus cross the hills so much more rapidly than we could—or philosophical, concerning this close union of far-off quarters and annihilation of distance; but that somehow there suddenly appeared before me a vision of those other lofty telegraph-wires which leap over everybody's head into the high windows of the Tuileries, and that my fancy consolidated itself into one thought of that mysterious person called Napoleon the Third. To be sure, it was nonsense—for the telegraph is the nineteenth century in impersonation, and enlightenment, and progress, and all the rest of it; yet I am obliged to confess, I thought of none of these things as I watched, with a little thrill of almost awe and wonder, how that big Spy of the Emperor marched, swifter than any fiery cross, to the edge of his domains, and in his progress scaled, as if they had been so many mole-heaps, the everlasting hills.

And then came the beautiful Mediterranean, blue, blue— I cannot say how blue—like the blue of eyes—and Cannes on the beach, marketing and pleasuring—and the grey olives and the green pines standing out against the sea— and the sun sinking, with no clouds to attend him, making once more, in lack of these, the steadfast sky itself gorgeous with those marvellous indescribable gradations of colour. I wonder what those priggish people mean who babble of complimentaries and primaries, and say there is no true harmony of colour but red and green. Was ever sweeter harmony than the young spring green of those pine branches falling, without any help or intervention, upon the full blue of that sea? Did ever fairy combination show sweeter than that rosy pink, that angelic bluish, which melts and melts into that other blue, the blue of the sky? Never mind—the theory of colour does famously for talk, which is something—Nature and we know better, and so there is no need of making a disturbance about it. Sleep, child, upon our knees, with the twilight on your face—with tiny roses on your cheeks, and some dim gold gleaming among the stray locks of your hair—thank heaven there is no green in your complexion to complete the harmony—and now let the sea fall darkling in the midst of its beatitude—and welcome night.

Welcome night, and oh the delight, after a night-journey, of—one cannot pause for refined expression—going to bed. I trust nobody is shocked. Baths and bread-and-milk for the bairnies—and then the delicious rest, quickened by the knowledge that fragrant oranges grew under their windows, which their happy hands might pluck tomorrow. I think, if I were an invalid—which, alas, there seems little hope of—I should choose Nice for my winter quarters. It is not in the least interesting, my dear connoisseur! I do not believe there is a picture in the town, and the architecture is, as a Cockney tradesman would say, " beneath contempt ", but then there is that Mediterranean, that sea of suns, rippling as if it loved it on the peaceful beach—and the hills beyond, grey and dark and silent, relieving all this light; and something like an island lying on the water far off, which, after all, is only the point of San Ospizio, and showing against its solid darkness the misty glory of the sunbeams, and the transparence of the sea.

I think it was at Nice that Johnnie distinguished himself by trying to catch the dust in the sun—as it was on the road to Nice that poor little Mary immortalised her simplicity by bestowing her half-franc, her whole worldly store, upon a little beggar-boy who besieged the diligence. Talk of invalids, those children, who are not at all given that way, expanded like flowers in the delicious May weather which we found waiting for us there. People come to be epicures in climate as in other things. It was the fashion in Nice at that moment to shiver and complain of cold with that dear English look of discontent which seems to upbraid Providence with leaving something short of perfection wherever our delightful country people go. If I could only have taken a phial out of my pocket, and produced for their benefit an hour of that day on which we left London, or a whistle full of that wind which cut us into little pieces on the heights of Fourvières. But certainly it is our national privilege—the safety-valve of the savage insular nature. Grumble then, oh excellent exiles, and carry your grey parasols, and dangle in your hands those fresh oranges with stalks and green leaves to them, and forget that it is January. It is very easy to do so where you are.

Nice, like all the other towns of the Mediterranean, occupies a bay, the high headlands of which, stretching out like protecting arms half round that semicircle of blue water, aid the darker hills behind in preserving from storms and chills the bright little town upon its beach. It is divided by a river, or rather by the bed of a river, a wide dry channel duly bridged over, and of an imposing breadth, through which there straggles a little rivulet of clear water, quite inadequate to the task of moistening a quarter part of the gravel bed which calls itself the Paglione. Great square houses, painted either white or in light tints akin thereto, with row upon row of green shutters to make them gay, have begun to stray in little detachments out of the town towards the hills; and vast hotels seem to the eye of a stranger to form half the bulk of the town itself, which has no features of nationality whatever, but is like every other place subjected to a yearly invasion of visitors. The table-d'hôte is full and gay, filled up by *habitués*, as one can easily perceive, who know what they are about, and the best way of making themselves comfortable. There is even a public breakfast at half-past ten o'clock where one begins the day with cutlets and fried potatoes, and where weak-minded English strangers interject their little pots of coffee and boiled milk, their orthodox bread and butter, into the midst of the wine bottles and stronger fare of their neighbours.

At this same table-d'hôte we were a little startled to hear an Englishman declare his intention of remaining " till the war began ". The war—what war? Then we, who had been shut up from newspapers for a week or two, heard for the first time those new-year's compliments of the French Emperor, which seem to have stirred all England into the delightful excitement of gossips over an impending quarrel. " There cannot be a doubt about it," said our informant, loftily. I do not know what this gentleman meant to do with himself " when the war began ", but for us, who were bound for Italy, and meant to remain there, this suggestion was rather exciting. " If one could only see a *Times*," cried Alice, who had unbounded faith in the Thunderer; but instead of a *Times*, we could but lay our heads together over a *Galignani*, which respectable old lady was in a high state of fuss and nervous excitement.

However, we had no further information of this supposititious war in leisurely Nice, where everybody took everything very quietly. We, too, enjoyed the sunshine and the rest with all our hearts, and climbed the rock on which perches a little old castle, to look over a widened horizon of sea and sun upon one side, and on the other to look down upon breaks of garden among the houses, where the foliage suggested nothing so strongly as a bush of gorse in full bloom, so full were the oranges among their leaves. The hills beyond were heavy with olives, a grey and misty cloud of vegetation upon the slopes, which rose dark and sombre in the light, though scattered everywhere with white houses, rising at different elevations almost to the summits of those hills.

Let us turn down to the beach; it is entirely occupied, but not by young ladies in pretty hats, or groups of children. That sea, which knows no tide, ripples with a soft regularity upon its ridge of pebbles, but does not send its music, thus near at hand, into the faces of any of those seekers of health or pleasure who keep upon the terrace yonder, out of reach of this tender foamy spray. No, for the beach has homelier tenants. Here comes a freshwater brook, briskly rattling into the sea, and in possession of a host of washerwomen, who kneel on each side as close as so many flies, animated by the liveliest industry, and beating their linen with an energy which, in this calm country, it is pleasant to hear; and yonder stray their mistresses or assistants, in careful superintendence of the long lines stretched from pole to pole along the beach, where the said linen hangs to bleach or dry in the sun. How these poor women manage, day after day and all day long, to work upon their knees, half dropping into the water, with that fervid sun beating on their heads, I cannot tell. The labour in such a constrained position must be prodigious; but the scene is extremely cheerful, and odd, and amusing. I wonder who wears all those clothes? I wonder if it is true that the Italians are not very remarkable for their love of clean linen. Oddly enough, these picturesque public washings only exist among people who are reported, falsely or truly, to be a little indifferent in this respect. I never saw a more cheerful sight than I saw one day upon the Green at Glasgow, where the little wild savages of girls sat under the sun, watching the clothes laid to bleach upon the grass, while their mothers washed hardby within reach of the Clyde; yet one understands that Glasgow is not a model of cleanliness. However, I have homely tastes. I like to see the linen swept through that pure running water, and dried among those breezes. But I suppose that is why the genteel people in Nice—the visitors and promenaders—keep up upon the dusty terrace, and never spread themselves in groups upon the shingle, as we do at home.

From Nice we started early in the morning for Genoa, another twenty-four hours' journey, which we arranged to break by stopping for the night half-way, and being taken up next morning by the night diligence. This road is like a road in fairyland, or in one's dreams. Up spur and straight over fold after fold, and slope after slope, of those continuous hills, dashing round sharp curves of road which follow the line of those deep and narrow ravines which divide them, finding out at every turn another and another bay lying calm within the shelter of those vast projecting and protecting arms, each with its little town smiling like a princess from the beach, calmly ripening her oranges, cultivating her palms, and tending her vineyards with such care as Eve bestowed on her flowers in Milton's Eden, where every plant and blossom brightened to her presence. Pines green with the green of spring; great olive-trees, grey and rich; rows of little aloes hanging over in miniature hedges from the garden walls; orange-trees, low and green, and golden with showers of fruit; pale little lemons hiding among their leaves—interpose between us and the sea, as we come dashing down from the heights almost at a gallop towards the Mentone or San Remo of the moment—when amidst all this wealth of nature our momentary stoppage collects a crowd of importunate beggars not to be repulsed.

Then up again, as the morning brightens towards noon, labouring up the hills, sweeping once more through the sharp double of the road which rounds those ravines—ravines terraced step by step from the deep bottom yonder, where a mountain stream has scarcely room to flow, up to the verge of this lofty road, sometimes higher, to the very hilltops, and terraced in a dainty and sumptuous fashion unknown to less favoured and luxuriant lands. One could fancy, in the absence of the vines, that these smooth green terraces were so many grassy benches which some benevolent giant had amused himself with making, out of a tenderly contemptuous kindness for the feeble little pygmies who surrounded him. Here is one of these ravines, not a valley, but a cleft between two hills, with a narrow stony watercourse marking its centre, pressed into very slender bounds by the grass and the young trees which almost meet over its rugged line, and rising in a succession of lines not so regular as the seats of an amphitheatre, but adapted to the inequalities of the soil. Here delightful little corners, where two people could sit together looking down upon the Mediterranean through its fringe of trees. Here prolonged is a lordly bench which could hold a score of spectators, all living green, as velvety (in the distance) as an English lawn, solitary, without even a cottage within sight to mark where someone watched over those sunny gardens—

sheltered on either side so deeply and warmly that wind can never reach them, save that soft wind which whispers over the herbage, the hush of the calm sea. Ah, troubled human people, sweeping past, glad of the momentary level of the road, and with no leisure to linger, or to see how nature smiles out of her superior happiness at you and your walletful of cares! I wonder why it is that Nature does look happiest in those solitary places, and in the early mornings, and the summer midnights, when there is no human eye about to spy upon the secret of her joy.

These valleys are not always vineyards, but sometimes orange-gardens; and though there is not a creature visible, nor apparently the least need of any common vulgar appliances of husbandry where everything is so perfect, yet the labour bestowed upon them must be immense. Notwithstanding, when we come to the next in succession of those picturesque towns which dot the whole road, here is again the same crowd of beggars, pathetic, and not to be denied. Such richness of country, such poverty of people. I do not understand how it is accounted for; for certainly there is no appearance of indolence in the dainty and extreme cultivation of those clefts among the hills.

When there is a little pause from the perpetual ascent and descent of the road, and the country spreads into a plain, where here and there a tall black cypress shoots straight up into the sky, looking like an attenuated spire, the aspect is said to be Oriental—chiefly, I presume, because here they cultivate the date-palm, which, like other things which ought to be imposing, does not strike one half so much as an orthodox imagination desires it should. I humbly conceive that Oriental means dull, and long for the hills and hollows which reveal in glimpses, like visions of enchantment, the further course of the coastline, which is too costly a pleasure to be enjoyed all at once, and which one prefers to have hoarded up among the mountains, and dispensed bit by bit as the occasion offers.

But, alas, this darkness; in which one has only the gratification of knowing that one is ever so many hundred feet above the sea; that below the descent is straight into the rocks which edge the Mediterranean; that this jar of the wheel was against the bit of wall which is our sole protection; and that this mad diligence gallops, *sans* drag, *sans* caution, down a slope which an English coachman would take with the most serious precautions, and would not like even then. But fortunately no accident befalls us, and everybody has fallen into an uncomfortable doze, when we dash along the stony street of Alassio, where we are to stop for the night. Oh night of chill and misery! There are two babies, four bags, a dozen shawls, a *Murray*, a basket, and a French novel to be produced in the dark out of the dust of the diligence; every article is handed out separately to the applause of the group of idlers, who stand by, and who are all prepared to escort us to our hotel, where we are safely delivered. Then the hotel itself, where there are some five or six rooms, all opening out of each other, and into somewhere else, with one solitary fireplace in the last one, with tiled floors, and ceilings half as high as St Paul's, and a bit of carpet the size of a small tablecloth spread in the centre of each; and a voluble landlady, with a coloured handkerchief tied over her head, who speaks a great deal of French, and will not understand that we speak very little, and are tired enough and stupid enough to have forgotten that. How we all nursed the fire in that one fireplace—the fire which was not disposed to burn—and meekly swallowed our coffee, and crept under the quilted coverlids with a dire anticipation of the diligence which was to pick us up at six o'clock next morning. Then the bill, which came in at dawn, our first true Italian bill, at sight of which the British lion stirred within the bosom of my brother. Let us not think of these agonies of travel; but, dearest traveller, fight like a true Briton over every bill they produce to you at an Italian inn.

We resumed our journey next day in a vehicle still less comfortable and still more daring than that which had brought us to Alassio, when we had for our travelling companion a merry Genevese, on commerce and on politics intent, hastening to Genoa full of expectation, and with a story on his lips which roused in all our minds once more the slumbering terror of the war. The Austrian flag had been burnt by the crowd—the Austrian consul, roughly treated, had left the city. Telegraphic information, sent immediately to Turin, had been answered by the despatch of five vessels bearing troops from Nice, said our informant, who, noways discouraged by his news, proved himself a famous playfellow for the children during the day's journey.

Of course, this story being true, and the Genoese mob having thus the support of the authorities, war was all but declared. Thus we went dashing on towards Genoa by just such a road as we had traversed yesterday, but under a light less favourable, the day being dark, wet, and cloudy, with at least one blast of snow, and our minds being somewhat roused by the possibility of finding ourselves actually in the presence of war, or at least of war impending. Coloured by our own fancies, we found excitement in the aspect even of the languid market-place crowd of the coast towns through which we passed, and discovered a quickened pace and a more important mien among the sturdy little grey soldiers, looking so clean and comfortable, whom one sees in the Sardinian states. Even the Mediterranean partook of the sentiment, and, though there was no storm, undulated in a strong swell and current, such as one would rather look at than feel, and threw a heavy angry surf upon the rocky beach. As we drew towards the end of our journey too—for even admiration and the love of beauty have their limits—I rather think we began to be more interested in the progress we made, and more pleased by the speed of our conveyance than by the loveliness of the landscape.

Rattling down the hills, turning sharp corners with a jerk, dashing and crunching through the broad gravelly course as wide as a Thames, through which meanders a pitcherful of fair water bearing a big name, and calling itself a river—we hurried on to the famous old republic, the superb —Genoa. Fine as this road and country are at all times, it must be still finer during the brief period when these Pailiones and Polceveras, of which we have crossed so many, are really rivers, and not mere beds of gravel. But there seems rain enough in these clouds to fill them up. Farewell, summer country, sleeping mid-world on the tideless beach of that bright sea. We are going south, it is true, but we are going back to winter—back to winter, back to war, back to tumults, cares, and labours—back to the world. I conclude that the world stopped somewhere on the other side of Nice, and begins again here as we draw near the gate of Genoa.

Farewell, beautiful Riveria. We think of you no more as yonder crescent of a city piles upward to the sky before our eyes, and throws her arms into the sea—nor of the splendour of that noble bay, nor of ' the Doria's pale palace ', nor of any beauty here—but look up with a shudder, half of excitement, half of terror, at the fortifications, and regard with an unusual interest the brisk little soldiers, and think of the flag burned, and the consul fled, and big Austria bristling her bayonets and setting her moustache; and brave little Sardinia blowing her trumpet from the hills, and rousing one cannot tell what echoes from the rich Lombard plains, the canals of Venice, and the streets of Milan. We saw excitement in every face we passed in the lamplight, as we threaded our way through the streets of Genoa, and thought of nothing less than Italy in arms.

But alas for English credulity and human weakness, that we should have to tell it! Though the evening gun that night startled us all to the windows with a sudden thrill, half fearing, half hoping the commencement of hostilities—alas, it was all a canard. The Black Eagles had suffered no violence from the mob of Genoa—the Austrian consul remained in the calmest security. I do not remember at this moment how the five ships carrying troops were accounted for—whether they too were inventions like the mob, or whether it was merely a common military transfer from one place to another. I think the latter was the truth. But we were " regularly sold ", according to Harry's vulgar exclamation. Of course we were much relieved, and, if the truth must be told, just a little disappointed, to find everything pacific, and the warlike rumour just as vague here as in other places. However, there was an indisputable excitement in Genoa—more than once, during that first evening, a distant echo of the ' Marseillaise ', that common Continental language of political passion, ascended to our high windows; and even the common operation of changing guard was certainly performed with an importance and *afflatus* which whispered of something in men's minds deeper than sentry-boxes. The streets were full of groups in eager discussion—the cafés crowded—and still, ever and anon, came dropping from this colonnade or yonder piazza that ominous echo of the ' Marseillaise '.

Genoa, as seen from these aforesaid high windows of ours, consisted, in the first place, of a high terrace balustraded with marble, which ran in a curve, not sufficiently bold to be called a semicircle, round the middle of the harbour, and beyond which appeared the masts—of which there certainly did not seem to be a forest—of vessels lying in the port. Round these ships, only partially visible, ran on either side a long arm of solid masonry with a light at each end, shutting in to the dimensions of a doorway this great calm basin, so well enclosed and sheltered that a storm without could hardly send a hint of its presence to the refugees who harboured here. Beyond the line of the terrace, straight up from the water's edge, in lines of building rising over each other so that the foundation of one is little more than level with the roof of the other, the town piles upward on either side, continuing, in a wider crescent than the harbour, the grand and irregular natural line of the coast. This bay or gulf of Genoa is the complete work for which all these lovely little bays, these Villefranches and Monacos and Mentones on the road, were the studies; for the divine artist does not scorn that principle of repetition full of infinite gradations of contrast which human art has groped its way to, as one of its laws.

This deepest crescent is the centre and climax whether you come from one side or the other—from Rome or from France—of a coast which doubles into innumerable recesses, and of a sea which luxuriates in bay after bay; and is well worthy to gather together and perfect with the superb seal of all its clustered palaces the two wonderful lines of sea and of mountain which have their common issue here. But as for the city of palaces, or anything which warrants that name, we can see nothing of it from these same high windows—high, not because they are shabby, for look at those walls where Aeneas, with legs which would have carried a dozen fathers, bears off old—was it Anchises? —on his sturdy shoulders. I humbly hope I am correct in supposing it to be Aeneas, though there is a lady in pink (also with legs) beside him, whom I do not remember in the tale, and one dreadful hero killing another in the foreground of the piece, towards whom the principal personages show the most profound indifference. However, never mind the story; the room is magnificent, and the frescoes are by Piola—a local greatness.

Dearest Reader, when you go to Genoa (if you can afford it), go to the Hotel de la Ville, and ask for the suite of apartments which opens from the right-hand side of the *salle-à-manger*. *We* could not afford it; but we have all come under a solemn vow never to reveal, under any circumstances, the rate at which the respectable Monsieur Schmidt gave us those magnificent rooms. With all the harbour before, and a good supply of bedrooms behind— bedrooms splendid with satin quilts, with pillows frilled with embroidery, with lace curtains, with walls and alcoves rich with elaborate ornament in stucco; and last, but greatest, doors that closed as fast as if they were English; with fires that were perfection—coal—the first coal that we had seen on the Continent—English coal mingled with wood, what could mortal desire further? But I dare not for my life—as I have told you—betray the moderate amount of francs for which, the house being only moderately full at the moment, we had them by the day.

The wonders of Genoa lie, however, in the principal line of street, which is quite behind and above our present quarters. Let us descend our glistening marble staircase, and close our eyes to the fact that it leads out under a ruinous-looking colonnade, in which dwell whiffs innumerable which are not of Arabian sweetness. One thinks involuntarily of those two-and-seventy different smells which immortalise Cologne, when one comes out under those heavy old arches. But now for the Via Balbi, the Strada Nuova, the streets of palaces. There they rise with that pale Italian blue above them, the momentary shining of a sky which is full of rain. Some half-dozen of those vast mansions on either side are quite enough to form a street; and as you pause at door after door of the six, you look in upon a splendid vista of arches and columns perhaps enclosing a green nest of orange trees, or widening into a magnificent court, from the ample marble sides of which rise the staircases which lead to the house. Then, though they are alike, there is a variety in each; one springs upwards on graceful marble columns to a domed roof, and beyond throws only some three or four broad low steps between you and the orange garden, against the fresh green of which the pillars shine. Another reveals to you its miniature quadrangle cloistered round, at the top of a short but princely staircase, down which on either side a pair of gigantic lions have been rushing, when some sudden spell arrested their course and fixed them there.

Next door the prospect widens, and one court draws itself out within another, with perhaps a gallery and grand balustrade behind, from which the inmates, cool in the shadow of their own lofty roof, could hear their fountain trickle as it played. Whosoever would see the fountain, if it chances to be a work of note, or would examine the frescoes, if there happen to be any about hiding among the columns, or would simply look at a kind of architecture so liberal and princely, may enter as he will; and if there is a collection of pictures above, which is exceedingly probable, is free to penetrate into the *salons* without either fee to pay or warrant of respectability to offer. I think these open courts and columns are a somewhat handsomer way of withdrawing oneself from the street than the Burlington House fashion of building a dead brick wall between the thoroughfare and one's gentility; and it is these princely entrances which gain for Genoa her distinction of *la superba*. The buildings themselves are no doubt grand and imposing; but in this is the characteristic and remarkable feature.

There are various picture-galleries, too, in Genoa, though I am half disposed to think that is something of a vulgar enthusiasm which rushes upon every picture within its range, and must see all the questionable Titians and second-rate Dolces to be found in *Murray*. But we went into the Red House in the Strada Nuova—the red house, more euphoniously the Palazzo Rosso—and saw a little wilderness of fine pictures, and some portraits which immediately took possession of the stately house, and revealed (to me at least) the Genoa of the past. I do not find much interest in portraits, as a general rule; but there was something in those fine Van Dycks, those princely gentlemen and noble ladies, with the small heads full of intelligence, the dainty hands, and sumptuous dress in which that courtly painter delights, which somehow gave a living expression to the sentiment of magnificence which pervaded all these palaces. No, they do not belong to our age, these echoing courts and columns—not to the lounging Italian out of doors, who is more than half a Frenchman, nor to the ladies in crinoline, but to those princely figures on the canvas, those refined and thoughtful faces looking down as if they had been observing all this course of ages from their pensive places on the ancestral walls.

Still anxious for news in our remaining flutter of excitement about the problematical war, we made several desperate but ill-rewarded efforts to get papers. There was not a single syllable of Italian among our party. Our sole hope was in the possibility that Genoa might have newspapers published in French; and so I suppose there are some one or two; but the sole French-Italian broadsheet which we had the luck to light upon was a very amazing little publication—a journal of Monaco, called, I think, the *Eden*. To us, who were eager for news of the possible outbreak of a war which would be European, it was wonderfully ludicrous to light upon this tiny champion of the tiniest principality in Christendom—I suppose in the world. To hear this odd little ' organ ' entering into the historical antecedents of its ' country '—to behold its rebukes to the rebellious towns of Mentone and Roccabruna, which ' in forsaking the rule of Prince Charles, forsook the march of progress and national advancement ', was the oddest anticlimax in the world. Monaco, as perhaps everybody does not know, is a tiny pleasure-town in one of those bays of the Mediterranean, along which the other day we were travelling—a nominal little monarchy, or rather princedom, to which Mentone, a vassal bigger than the master, and Roccabruna, a village among the hills, once belonged. These unprincipled places have withdrawn themselves from under the mighty sceptre of Charles XIII or XIV of Monaco,—and oh, to witness the rampant patriotism of the *Eden*! Poor little *Eden*, I daresay it had a great soul; but when, in answer to anxious questions about Austria and France, one read that article about those two deserters of towns, the result was an explosion of laughter which quieted everybody's political anxieties for the night, better than *Galignani*, perhaps even better than the *Times*.

And next evening we went to sea—the length of Leghorn

—a whole ten hours' voyage along the coast of the Mediterranean—a night when the flags hung down limp and motionless from the mastheads, without a breath to stir them—the rain over, the clouds promising to break, the moon known to be yonder, if the clouds would but let her forth. Yet my sister-in-law, Alice, had her misgivings. The evening gun darted with a flash and roar into all the echoes—the pale water glistened round us lying in the harbour—the lights ran twinkling line above line into the windows in the town—dark boat-loads of opaque objects, afterwards recognised to be men and women, came dropping out to us one by one; and by and by, when we had lost our patience and recovered it again, we sailed at last, sweeping out of that sea-gate of Genoa into the brimful and glistening sea—out of sight of the last arm of the crescent and its towered and clustered pile of houses, across another and another bay, with great dark hills stealing out round and beyond them, opening in black and dim perspective out of the night. The moon broke out at last—the night was lovely. I dare say, had we been in England, half the passengers would have stayed on deck all night. But here people love to be wretched when they are travelling. When we went down at midnight there was not a soul visible on the whole length of the vessel save the man at the helm, the look-out man, the officer on his watch, and a heap of dark figures on the boiler and about it, laid out at full length dead asleep.

We got into Leghorn before we were aware, so smooth and rapid was the voyage—got into Leghorn—that is to say, got into a great basin, with various ships, some fortifications, and a house in sight, all of which we had the great gratification of gazing at for an hour or two, as it was quite impossible we could land till the police had come to look at us. I do not know when the police did arrive. Words have different significations—that which means a solemn procession of bluecoats and batons in London, and a rush of *gendarmerie* and cocked-hats in France, may perhaps mean a secret missive from the shore at Leghorn. At all events, our permission came at last, without any visible appearance of the much-to-be-respected police; and we ' disembarked '. To disembark means, at Leghorn, to go out for a half-day's excursion in a little boat which will call at the custom-house in passing, and after getting through the necessary ceremonials there, will carry you on to your destination, at which you are pretty sure to arrive some time, hour not specified. Through the strangest passages and alleys of water, which were not docks, I suppose—at least there was not a vessel of any kind in them—we reached at last a dreary hotel, where there was no more appearance of a town than of the pyramids. I presume there is a town of Leghorn, but I can testify by experience that one may safely arrive at the port bearing that name, find some breakfast, and make one's way to the railway station, without being at all aware of the existence of a seafaring and laborious population anywhere in one's vicinity. That is to say, we all believe in Leghorn, but we could not see it.

One thing, however, we did see abundantly, and that was the custom-house. We were all examined, it is true, in the middle of our little water-excursion on our way to the hotel. But that does not matter; we must all be examined again at the gate of the railway, little bags and all, when the wary officers of La Dogana examine whether there are any creases in poor Alice's best silk gown (creases, have I not seen mud upon it? classic mud, thy venerated dust, oh ancient Trinity, moistened by thy perennial rains!) and go over all our united wardrobe with a conscientious inspection. But courage, we are safe at last; here they come, all the boxes nicely tied up with official string, with little pewter seals hanging at each—virtuous boxes, warranted and done for; and here we are once more in a railway carriage—our last conveyance—hurrah! almost at the end of our long journey. When the children are lifted into the carriage (by a hand-some fellow in a grey uniform, who lets us know *par paren-thèse* that he has four of his own, for which piece of information our universal heart warms to him, though his soldier-ship is an odd railway porter)—when the children, I say, are lifted in, Alice kisses them clandestinely with a little sentiment in her face. Yes, here they are, those little creatures, beyond price or value—those two only ones surviving (and the fathers and mothers know what *that* word means and implies) safe upon the Tuscan soil, and no harm taken, I do not wonder, for my part, that their mother is very quiet for a little, and has something in her eyes.

And so here we go, moderately, yet quickly, through the long flat, when at last one finds out the Arno by the sails of a line of boats perfectly relieved against the grassy plain beyond—nay, not the sails alone, but almost the entire hull as well, so level is the landscape—and where our road is bordered by fields covered with water, which we find out with wonder to be fields of rice, and draw up gently to a town from which that tower, which is to all the world the sign of Pisa, projects its leaning side towards us. Then on again into a true Italian landscape—that landscape which in old pictures one supposes a composition, and looks on with doubt accordingly—where the little hills slope softly up and down, bearing each upon its crest its house or little cluster of houses, and its town, and where all the unequal heights and varieties of soil, coupled with those unfailing resemblances, make up a scene so rich, and soft, and novel, so rural, and nevertheless so refined and delicate, and with such a dainty gentle animation and cheerfulness in its aspect, that one is startled with a landscape altogether out of one's experience—nature fresh and living, yet not the nature one has been accustomed to see. So that it is not the towns or the people principally, but perhaps, chiefest of all, this fresh and unaccustomed scenery, which convinces us that we are no longer among the Gauls and Teutons, but are where the old world lived in the old ages, and where the modern arts were born. And here is Florence in the dark— Florence, our journey's end and temporary habitation—the Florence of Dante and Michael Angelo—the Florence of the Medicis—the City of Imaginations! Can anyone see anything in the darkness? Hark, there is a rustle of water—the Arno running full under its bridges. Is there no *campanile* visible over the house-tops?—no shadow of the great Dome upon our road? Dome—*campanile*! I wonder what anybody is thinking of—as for the house-tops, there is no such thing to be seen anywhere—and, lo, we plunge out of our *fiacre*, the whole bundle of us, into the doorway of a hotel, it is true, in the second place; but, firstly, into the white abyss, profound and impenetrable, of—a fog!

From the depths of which, oh kindest reader, a slowly receding voice, with passive despair in its accents, bids you farewell!

[April 1859

4

THE INLAND SEA OF JAPAN

Andrew Wilson

It was not unpleasant to be at Talien, or ' Great Girdle Bay ', in Manchuria, when the British expedition against China was collected there, in the summer of last year, previous to its advance on the Taku forts.* It was pleasant to be there, because, in anticipation, we could always put down any travelled bore with the crushing phrase, " When I was in Manchuria." Then the clear brilliant sky and life-giving air of the north were themselves a pure enjoyment after the steam-bath of Hong Kong, which place I had described to myself a few weeks before, when in an atrabilarious mood, as—

' A mount of desolation
   Upraised in steaming air,
With views of rotten granite rocks,
   Salt water, and despair.'

It was something to see that magnificent bay—hitherto known to junks alone—covered with nearly two hundred

* This followed the attack on Admiral Hope's squadron by the forts at the mouth of the Peiho on 24th June 1859.—Publisher's note.

vessels flying the English flag, from the little rolling gun-boat to the fifty-gun steam frigate, or the not less magnificent chartered steamer of two or three thousand tons. The utmost harmony prevailed throughout the expedition. Entire confidence was placed in Sir James Hope Grant and its other chiefs. The water of the bay became a pleasant green plain, over which we hastened daily to pay pleasant visits from ship to ship. The little villages on shore gave occasion for lively foraging excursions, on which good Mexican dollars were exchanged for very porcupine-like pigs and ancient fowls. It was extensively rumoured that some man had shot a hare, which led to a general furbishing-up of fowling-pieces. But our gallant allies were not ready; their saddles had been sunk somewhere near Saddle Island, on the coast of China. Further delay was inevitable, and I began to tire of Talien.

The captain of the steamer *Carthage* had some very amusing stories of old times, when he and British rule in India were both a good deal younger than they are at present. Among others, he used to tell of an Indo-Portuguese steward he once had, who, as a deadly act of revenge for some real or fancied insult, filled his pocket with silver spoons, jumped overboard, and so drowned himself.

But such stories were insufficient to make the time pass profitably, and as vessels were running down to Japan for horses and fodder, I took the opportunity of visiting that country of paradisaical renown, and of determining with my own eyes the truth of the marvellous accounts concerning it.

The first half of the passage was a dead calm, over an oily sea, in which numerous sharks were swimming down the coast of the Corea; and we sighted one or two of the

Russian frigates that abound in these waters. But as we approached Nagasaki, there came storm and rain, which greatly improved the wonderful appearance of that picturesque harbour. After the sterile hills of China, it appeared as if we had reached something like the Highlands of Scotland clothed with tropical vegetation, or the Ghauts of Western India in a temperate climate. From the dark-blue sea and white line of foam there suddenly rose dark precipices, fringed with trees and streaked with waterfalls. Above these were hills clothed with the richest dark-green verdure, and varied with wood, or else by terraced gardens and fields; while still beyond rose pine-covered mountains, breaking through white mists, and capped with dark slate-coloured clouds. Like Tennyson's Ida, it was—

' Lovelier

Than all the valleys of Ionian hills.
The swimming vapour slopes athwart the glen,
Puts forth an arm and creeps from pine to pine,
And loiters, slowly drawn. On either hand
The lawns and meadow ledges, midway down,
Hang rich in flowers, and far below them roars
The long brook, falling through the cloven ravine
In cataract after cataract to the sea.'

Shortly after casting anchor, we were put in charge of a couple of sworded custom-officers, who placed in our hands the following interesting specimen of Japanese English, which will be acceptable to all students of idiom:

' THE PROHIBITION.

' To be throwed ballast out of all ships in this port.

' To be done any remain of ships at the outside of this
   port, and
' To be fished and hunted in this port and shore.
   1st year of banyan.
     The Government
       at
     Nagasaky.'

This singular mixture of English, Dutch, and Japanese
idioms will be found quite intelligible after a little study, but
it stands in very unfavourable contrast with the English
spoken by the Japanese officials who have been told off for
that purpose. They are not like the Chinese in this respect,
for the English which they do speak is wonderfully accurate
and pure, and is used by some of them with considerable
fluency. On the other hand, Japanese is infinitely easier to
learn than the Celestial tongue. It is almost impossible to
help picking up a little of it, so characteristic, and yet so easy
of pronunciation, are many of its words and phrases. In this
respect it is even easier than Italian and Hindustani, though,
as with the former language, difficulties accumulate upon the
learner as he proceeds. It would be hard to avoid, even if
one wished it, picking up such words as *O-ha-yo*, ' Good
day ', or rather equivalent to that; *Jigi jigi*, ' Make haste ';
Pigi pigi, ' Go away '; *Ip-iocha*, ' Very good '; *Kore wa gin
sen nan mu i ka?* ' How many dollars is this?'

The little artificial island of Desima, to which the
Dutch were formerly confined, the wrestlers, the tea-
houses, and the other lions of Nagasaki, have been already
sufficiently described, and I need only say that the houses
are scrupulously clean; the ladies are indubitably fine-
looking; and a bull-necked wrestler sufficiently proved that
he could throw me over his head, though the operation was

not entirely carried out. At this time a number of horses were being conveyed for the China expedition from Kanagawa, in the neighbourhood of the capital, and it had been found that they fared ill upon the long and rough outer sea-passage. Consequently it was resolved, with the not very willing permission of the Japanese authorities, but under the guidance of pilots which they provided, to try if a sailing vessel could be towed through the Suwo Nada, or Inland Sea of Japan—a passage which had been already explored by a Dutch steamer, and by H.M. steamer *Cruizer*. This inner passage runs from Nagasaki up the west and north coasts of Kiusiu [Kyushu], among the innumerable small islands which lie between it and the Goto Islands. After a narrow strait at Hirado Island, there is a piece of clear sea on the north stretching out into the Corean Straits; thence by Wilson Island, and about the 34th parallel of north latitude, the course lies through a very narrow passage, not more than a quarter of a mile in breadth, between Kiusiu and Nippon [Honshu], into the Inland Sea, which is formed by these islands and that of Sikok [Shikoku], the principal ones of Japan. This Suwo Sea stretches from nearly 131° longitude to a little beyond 135°, and is from sixty to ten miles in breadth. It is scattered over with numerous islands, and has two other entrances besides that just mentioned—the Bungo Channel on the west, and the King [Kii] on the east, of Sikok. At its eastern extremity there is the most important port, Hiogo, which is to be opened to foreigners in 1863, beside Ohosaka [Osaka], the greatest port of the empire, and at the mouth of the River Engawa, on which stands the city of Miako, the residence of the Mikado or Spiritual Emperor, and the greatest commercial emporium in the ' Land of the Rising Sun '. I gladly embraced the opportunity of going through this sea, as that was really passing through a great portion of the interior of the country without encountering the almost insuperable obstacles to which the traveller would otherwise be exposed. It was also of great interest to be able to see Ohosaka, which had not then been visited by any European in modern times, and which must afford by far the greater part of our future trade with Japan.

The vessels selected for this somewhat doubtful trip were the steamer *Sydney* of the Indian Navy, and the American ship *Fanny M'Henry*, chartered to the British Government, but commanded by Captain Smith, a young Virginian, and a most courteous and agreeable specimen of the ' Old Dominion '. Leaving Nagasaki, or ' Long Cape ', as its meaning implies, we soon reached Hirado Island, and proceeded through a narrow passage of two or three miles in length, with a pretty sharp turn in it, a fort on either side, and barely room for large vessels to pass. Here a rather exciting incident occurred. When we were about two-thirds through, and opposite one of the forts, the tiller-chains of the steamer got jammed, and it came to a dead stop in the middle of the channel. That was all very well for the steamer, which could keep itself pretty stationary; but the twelve-hundred-ton ship behind had not only a great deal of way on it, but had also its topsails set; so there was no rest for it, and down it came towards the steamer, almost justifying the exclamation of a startled Irish sailor—" Jasus, we're into her! " It seemed as if the *Fanny* had no choice between running down the tug or running herself upon the rocks; but by the narrowest shave she managed to get past without doing either. One of the hawsers by which the two vessels were attached was cut away in time, but in the confusion of the moment the other was allowed to remain until it turned the head of the ship towards one of the sides of the passage, and shaved off the cabin windows of the steamer before it snapped, from the strain upon it, with a noise like the report of a small cannon. Then there came a trying manœuvre for the ship in which I was. With the wind still in her topsails, she flew across the narrow channel like a thing of life determined to dash itself in pieces against the opposite shore. But luckily our captain was a thorough seaman, and his crew were all active able-bodied English sailors. Never have I seen even a man-of-war more smartly handled. The men flew to the different ropes with wonderful speed, and the vessel was put about just in time to escape destruction; for, on looking over the stern, I saw it was only two or three feet from the sharp-pointed rocks which lined the shore.

Even there the danger did not end. The water of the channel was too deep to allow of anchoring, and the current was too strong to allow of our lying-to; so there was nothing for it but to make a bold attempt to sail on, though the three Japanese pilots were all on board the steamer; and across the further entrance, through which we had to take our perilous way, there was an ugly line of reefs. Fortune, however, was in our favour, and we sailed safely through into more open water, where anchorage was found until the steamer again took us in tow. This adventure rather interfered with observations; but I saw there was a large town on the island of Hirado, with the residence of a Damio or prince, surrounded with trees and fortifications. The people on shore appeared quite stupified by the extraordinary, and, to them, inexplicable nature of our manœuvres. Perhaps they thought that a sudden fit of insanity had attacked the *Fanny M'Henry*, or that our motions were preliminary to an attack upon their position.

Towards evening we got pretty well clear of islands, and on our left—

' There gloomed the dark broad sea '

of the Corean Strait. As it was too dark then to proceed farther, we steamed round and round till daylight, when we found ourselves beside Iki Island, and off the western entrance of the Inland Sea. The mountains which stretched round were bolder, and with less wood upon them, than those passed on the previous day. The passage we had now to go through was that between the great islands of Kiusiu and Nippon; and the abundance of population began to show itself. There were numbers of large junks, perfectly clean, elaborately carved, and each carrying a large beautiful white sail on a mast composed of various pieces of wood bound together with rings of iron, as is the case with the best class of English and American ships. The lower hills had plenty of wood; the sandy gravel of the shore was covered with trees and bushes to where it abruptly broke at the water's edge; and there was sufficient bright blue sky, with a few white clouds floating across it, to give fine effects of light and shade on the forests and green fields which stretched up the hills behind, and on the great green rolling mountains beyond. On the right, as the passage began to narrow, there was a Damio's palace, and a large town, or a succession of villages, extending for several miles, and larger than Nagasaki. The junks which we saw did not appear to have any guns or stink-pots like those of China; for foreign trade, with its disorganising influence, had not been there to prepare the way for native piracy. The snug little bays and villages had quaint vessels lying before them, some of which were painted, gilded, and adorned with fine carved filigree work. The cottages of the smaller villages were shaped somewhat like the huts of the islands of the Pacific; but in the other villages there were good large houses, some of them double-storeyed, others with verandas round, and steps leading up to them. Every turn of our ship gave some new effect of scenery; and the chief impression conveyed was the beauty, the quietness, the peacefulness of this entrance to the Inland Sea. Surely we had reached ' the haunts of ancient peace '.

> ' I stood upon a shore, a pleasant shore,
> Where a sweet clime was breathed from a land
> Of fragrance, quietness, and trees and flowers.
> Full of calm joy it was . . .
> Too full of joy and soft delicious warmth;
> So that I felt a movement in my heart
> To chide and to reproach that solitude
> With songs of misery, music of our woes.'

Such were the lines which occurred to my recollection in connection with this new sea and these pleasant isles: for it is not likely that the Japanese will long be left undisturbed in the happiness which they evidently enjoy beyond any other people. The rude music, not of our woes, but of Western activity, will soon disturb, and are already disturbing, the ancient arrangements of those happy isles.

The town upon the right, on entering the channel, is called Kokura, and after passing it the sunken rocks in the way are pointed out by tall erect stones, hat-shaped at the top. Indeed, all through the Inland Sea, sunken rocks are marked by stone shafts; and other means, such as light-houses, have been employed to render navigation safe.

After passing a junk-building yard, we came on another large town upon the left, called Simonosaki, with fine temples behind it embosomed in wood. In front there was an excellent stone sea-wall, with convenient piers, which might put Hong Kong to shame, with large junks lying alongside of them. The whole town seemed to have turned out to gaze at us, and the wonder-struck crews of the native vessels raised their arms to us by way of saluta-tion. Large as the town was, one cannot go a day's sail up the waters in the neighbourhood of Canton without meeting half a dozen of the same size, or even larger. Japan by no means struck me as being so thickly populated as China; and I should think Dr Williams's estimate of about twenty millions of people to be probably near the truth.*

After leaving Simonosaki, the passage began to open up into a wide loch, with lower, but still picturesque, hills on either side. It reminded me strongly of Lake Windermere, but had quite a number of beautiful wooded islets. Then it was that the Suwo Nada opened before us, and the moun-tains became dim in the distance, while a fresh cool breeze ruffled its inland waters, which had then scarcely been vexed by any foreign keels. It was something to get into what, by a certain stretch of phraseology, might be called ' a new sea '; but I believe we went downstairs to discuss Shanghae fowls and drink claret-and-water.

Proceeding down the Inland Sea, the south shore was about ten miles distant, and the north about fifteen. The white puckered sails of junks were plentifully scattered over the blue water, and their seamen examined us through rather dim telescopes of native manufacture. On the south

* S. W. Williams: *The Middle Kingdom* (1848).—Publisher's note.

side the mountains were very high, rising up occasionally into volcano-like peaks. There was a good deal of wood and pasture upon them, but also many barren streaks, especially near the shore, and the country was not so rich as it is on the other side of the Iki Passage. Still, everywhere in Japan the amount of wood excites attention. The fields are surrounded by thick belts of tangled trees and brush-wood, and the growth is preserved by a Japanese law, which requires every person who cuts down a tree to plant another instead.

On the second day after entering we were surprised by observing an English-rigged cutter in the distance, and for a moment entertained the fancy that perhaps Lord Dufferin, or some other adventurous English yachtsman, might be trying to grope his way before us ' into the bowls of Japan '; but it proved to be a vessel which one of the Damios had got on a foreign model. The Japanese have some wonderful antique-looking large vessels, in imitation of what must have been the Dutch build about two centuries ago; but they are by no means backward in adopting improvements which increase their command over their own seas. Already they have several steamers, which they know well how to manage, and very lately one of these crossed the Pacific, from San Francisco to Yedo [Tokyo], managed entirely by Japanese officers and engineers. This disposition of theirs to adopt the machinery and also the arms of the West is very laudable; but it will enable them to keep their own internal trade by water in their own hands; and it will evidently make them much more formidable in war than the Chinese have ever been. In such a case they would probably draw further supplies of arms from Holland or America; and it is to be noticed that the policy of the United States in Japan—which country they were the first to open up in recent times, and which they are disposed to claim as a special field of their own—has been latterly in opposition to that pursued by the representatives of England and France.

After passing, on our right, the entrance of the Bungo Channel, which runs southwards to the open ocean, the Suwo Nada appeared to close up altogether, owing to the immense number of islands and islets—

> ' Summer isles of Eden lying
> In dark purple spheres of sea.'

Many of these were almost pyramidal-shaped, and yet terraced, for purposes of cultivation, in an almost impossible manner. We tried to anchor for the night quite close to a village on one of these islands, but could not get sufficiently shallow water, though we almost brushed the shore. The people, and especially the women and children, came out in great numbers in boats to see us, and were not backward in their salutations and exclamations of gratified surprise. They raised so loud a laugh when ' the Doctor ', our black cook, showed his head over the bulwarks, that even that hardened individual was abashed, and withdrew, cursing, to his own sanctuary. A little way beyond, there was anchorage in ten fathoms, and the passages opened up into pretty broad stretches of water between numerous islands, which sometimes formed quite a labyrinth. Every little bay had a village in it, and the bright verdure came down close to the water's edge; but here and there a red barren hill looked as if it had been peeled of its vegetation. A sky so bright and blue, and an air so dry and pure as that we then enjoyed, are rarely to be found anywhere. On the southern side the hills seemed to be composed chiefly of marl and limestone, with quarries in them; but as this, the fourth day of our voyage, drew on, the hills became very barren, being of hard rounded sandstone, only very imperfectly sprinkled over with bushes and trees. Some spots, however, were very beautiful, with wood running up grass-covered hills, like strips of dark embroidery on a light-green velvet mantle, while in the sandstone above the water's edge there were wave-worn caves, which Don Juan and Haidée would not have despised.

On the south, the high mountains of Sikok, crowned with white clouds, marked the coastline. Possibly the pilots went unnecessarily about among the islands in order to make the navigation appear as intricate as possible; but, if not, they must have had the bump of locality most enormously developed in order to remember the way. On some of the more richly wooded hills there was table-land at the top, with green cultivated fields and tracts of warm sunny pasture spotted with little black cattle. It being just after the close of the wet season (which was late this year), and in the middle of summer, the country looked exceeding fresh and green. The variety and succession of views were too great to allow many of them being impressed upon the mind: and we felt as if making a rapid survey of a large picture-gallery or a long moving panorama. This kind of work is, after all, not very satisfactory. Goethe has said that, when he desired to understand the power of nature, he selected an *eckchen*, or little corner, for contemplation. A certain repose is necessary if we are to realise the life, the power of nature, when manifested in the translucent depth of air, the calm sleeping sea, the awful mountain-forms; and to appreciate her wilder moods, she must be seen when shaken by her own fury, driving the clouds across the sky, lashing the waves into foam, and tossing the arms of the trees toward the darkened heaven.

Passing into a picturesque loch, with high dark wooded hills around, and a mile or two in breadth, we noticed many fields interspersed among the trees and jungle. In a small bay, just beyond, there was a large dock, substantially walled in, and a gently shelving sandy shore affording good anchorage. Here a number of old women came out to gaze at us in fishing sampans, looking out of their bleared old eyes in mute amazement at having lived to see the day. In a larger sea, on which we soon entered, bounded on the south by the high mountains of Sikok, and on the north by innumerable islands, and with no visible outlet to it, the barren redness of some of the hills rather augmented the brilliancy of the scene by adding another colour to the deep blue of the water, the bright blue of the sky, the forests' dark green hue, and the white shining clouds lying along the mountaintops. As we got on, however, not even the coast of southern China could have presented a more sterile appearance; and from one of the mountains on the south there rose the yellow smoke of a volcano.

Suddenly another change: we were among small islands, lying close together, of soft rock worn by the sea into fretted caves, and covered thickly with green ferns. There were little bays with sandy beaches, and little cottages where one would gladly have made selection for a summer residence. The larger villages had breakwaters and piers before them, indicating no small amount of enterprise and trade. From inquiries afterwards made, I found that the shores of this Inland Sea might afford large quantities of oil and sugar—the former at three dollars for a tub of about sixteen gallons, and the latter (refined and white) at about six cents a pound. Firewood is also exceedingly cheap, is in abundance, and might be profitably taken over to China.

The morning of our fifth day, as the anchor was being raised, presented a most wonderful dawn. First a pale translucent green light filled the whole heaven, gradually changing into a deep ruddy brown, which seemed not so much to colour as to permeate water, islands, and sky, and from that softening into a celestial rosy red. Beside the white castle of a Damio, near which we had anchored, there was the tree-fringed *Tocaido*—the great road which runs the entire length of the three large islands of Japan. Here as elsewhere, where I had the opportunity of travelling upon it, it is a fine white broad road, in excellent repair, with side-walks for foot-passengers, lines of trees on either side, and tea-houses at convenient distances for the refreshment of travellers. These houses have no furniture beyond the beautifully clean matting of their floors; but, when required, the wearied wayfarer will be provided with a stool of some kind, and with a quilt and a small bamboo pillow. Tea, rice, fish, and sweet cakes are served by young female attendants, who take pleasure in making themselves as agreeable as possible, and whose appearance is often very charming, if not strictly beautiful in Western eyes, from their ruddy complexions, finely-developed forms, desire to please, and over-beaming cheerfulness. Indeed there was nothing which struck me so much everywhere, and with all classes in Japan, as the unmistakable and unvarying happiness of the people. Certainly, if that is to be the test of national success, they have surpassed all nations. Never did I hear a word spoken in anger, or behold a cross, uncomfortable look; and their faces present either aspects of calm complacency, or smiling enjoyment, or of hearty amusement. If this be sometimes hypocrisy, it is a hypocrisy so like reality as to be quite as good as it, and quite undistinguishable from it. If hypocrisy, it is even more wonderful, and quite as admirable, as the reality could be; for the display of suffering and annoyance is very disagreeable to others, and society owes much to those who always present a smiling face, whatever their internal feelings may be. In this respect our highest and most civilised classes resemble the people of the far East.

' It may be we shall touch the Happy Isles,'—

when our spirits shall float into the serenity of other airs than those we breathe on earth; but he who has visited the country of the ' Sun's Origin ' has already had a foretaste of what they may be.

Towards the east end of the Suwo Nada the sea opened out widely, and leaving the King Channel on our right, we found ourselves in a vast bay, the shores of which were crowded with towns, villages, and white palaces, and the water all dotted over with innumerable junks making their way to or from the great port Ohosaka. The end of this bay forms a large semicircle, across which ran a ripple-line marking the influence of the fresh water from the River Engawa, which falls into it. On shore the semicircle was occupied by the town of Ohosaka, extending apparently about ten miles, and diversified by large white palaces surrounded with trees. A thick line of junks kept advancing into the river, showing that the trade of the place must be enormous; and as they followed the windings of the stream, their sails appeared to be moving among the trees on land. The fields to the left of the river as we faced the town were very low, and protected by large substantial sea-walls. Numerous junks were lying at anchor beside similar walls raised for their protection, and lines of stakes pointed out the way of entrance. Many of the junks were lying beside a large building, probably the custom-house; and near it there was a strong fortification, armed with cannon. The river appeared to be run off into numerous canals, which traversed the town in all directions, and were frequently crossed by elegant bridges, over which streams of passengers were passing. Though foreigners have not been at Ohosaka for long, it was visited by Jesuit missionaries in the sixteenth and seventeenth centuries; and it was in 1614 that the Emperor Xogunsama drove away all Christians from it. A curious and interesting work, entitled *Ambassades vers les Empereurs du Japan*, published at Amsterdam in 1680, mentions that at Ohosaka there was a ' *temple des diables* ', where the Japanese adore a frightful statue, who wears a crown full of diamonds on the head of a bear. The narrator makes the important statement that ' *Les Japonnais honorent les diables, et leur font toutes sorte d'offrandes et de cultes religieux, afin qu'ils ne leur fassent point de mal.*'

We steamed within two miles of the shore, and found there a depth of about five fathoms; but for many miles before that the lead had given only from seven to five fathoms; so, though the bay is exposed to the south-west, no very heavy sea could get into it; large vessels might ride out a storm from that quarter, and on other sides they are effectually protected. In the distance the mountains converge, forming the valley of the Engawa, on which, forty miles off, is Miako—'the Capital'—where the Mikado—'the Lord of the World'—or Spiritual Emperor, resides in a state of deified isolation, which would be perfectly intolerable were it not relieved by a large number of wives. The Siogoun, or Temporal Emperor, of course, resides at Yedo—'River's Door'—where the temporal business of the country is chiefly transacted; but Miako is the greatest manufacturing place and commercial emporium of the whole empire. None of the other ports can for a moment compare in size and importance with Ohosaka, or 'Great Board', which had been rightly described, shortly before, by Dr Williams, as 'one of the largest cities in the empire, but not yet visited by any foreign ships'. Its great extent was not less striking than its appearance, so far as our glasses could determine, of prosperity and wealth.

It was extremely provoking not to be able to land in order to visit this place, but that was strictly forbidden to us. I have no doubt it could have been done, notwithstanding the objections of Japanese officials; and they would probably have allowed us to proceed *nay-boen*, or being there as if we were not there; but 'the expedition'—to dignify our two vessels—had received orders not to allow any parties to land from it. So there was no help for it; and after going in as close as was deemed safe, we steamed for about ten miles along the north side of the bay to Hiogo, the place which is to be opened to foreign trade in 1863, or even earlier if her Majesty's Plenipotentiary can prevail on the Government to do so.

The shore, as we went along, was almost a continuous stretch of villages, but soon rose up behind into mountainous cliffs, on one of which were two white houses that might have been the abodes of hermits. The port of Hiogo is formed by a neck of land running southward from the north shore, and so effectually protected from the south-west winds, to which Ohosaka is exposed. There is very good anchorage at about four or five fathoms, and this depth of water is found quite close to the shore.

Indeed, a platform might almost be run from the beach on to a vessel lying at anchor with short chain; and a few stone piers, such as the Japanese know so well how to construct, will make it one of the most commodious places in the world for shipping. It is quite close enough to Ohosaka for the purposes of trade, and yet far enough off to allow the foreign residents plenty of room to move about without annoying the inhabitants of the large town by their peculiar habits, and their disregard of all the manners which the Japanese regard as constituting politeness. The Japanese represent Ohosaka to be subject to very violent earthquakes, but the extent of the town and the size of many of the buildings go to contradict the statement.

When anchoring for the night at Hiogo, our vessel, through mismanagement on board the steamer, got in among some junks that were lying at anchor, and threatened to do them damage. It was very interesting to notice the extreme coolness and quietness displayed by the Japanese boatmen on this occasion. They exerted themselves manfully and ingeniously; but it was without any bustle, outcry, or apparent excitement. Even the author of *Guy Livingstone** would have been satisfied with their conduct, and must have set them down, according to his theories, as aristocratic braves. During the evening a number of people from shore paid us visits, but they were all of the lower class; and one of them, I am sorry to say, demeaned himself so far as to steal a pepper-box. That, however, was the only thing taken, and otherwise no fault could be found with their demeanour; nor was their natural curiosity displayed in any impertinent manner. They seemed to know something about us, for many of them accosted us with the phrase, " *Ingleese Ipiocha* ", and

* G. A. Lawrence (1827-76).—Publisher's note.

appeared to rejoice at the prospect of the very good English being settled in their neighbourhood. Nothing was to be got from them, even for itzebues, except some fish of an inferior kind.

On leaving in the morning we had a practical illustration of the closeness with which vessels might approach the shore; for, when attaching the hawsers and getting under way, the *Fanny* was allowed to drift so close in that it really looked as if one could jump from her on to the beach. Certainly Hiogo is to be the place for foreigners in Japan, and Nagasaki and Yokohama must hide their diminished heads before it. The mercantile houses will have their headquarters there, and the waters of the Inland Sea will afford them delightful opportunities for boat and yacht excursions. But it will not do to anticipate, for the prospects of foreign trade in Japan have been all along somewhat doubtful, and now the recent attack on the residence of the British Minister at Yedo threatens new difficulties. The fact is, that the people of these islands are able to supply themselves with all that they know or wish for without going abroad for a single article, and their rulers are by no means anxious that wants should be created which can only be supplied from other countries, nor do they see that they are called on to supply silk or anything else to the rest of the world. The state of isolation in which their beautiful country has lain for two centuries has evidently been highly favourable to its internal development and enjoyment, so it is no wonder that they look upon the foreign intruders with disfavour, and throw very puzzling obstacles in our way, without committing themselves, as yet, to acts which would lead to open war.

Their policy at present is, to weary out foreigners by

affected slowness of comprehension and difficulty of movement. *Elle est pleine de finesse sous l'apparence de bêtise.* This *vis inertiae* of theirs has been calculated and used with great skill. They have not been able to understand the most simple matters, and the most urgent affairs have been treated with forms and ceremonies involving an enormous loss of time. Yet care has been taken to avoid giving open ground of offence. My individual opinion, however, is not only that the Japanese are ready to go to war with us, if they find they cannot otherwise protect their peculiar institutions from our innovating influence, but that, owing to their warlike character and the nature of their country, we shall find it no joke to deal with them on that platform. Perhaps it may be as well for us to consider, before having recourse to that *ultima ratio* sometimes of fools as well as of wise kings, whether our representatives there, both officials and merchants, have not been rather putting the cart before the horse, fancying they had only to cry out " Sesame!" in order to open up the country and obtain all they desired.

After leaving Hiogo we steered across the bay in a south-westerly direction toward the large island of Awadsi [Awaji] and the King Channel. The weather this day rather increased in heat, but still, though the 19th of July, it was never uncomfortable, the thermometer not rising above 80° in the cabin. At the inner entrance of the King Channel there were some forts of substantial masonry commanding it, and a very large one in course of construction. Some officials came out from these forts to make a report upon us, and kept up with us for some time in a four-oared boat. We could see that they not only wrote down long descriptions of the foreign vessels, but also made drawings of them. Through the King we passed into the open sea on the southern coast of Japan, and on the second day saw the snow-streaked peak of the volcano Fusi-yama, the holy mountain of Japan, rising above high distant clouds. The white palaces of the Damios which we saw from the Inland Sea may have had their traditions and dread memories, the villages their simple but affecting tales, and the mountains their ancient legends; but to us these things were a sealed book. All that was open to us on which to report was the beautiful scenery of a succession of sea lochs unparalleled in any other part of the world, and the indications of the existence of a large, industrious, comfortable, and almost wealthy population such as mountains and islands nowhere else present.

[November 1861

5

EVENING ON THE VELD

John Buchan

We leave the broken highway, channelled by rains and rutted by ox-wagons, and plunge into the leafy coolness of a great wood. Great in circumference only, for the blue gums and pines and mimosa bushes are scarcely six years old, though the feathery leafage and the frequency of planting make a thicket of the young trees. The rides are broad and grassy as an English holt, dipping into hollows, climbing steep ridges, and showing at intervals little side-alleys, ending in green hills, with the accompaniment everywhere of the spicy smell of gums and the deep rooty fragrance of pines. Sometimes all alien woodland ceases, and we ride through aisles of fine trees, which have nothing save height to distinguish them from Rannoch or Rothiemurchus. A deer looks shyly out, which might be a roebuck; the cooing of doves, the tap of a woodpecker, even the hawk above in the blue heavens, have nothing strange. Only an occasional widow-bird with its ridiculous flight, an ant-heap to stumble over, and a clump of scarlet veld-flowers are there to mark the distinction. Here we have the sign visible of man's conquest over the soil, and of the real adaptability of the land. With care and money great tracts of the high-veld might change their character. An English country-house, with deer-park and coverts and fish-ponds, could be created here and in many kindred places, where the owner might forget his continent. And in time this will happen. As the rich man pushes farther out from the city for his home, he will remake the most complaisant of countries to suit his taste, and, save for climate and a certain ineradicable flora and fauna, patches of Surrey and Perthshire will appear on this kindly soil.

With the end of the wood we come out upon the veld. What is this mysterious thing, this veld, so full of memories for the English race, so omnipresent, so baffling? Like the words ' prairie ', ' moor ', and ' down ', it is easy to make a rough mental picture of. It will doubtless become in time, when South Africa gets herself a literature, a conventional counter in description. Today every London shop-boy knows what this wilderness of coarse green or brown grasses is like; he can picture the dry streams, the jagged koppies, the glare of summer and the bitter winter cold. It has entered into patriotic jingles, and has given a *mise-en-scène* to crude melodrama. And yet no natural feature was ever so hard to fully realise. One cannot think of a monotonous vastness, like the prairie, for it is everywhere broken up and varied. It is too great for an easy appreciation, as of an English landscape, too subtle and diverse for rhetorical generalities—a thing essentially mysterious and individual. In consequence it has a charm which the common efforts of Mother Earth after grandiloquence can never possess. There is something homely and kindly and soothing in it, something essentially humane and fitted to the needs of human life. Climb to the top of the nearest ridge, and after a broad green valley there will be another ridge just the same: cross the mountains fifty miles off, and the country will repeat itself as before. But this sameness in outline is combined with an infinite variety in detail, so that we readily take back our first complaint of monotony, and wonder at the intricate novelty of each vista.

Here the veld is simply the broad green side of a hill, with blue points of mountain peeping over the crest, and a ragged brown road scarred across it. The road is as hard as adamant, a stiff red clay baked by the sun into porphyry, with fissures yawning here and there, so deep that often it is hard to see the gravel at the bottom. A cheerful country to drive in on a dark night in a light English cart, but less deadly to the lumbering wagons of the farmer. We choose the grass to ride on, which grows in coarse clumps with bare soil between. Here, too, are traps for the loose rider. A conical ant-heap with odd perforations, an ant-bear hole three feet down, or, most insidious of all, a meerkat's hole hidden behind a tuft of herbage. A good pony can gallop and yet steer, provided the rider trusts it; but the best will make mistakes, and on occasion roll over like a rabbit. Most men begin with a dreary apprenticeship to spills; but it is curious how few are hurt, despite the hardness of the ground. One soon learns the art of falling clear and falling softly.

The four o'clock December sun blazes down on us, raising hot odours from the grass. A grey African hare starts from its form, a meerkat slips away indignantly, a widow-bird, coy and ridiculous like a flirtatious widow, flops on ahead. The sleepy, long-horned Afrikaner cattle raise listless eyes as we pass, and a few gaudy butterflies waver athwart us. Otherwise there is no sound or sight of life. Flowers of rich colours—chrysanthemums, gentians, geraniums—most of them variants of familiar European species, grow in clumps so lowly that one can only observe them by looking directly from above. It is this which makes the veld so colourless to a stranger. There are no gowans or buttercups or heather, to blazon it like a spring meadow or an August moorland. Five yards off, and nothing is visible but the green stalks of grass or a red boulder.

At the summit of the ridge there is a breeze and a far prospect. The road still runs on up hill and down dale, through the distant mountains, and on to the great pastoral uplands of Rustenburg and the far north-west. On either side the same waving grass, now grey and now green as the wind breathes over it. Below is a glen with a gleam of water, and some yards of tender lawn on either bank. Farmhouses line the sides, each with its dam, its few acres of untidy crop land, and its bower of trees. Beyond rise line upon line of green ridges, with a glimpse of woods and dwellings set far apart, till in the far distance the bold spurs of the Magaliesberg stand out against the sky. A thin trail of smoke from some veld-fire hangs between us and the mountains, tempering the intense clearness of an African prospect. There is something extraordinarily delicate and remote about the vista; it might be a mirage, did not the map bear witness to its reality. It is not unlike a child's conception of the landscape of Bunyan, a road running straight through a mystical green country, with the hilltops of the Delectable Mountains to cheer the pilgrim. And indeed the land is instinct with romance. The names of the gorges which break the mountain line—Olifants' Port, Crocodile Port, Commando Nek—speak of war and adventure and the far tropics beyond these pastoral valleys. The little farms are all ' Rests ' and ' Fountains ', the true nomenclature of a far-wandering, home-loving people. The slender rivulet below us is one of the topmost branches of the great Limpopo, rising in a marsh in the wood behind us, forcing its way through the hills and the bush-veld to the north, and travelling thence through jungles and fever-swamps to the Portuguese sea-coast. The road is one of the old highways of exploration; it is not fifty years since a white man first saw the place. And yet it is as pastoral as Yarrow or Exmoor; it has the green simplicity of sheep-walks and the homeliness of a long-settled rustic land. In the afternoon peace there is no hint of the foreign or the garish; it is as remote as Holland itself from the unwhole-some splendours of the East and South.

No landscape is so masterful as the veld. Broken up into valleys, reclaimed in parts by man, showing fifty varieties of scene, it yet preserves one essential character. For, homely as it is, it is likewise untameable. There are no fierce encroachments about it. A deserted garden does not return to the veld for many years, if ever. It is not, like the jungle, the natural enemy of man, waiting for a chance to enter and obliterate his handiwork, and repelled only by sleepless watching. Rather it is the quiet spectator of human efforts ready to meet them half-way, and yet from its vastness always the dominant feature in any landscape. Its normal air is sad, grey, and Quakerish, never flamboy-ant under the brightest sun, and yet both strenuous and restful. The few red monstrosities man has built on its edge serve only to set off this essential dignity. For one thing, it is not created according to the scale of man. It will give him a home, but he will never alter its aspect. Let him plough and reap it for a thousand years, and he may beautify and fructify but never change it. The face of England has altered materially in two centuries, because England is on a human scale—a parterre land, without intrinsic wildness. But cultivation on the veld will always be superimposed: it will remain, like Egypt, ageless and immutable—one of the primeval types of the created world.

But, though dominant, it is also adaptable. It can, for the moment, assume against its unchangeable background a chameleon-like variety. Sky and weather combine to make it imitative at times. Now, under a pale Italian sky, it is the Campagna—hot, airless, profoundly melancholy. Again, when the mist drives over it, and wet scarps of hill stand out among clouds, it is Dartmoor or Liddesdale; or on a radiant evening, when the mountains are one bank of hazy purple, it has borrowed from Skye and the far West Highlands. On a clear steely morning it has the air of its namesake, the Norwegian fjells—in one way the closest of its parallels. But each phase passes, the tantalising memory goes, and we are back again upon the aboriginal veld, so individual that we wonder whence arose the illusion.

A modern is badly trained for appreciating certain kinds of scenery. Generations of poets and essayists have so stamped the ' pathetic fallacy ' upon his soul that wherever he goes, unless in the presence of a Niagara or a Mount Everest, he runs wild, looking for a human interest or a historical memory. This is well enough in the old settled lands, but on the veld it is curiously inept. The man who, in Emerson's phrase, seeks ' to impress his English whim upon the immutable past ', will find little reward for his gymnastics. Not that there is no history of a kind—of Bantu wars, and great tribal immigrations, of wandering gold-seekers and Portuguese adventurers, of the voortrekker and the heroic battles in the wilds. But the veld is so little subject to human life that had Thermopylae been fought in yonder nek, or had Saint Francis wandered on this hillside, it would have mastered and obliterated the memories. It has its history; but it is the history of cosmic forces, of the cycle of seasons, of storms and suns and floods, the joys and sorrows of the natural world.

> ' Lo, for there among the flowers and grasses,
>   Only the mightier movement sounds and passes;
>   Only winds and rivers,
>   Life and death.'

Men dreamed of it and its wealth long ago in Portugal and Holland. They have quarrelled about it in London and Cape Town, fought for it, parcelled it out in maps, bought it and sold it. It has been subject for long to the lusts and hopes of man. It has been larded with epithets; town-bred folk have made theories about it; armies have rumbled across it; the flood of high politics has swept it—

> ' That torrent of unquiet dream
>   That mortals truth and reason deem.'

But the veld has no memory of it. Men go and come, kingdoms fall and rise, but it remains austere, secluded, impenetrable, the ' still unravished bride of quietness '.

As one lives with it the thought arises: May not some future civilisation grow up here in keeping with the grave country? The basis of every civilisation is wealth—wealth to provide the background of leisure, which in turn is the basis of culture in a commercial world. Our colonial settlements have hitherto been fortuitous. They have fought a hard fight for a livelihood, and in the process missed the finer formative influences of the land. When, then, civilisation came it was naturally a borrowed one—English with an accent. But here, as in the old Greek colonies, we begin *de novo*, and at a certain high plane of life. The Dutch, our forerunners, acquired the stamp of the soil, but they lived on the barest scale of existence, and were without the aptitude or the wealth to go further. Our situation is different. We start rich, and with a prospect of growing richer. On one side are the mining centres—cosmopolitan, money-making, living at a strained pitch; on the other this silent country. The time will come when the rich man will leave the towns, and, as most of them are educated and all are able men, he will create for himself a leisured country life. His sons in turn will grow up with something auto-chthonous in their nature. For those who are truly South Africans at heart, and do not hurry to Europe to spend their wealth, there is a future, we believe, of another kind than they contemplate. All great institutions are rooted and grounded in the soil. There is an art, a literature, a school of thought implicit here for the understanding heart—no tarnished European importation, but the natural, spontaneous fruit of the land.

As we descend into the glen the going underfoot grows softer, the flinty red clay changes to sand, and soon to an irregular kind of turf. At last we are on the streambank, and the waving grasses have gone. Instead there is the true meadow growth, reeds and water-plants and a species of gorgeous scarlet buck-bean, little runnels from the farm-dams creep among the rushes, and soon our horses' feet are squelching through a veritable bog. Here are the sights and sounds of a Hampshire water-meadow. Swallows skim over the pools; dragon-flies and bees brush past; one almost expects to see a great trout raise a sleepy head from yonder shining reach. But there are no trout, alas, none, I fear, nearer than Natal; only a small greenish barbel who is a giant at four to the pound. The angler will get small satisfaction here, though on the Mooi River, above Potcherfstroom, I heave heard stories of a golden-scaled monster who will rise to a sea-trout fly. As we jump the little mill-lades, a perfect host of frogs are leaping in the grass, and small bright-eyed lizards slip off the stones at our approach. But, though the glen is quick with life, there is no sound: a deep Sabbatical calm broods over all things. The cry of a Kaffir driver from the highroad we have left breaks with an almost startling violence on the quiet. The tall reeds hush the stream's flow, the birds seem songless, even the hum of insects is curiously dim. There is nothing for the ear, but much for the eye and more for the nostril. Our ride has been through a treasure-house of sweet scents. First the pines and gum-trees; then the drowsy sweetness of the sunburnt veld; and now the more delicate flavour of rich soil and water and the sun-distilled essences of a thousand herbs. What the old Greek wrote of Arabia the Blessed might fitly be written here: ' From this country there is a smell wondrous sweet.'

Lower down the glen narrows. The stream would be a torrent if there were more water; but the cascades are a mere trickle and, only the deep green rock-pools, the banks of shingle, and the worn foot of the cliff, show what this thread can grow to in the rains. A light wild brushwood begins, and creeps down to the very edge of the stream. Twenty years ago lions roamed in this scrub; now we see nothing but two poaching pariah dogs. We pass many little one-storeyed farms, each with a flowergarden run to seed, and some acres of tangled crops. All are deserted. War has been here with its heavy hand, and a broken stoep, empty windows, and a tumbled-in roof are the marks of its passage. The owners may be anywhere—still on commando with Delarey, in Bermuda or Ceylon, in Europe, in camp of refuge, on parole in the towns. Great sunflowers, a foot in diameter, sprawl over the railings, dahlias and marigolds nod in the evening sunshine, and broken fruit-trees lean over the walks. Suddenly from the yard a huge aasvogel flaps out—the bird not of war but of unclean pillage. There is nothing royal in the creature, only obscene ferocity and a furtive greed. But its presence, as it rises high into the air, joined with the fallen rooftrees, effectively drives out Arcady from the scene. We feel we are in a shattered country. This quiet glen, which in peace might be a watered garden, becomes suddenly a desert. The veld is silent, but such secret nooks will blab their tale shamelessly to the passer-by.

The stream bends northward in a more open valley, and as we climb the ridge we catch sight of the country beyond and the same august lines of mountain. But now there is a new feature in the landscape. Bushes are dotted over the far slope and on the brow cluster together into something like a coppice. That is a patch of bush-veld, as rare on our high-veld as are fragments of the old Ettrick forest in Tweeddale. Two hundred miles north is the real bush-veld, full of game and fevers, the barrier between the tropical Limpopo and these grassy uplands. Seen in the splendour of evening there is a curious savagery about that little patch, which is neither veld nor woodland, but something dwarfish and uncanny. That is Africa, the Africa of travellers; but thus far we have ridden through a countryside so homely and familiar that we are not prepared for a foreign intrusion, which leads us to our hope of a new civilisation. If it ever comes, what an outlook it will have into the wilds! In England we look to the sea, in France across a frontier, even in Russia there is a mountain barrier between East and West. But here civilisation will march sharply with barbarism, like a castle of the Pale, looking over a river to a land of mists and outlaws. A man would have but to walk northward, out of the cities and clubs and the whole world of books and talk, to reach the country of the oldest earth-dwellers, the untameable heart of the continent. It is much for a civilisation to have its background—the Egyptian against the Ethiopian, Greek against Thracian, Rome against Gaul. It is also much for a race to have an outlook, a far horizon to which its fancy can turn. Even so strong men are knit and art is preserved from domesticity.

We turn homeward over the long shoulders of hill, keeping to the track in the failing light. If the place is sober by day, it is transformed in the evening. For an hour the land sinks out of account, and the sky is the sole feature. No words can tell the tale of a veld sunset. Not the sun dipping behind the peaks of Jura, or flaming in the mouth of a Norwegian fiord, or sinking, a great ball of fire, in mid-Atlantic, has the amazing pageantry of these upland evenings. A flood of crimson descends on the world, rolling in tides from the flagrant west, and kindling bush and scaur and hill-top, till the land glows and pulsates in a riot of colour. And then slowly the splendour ebbs, lingering only to the west in a shoreless, magical sea. A delicate pearl-grey overspreads the sky, and the onlooker thinks that the spectacle is ended. It has but begun; for there succeed flushes of ineffable colour—purple, rose-pink, tints of no mortal name—each melting imperceptibly into the other, and revealing again the twilight world which the earlier pageant had obscured. Every feature in the land-scape stands out with a tender, amethystine clearness. The mountain-ridge is cut like a jewel against the sky; the track is a ribbon of pure beaten gold. And then the light fades, the air becomes a soft mulberry haze, the first star pricks out in the blue, and night is come.

Here is a virgin soil for art, if the art arises. In our modern history there is no true poetry of vastness and solitude. What there is is temperamental and introspective, not the simple interpretation of a natural fact. In the old world, indeed, there is no room for it; a tortured, crowded land may produce the aptitude, but it cannot give the experience. And the new lands have had no chance to realise their freshness: when their need for literature arose, they have taken it second-hand. The Australian poet sings of the bush in the rococo accents of Fleet Street, and when he is natural he can tell of simple human emotions, but not of the wilds. For the chance of the seeing eye has gone. He is not civilised but de-civilised, having borrowed the raiment of his elder brother. But, if South African conditions be as men believe, here we have a different prospect. The man who takes this country as his own will take it at another level than the pioneer. The veld will be to him more than a hunting-ground, and the seasons may be viewed from another than a commercial standpoint. If the art arises, it will be an austere art—with none of the fatuities of the picturesque, bare of false romance and preciosities, but essentially large, simple, and true. It will be the chronicle of the veld, the song of the cycle of Nature, the epic of life and death, and ' the unimaginable touch of time '. Who can say that from this land some dew of freshness may not descend upon a jaded literature, and the world would be the richer by a new Wordsworth, a more humane Thoreau, or a manlier Sénancour?

Once more we are in the wood, now a ghostly place with dark aisles and the windless hush of evening in the branches. The flying ants are coming out of the ground for their short life of a night. The place is alive with wings, moths and strange insects, that go white and glimmering in the dusk.

The clear darkness that precedes moonrise is over the earth, so that everything stands out clear in a kind of dark-green monochrome. Something of an antique dignity, like an evening of Claude Lorraine, is stealing into the landscape. Once more the veld is putting on an alien dress, till in this fairyland weather we forgot our continent again. And yet who shall limit Africa to one aspect? Our whole ride has been a kaleidoscope of its many phases. Hot and sunburnt, dry grasses and little streams, the red rock and the fantastic sunset. And on the other side the quiet green valleys, the soothing vista of blue hills, the cool woods, the water-meadows, and the twilight. It is a land of contrasts— glimpses of desert and barbarism, memories of war, relics of old turmoil, and yet essentially a homeland. As the phrase goes, it is a ' white man's country '; by which I understand a country not only capable of sustaining life, but fit for the amenities of life and the nursery of a nation. Whether it will rise to a nation or sink to a territory rests only with its people. But it is well to recognise its possibilities, to be in love with the place, for only then may we have the hope which can front and triumph over the many obstacles.

The first darkness is passing, a faint golden light creeps up the sky, and suddenly over a crest comes the African moon, bathing the warm earth in its cold pure radiance. This moon, at any rate, is the peculiar possession of the land. At home it is a disc, a ball of light; but here it is a glowing world riding in the heavens, a veritable kingdom of fire. No virgin huntress could personify it, but rather some mighty warrior-god, driving his chariot among trampled stars. It lights us out of the wood, and on to the highroad, and then among the sunflowers and oleanders of the garden. The night air is cool and bracing, but soft as summer; and as we dismount our thoughts turn home-ward, and we have a sudden regret. For in this month and in this hour in that other country we should be faring very differently. No dallying with zephyrs and sunsets; but the coming in, cold and weary, from the snowy hill, and telling over the peatfire the unforgettable romance of winter sport.

[May 1902

6

THE QUEST OF THE GOLDEN FLEECE

Hugh Clifford

All the wintry afternoon we had been worming our way
down the Thames, the big steamer filtering slowly through
the throng of craft like a bus moving ponderously amid
crowded traffic. When at last we won free of the river, the
Channel chop took us on its knee and rocked us roughly,
while the scud of wind and rain slapped us in the face with
riotous horse-play. As we came up from dinner and
struggled aft, our feet slipped and slithered over the wet
decks, and the shouts of the frozen lascars at the look-out
reached us through the sopping gloom, despairing as the
howls of souls in torment. The ugly, hopeless melancholy
of our surroundings accorded well with the mood which
possessed the majority of those on board, for we were out-
ward-bound, and men who leave England for the good of
their purses carry heavy hearts with them at the start.
In the smoking-room, therefore, with coat-collars tugged
up about our ears, and hands thrust deeply into our pockets,
we sat smoking with mournful earnestness, glaring at our
neighbours with the open animosity of the genial Briton.

Through the thickening fog of the tobacco-smoke the
figure of the man seated immediately opposite to me was
dimly visible, but presently his unusual appearance

claimed my closer attention and aroused my curiosity. His emaciated body was wrapped in a huge ulster, from the up-turned collar of which a head emerged that I can only describe as being like nothing so much as a death's-head moth. He was clean-shaven, and his cheeks were as hollow as saucers; his temples were pinched and prominent; from the bottom of deeply sunken sockets little wild eyes glared like savage things held fast in a gin. The mouth was set hard, as though its owner was enduring agony and trying his best to repress a scream. As much of his hair as his cap and his coat-collar suffered to be seen was of a dirty yellow white, yet in some indefinable way the man did not give the impression of being old. Rather he seemed to be one prematurely broken; one who suffered acutely and unceasingly; one who, with rigid self-control, maintained a tight grip upon himself, as though all his nerves were on edge. I had marked a somewhat similar expression of concentrated determination upon the faces of fellow-passengers engaged in fighting the demon of sea-sickness; but this fellow sucked at his pipe, and obviously drew a measure of comfort from it, in a fashion which showed that he was indifferent to the choppy motion. Yet though those buried eyes of his were glaring and savage—eyes that seemed to be eternally seeking some means of escape from a haunting peril— they were not restless, but rather were fixed in a venomous scowl, while the man himself, dead quiet save for the light that glinted from them, was apparently sunken in a fathomless abstraction.

All this I noted mechanically, but it was the extraordinary condition of his face that chiefly excited my wonder. It was literally pock-marked with little purple cicatrices, small oblong lumps, smooth and shining feebly in the lamplight, that rose above the surface of the skin, and ran this way and that at every imaginable angle. I had seen more than once the faces of German duellists wonderfully and fearfully beslashed, but the scars they wore were long and clean, wholly unlike the badly healed lumps which disfigured my queer *vis-à-vis*. I fell to speculating as to what could have caused such a multiplicity of wounds: not a gunpowder explosion, certainly, for the skin showed none of the blue tattooing inseparable from injuries so inflicted; nor yet the bursting of a gun, for that always makes at least one large jagged cut, not innumerable tiny scars such as those at which I was looking. I could think of no solution that would fit the case, and as I watched, suddenly the man withdrew his hands from his pockets, waggling them before his face with a nervous motion, as though he were warding off some invisible assailants. Then I saw that every inch of his palms, the backs, and as much of his wrists as were exposed to view, were pitted with cicatrices similar to those with which his face was bedecked.

" Evening, you folk! " said a nasal voice in the doorway, breaking discordantly upon the sulky silence which brooded over us, and I looked up to see the figure of a typical ' downeaster ', slim and alert, standing just within the room. He had a keen hard face on him, like a meat-axe, and the wet of the rain stood upon it in drops. He jerked his head at us in collective greeting, walked through the haze of smoke with free gait and swinging shoulders, and threw himself down in a heap on the horse-hair bench beside the man whose strange appearance had rivetted my attention. Seated thus he looked round at us with quick humorous glances, as though our British solemnity, which made each one of us grimly isolated in a crowd, struck him as at once amusing and impossible of endurance.

" Snakes! " he exclaimed genially. " This is *mighty*

cheerful!" His strident twang seemed to cut wedges out of the foggy silence. "We look as though we had swallowed a peck of tenpenny nails, and the blamed things were sitting heavy on our stomachs! Come, let us be friendly. I ain't doing any trade in sore-headed bears. Wake up, sonny!" And he dug his melancholy neighbour in the ribs with an aggressive and outrageous thumb.

It was for all the world as though he had touched the spring that sets in motion the clock-work of a mechanical toy. The man's cap flew from his head, disclosing a scalp ill-covered with sparse hairs and scarred like his face, as he leaped to his feet with a scream, torn suddenly, as it were, from the depths of his self-absorbed abstraction. Casting quick, nervous glances over his shoulder, he backed into the nearest corner, his hands clawing at the air, his eyes hunted, defiant, yet abject. His whole figure was instinct with terror —terror seeking impotently to defend itself against unnumbered enemies. His teeth were set, his gums were drawn back over them in two rigid white lines, a sort of snarling cry broke from him—a cry that seemed to be the expression of furious rage, pain, and agonisingly concentrated effort.

It all took place in a fraction of a second—as quickly as a man 'jumps' when badly startled—and as quickly he recovered his balance, and pulled himself together. Then he cast a murderous glance at the American, who at that moment presented a picture of petrified astonishment, let fly a venomous oath at him, and slammed out of the room in a towering rage.

"Goramercy!" ejaculated the American, limply. "I want a drink. Who'll join me?" But no one responded to his invitation.

That was the occasion of my first meeting with Timothy O'Hara; but as I subsequently travelled half across the world in his company, was admitted to his friendship, and heard him relate his experiences, not once but many times, I am able to supply the curious with the key to his extra-ordinary behaviour that evening. I regret that it is impos-sible to give his story in his own words, for he told it graphically and with force, but unfortunately his very proper indignation invariably got the better of his discretion, with the result that he frequently waxed blasphemous in the course of his narrative, and at times was rendered altogether inarticulate by rage. I flatter myself, however, that the version which I now offer to the reader is faithful and accurate in all essential details; and my own intimate knowledge of that gentle race called Mûruts, at whose hands O'Hara fared so evilly, has helped me to fill in such blanks as may have existed in the tale as it originally reached me.

Some years ago there was a man in North Borneo, whose name does not matter—a man who had the itch of travel in him, and loved untrodden places for their own sake. He undertook to explore the interior of the No-Man's-Land which the Chartered Company euphemistically describes as its 'property'. He made his way inland from the western coast, and little more was heard of him for several months. At the end of that time a haze of disquieting rumours, as impalpable as the used-up fever-laden wind that blows eternally from the interior, reached the little squalid stations on the sea-shore, and shortly afterwards the body of the explorer, terribly mangled and mutilated, was sluiced down-country by a freshet, and brought up on a sand-spit near the mouth of a river on the east coast. Here it was discovered by a couple of white men, who with the aid of a handful of unwilling natives buried it with becoming state, since it was the only thing with a European father and mother which had ever travelled across the centre of North Borneo from sea to sea since the beginning of time.

In life the explorer had been noted for his beard, a great yellow cascade of hair which fell down his breast from his lip to his waist, and when his corpse was found this ornament was missing. The Chartered Company, whose business it is to pay dividends under adverse circumstances, does not profess to be a philanthropical institution, and cannot spend its hard-squeezed revenues upon putting the fear of death into people who have made too free with the lives of white folk, as is the practice in other parts of Asia. Therefore no steps were taken by the local administration to punish the Mûruts of the interior who had amused themselves by putting the explorer to an ugly death; but the knowledge that the murdered man's beard had been shorn from his chin by some truculent savage, and was even then ornamenting the knife-handle of a Mûrut chief in the heart of the island, rankled in the minds of the white men on the spot. The wise and prudent members of the community talked a great deal, said roundly that the thing was a shame and an abomination, and took care to let their discretion carry them no further than the spoken word. The young and foolish did not say so much, but the recovery of that wisp of hair became to many of them a tremendous ambition, a dream, something that made even existence in North Borneo tolerable while it presented itself to their imaginations as a feat possible of accomplishment. With a few this dream became an *idée fixe*, an object in a life that otherwise was unendurable, and it may even have saved a few from the folly of immediate suicide. The quest would be the most hazardous conceivable, a fitting enterprise for men rendered desperate by the circumstances into the midst of which fate had thrust them; and a man might well feel that there was more satisfaction to be found in throwing away his life in an attempt to cleanse the stained honour of his breed than in pathetically blowing out his brains. The former was a romantic, nay, a glorious, venture; the latter earns a very general contempt, is even branded as an act of cowardice, and cowardice is the one sin of which the men of the outskirts fear to be accused.

Sitting at home in England, with pleasant things to distract the mind all about you, and with nothing at hand more dangerous than a motor-car, all this pother concerning the hairs off a dead man's chin may appeal to you as something absurdly sentimental and irrational; but try for the moment to place yourself in the position of an isolated white man at an out-station of North Borneo. Picture to yourself a tumbledown thatched bungalow standing on a roughly cleared hill, with four Chinese shops and a dilapidated police-station squatting on the bank of a black, creeping river. Rub in a smudge of blue-green forest, shutting you up on flanks, front, and rear. Fill that forest with scattered huts, wherein squalid natives live the lives of beasts—natives whose language you do not know, whose ideas you do not understand, who make their presence felt only by means of savage howls raised by them in their drunken orgies—natives whose hatred of you can only be kept from active expression by the fear which your armed readiness may inspire. Add to this merciless heat, faint exhausted air, an occasional bout of the black fever of the country, and not enough of work to preserve your mind from rust. Remember that the men who are doomed to live in these places get no sport, have no recreations, no companionship; that the long, empty, suffocating days trail by one by one, bringing no hope of change, and that the only communication with the outer world is kept up fitfully by certain dingy steam-tramps which are always behind time, and which may, or may not, arrive once a month. Can you wonder that amid such surroundings men wax melancholy, that they take to brooding over all manner of trivial things in a fashion which is not quite sane, and that the knowledge that their continued existence is dependent upon the wholesome awe in which white folk are held sometimes gets upon their nerves, and makes them feverishly anxious to vindicate the honour of their race? When you have let the full meaning of these things sink into your minds, you will begin to understand why so much excitement prevailed in North Borneo concerning the reported ownership of the deceased explorer's beard.

Timothy O'Hara and Harold Bateman had lived lives such as those which I have described for half a dozen years or more. They had had ample leisure in which to turn the matter of the explorer's beard over and over in their minds, till the thought of it had bred something like fanaticism, a kind of still, white-hot rage, within them. It chanced that their leave of absence fell due upon one and the same day. It followed that they put their heads together and decided to start upon a private raid of their own into the interior of the Mûrut country, with a view to redeeming the trophy. It also followed that they made their preparations with the utmost secrecy, and that they enlisted a dozen villainous little Dyaks from Sarawak to act as their punitive force. The whole thing was highly improper and very illegal, but it promised adventurous experiences, and both Bateman and O'Hara were young and not over-wise. Also, it must be urged in extenuation of their conduct that they had the effects of some six years' crushing monotony to work off, that they had learned to regard the Mûruts of the interior as their natural enemies, and that the ugliness and the deadly solitude of their existence had rendered them savage, just as the tamest beast becomes wild and ferocious when it finds itself held in the painful grip of a trap.

I am in nowise concerned to justify their doings: my part is to record them. O'Hara and Bateman vanished one day from the last outpost of quasi-civilisation, having given out that they were off up-country in search of big game—which was a fact. Their little expedition slipped into the forest, and the wilderness swallowed it. When once they had pushed out into the unknown interior they were gone past power of recall—were lost as completely as a needle in a ten-acre hay-field; and they breathed more freely because they had escaped from the narrow zone wherein the law of the white man runs, and need guide themselves for the future merely by the dictates of their own rudimentary notions of right and wrong.

They had a pretty awful time of it, so far as I can gather; for the current of the rivers, which crept towards them, black and oily, from the upper country, was dead against them, and the rapids soon caused them to abandon their boats. Then they tramped it, trudging with dogged perseverance up and down the hills, clambering painfully up sheer ascents, slipping down the steep pitches on the other side, splashing and labouring through the swamps betwixt hill and hill, or wading waist-deep across wastes of rank *lâlang*-grass, from the green surface of which the refracted heat smote them under their hat-brims with the force of blows. Aching in every limb, half-blinded by the sweat that trickled into their eyes, flayed by the sun, mired to the ears in the morasses, torn by thorn-thickets, devoured by tree-leeches, stung by all manner of jungle-insects, and oppressed by the weight of self-imposed effort that pride forbade them to abandon, they struggled forward persistently, fiercely, growing more savage and more vindictive at every painful step. The golden fleece of beard, which was the object of their quest, became an oriflamme, in the wake of which they floundered eternally through the inferno of an endless fight. Their determination to recover it became a madness, a possession; it filled their minds to the exclusion of aught else, nerved them to fresh endeavour, spurred them out of their weariness, and would not suffer them to rest. But the bitterness of their travail incensed them mightily against the Mûrut folk, whose lack of reverence for white men had imposed so tremendous a task upon these self-appointed champions of their race; and as they sat over their unpalatable meals when the day's toil was ended, they talked together in blood-thirsty fashion of the vengeance they would wreak, and the punishment they would exact from the tribe which was discovered to be in possession of the object of their search.

One feature of their march was that prudence forbade a halt. The Mûrut of North Borneo is a person of mean understanding, who requires time wherein to set his slow intellect in motion. He is a dipsomaniac, a homicide by training and predilection, and he has a passion for collecting other people's skulls, which is as unscrupulous and as fanatical as that of the modern philatelist. Whenever he encounters a stranger he immediately falls to coveting that stranger's skull; but as he is a creature of poor courage, it is essential to his comfort that he should win possession of it only by means that will not endanger his own skin. The question as to how such means may be contrived presents a difficult problem for his solution, and it takes his groping mind from two to three days in which to hit upon a workable plan. The explorer, as Bateman and O'Hara were aware, lost his life because, overcome by fatigue, he allowed himself to commit the mistake of spending more than a single night under a hospitable Mûrut roof-tree, and so gave time to his hosts to plot his destruction. Had he only held steadily upon his way, all might have been well with him: for in a country where every village is at enmity with its neighbours, a short march would have carried him into a stranger's land, which he should have been able to quit in its turn ere the schemes for his immolation hatched therein had had leisure in which to ripen. O'Hara and Bateman, therefore, no matter how worn out they might be by that everlasting, clambering tramp across that cruel huddle of hill-caps, were rowelled by necessity into pushing forward, and still forward, as surely as the day dawned. They felt much as the urchin Jo must have done when all men combined to keep him ' moving on '; and as they were less meek than he, their hatred of the Mûrut people, who here acted towards them the part of vigilant constables, increased and multiplied exceedingly.

Often the filth and squalor of the long airless huts—each one of which accommodated a whole village community in its dark interior, all the pigs and fowls of the place beneath its flooring, and as many blackened human skulls as could find hanging-space along its roof-beams—sickened them, and drove them forth to camp in the jungle. Here there were only wild beasts—self-respecting and on the whole cleanly beasts, which compared very favourably with the less attractive animals in the village huts—but a vigilant guard had to be maintained against possible surprise, and this, after a heartbreaking tramp, was hard alike upon white men and Dyaks.

The raiders had pitched their camp in such a place one evening, and as the party lacked meat, and the pigeons could be heard cooing in the tree-tops close at hand, O'Hara took his fowling-piece and strolled off alone into the forest, with the intention of shooting a few birds for the pot. The jungle was very dense in this part of the country, so dense indeed that a man was powerless to see in any direction for a distance of more than a dozen yards; but the pigeons were plentiful, and as they fluttered from tree to tree O'Hara walked after them without realising in the least how far he was straying from his starting-point. At last the fast-failing light arrested his attention, and as he stooped to pick up the last pigeon, the search for which among the brambles had occupied more time than he had fancied, it suddenly struck him that he ought to be returning to the camp, while a doubt as to its exact direction assailed him. He was in the very act of straightening himself again with a view to looking about him for some indication of the path by which he had come, when a slight crackle in the underwood smote upon his ear. He remained very still, stooping forward as he was, holding his breath, and listening intently. It flashed through his mind that the sound might have been made by one of the Dyaks, who perhaps had come out of the camp in search of him, and he waited the repetition of the snapping noise with eagerness, hoping that it would tell him whether it were caused by man or beast. As he stood thus for an instant with bowed shoulders, the crackle came again, louder, crisper, and much nearer than before, and at the same moment, before he had time to change his attitude or to realise that danger threatened him, something smote him heavily in the back, bringing him prone to the earth with a grunt. The concussion was caused by some yielding substance, that yet was quick and warm, and the litter of dead leaves and the tangle of underwood combined to break his fall. He was not hurt, therefore, though the breath was knocked out of him, and that unseen something, which tumbled and writhed upon his back, pinned him to the ground. He skewed his head round, trying to see what had assailed him, and immediately a diabolical face peeped over his shoulder an inch or two above it. He only saw it, as it were, in a flash but the sight was one which, he was accustomed to say, he would never forget. In after-years it was wont to recur to him in dreams, and as surely as it came it woke him with a scream. It was a savage face, brown yet pallid, grimed with dirt and wood-ashes, with a narrow retreating forehead, a bestial prognathous snout, and a tiny twitching chin. The little black eyes, fierce and excited, were ringed about by angry red sores, for the eyelashes had been plucked out. The eyebrows also had been similarly removed, but from the upper lip a few coarse wires sprouted uncleanly. The face was split in twain by a set of uneven teeth, pointed like those of a wild cat, and tightly clenched, while above and below them the gums snarled rigidly, bearing witness to the physical effort which their owner was making. The scalp was divided into even halves by a broad parting, on either side of which there rose a tangle of dirty, ill-kept hair, that was drawn back into a chignon which gave the creature a curious sexless aspect. All these things O'Hara noted in the fraction of a second, and as the horror bred of them set him heaving and fighting as well as his cramped position made possible, a sharp kneecap was driven into the back of his neck, and his head fell forward with a concussion that blinded him. For a moment he lay still and inert, and in that moment he was conscious of little deft hands, that flew this way and that, over, under, and around his limbs, and of the pressure of narrow withes, drawn suddenly taut, that ate into his flesh. Up to this time the whole affair had been transacted in a dead, unnatural silence that somehow gave to it the strangeness and unreality of a nightmare; but now, as O'Hara lay prostrate with his face buried in the underwood, the evensong of the forest insects, which rings through the jungle during the gloaming hour, was suddenly interrupted by an outbreak of queer sounds—by gurgling, jerky speech intermixed with shrill squeakings and whistlings, and by the clicking cackle which stands the Mûrut folk instead of laughter. Yet even now the voices of his captors were subdued and hushed, as though unwilling to be overheard, and O'Hara, understanding that the Mûruts feared to be interrupted by their victim's friends, made shift to raise a shout, albeit the green stuff forced its way into his mouth and choked his utterance.

Immediately the little nimble hands were busy, clutching him afresh, while the tones of those inhuman voices shrilled and gurgled and clicked more excitedly than before. O'Hara was heaved and tugged, first one way, then another, until finally his body was rolled over on to its back, falling with a dull bump. He shouted once more, putting all the strength that was in him into the yell, and the nearest Mûrut promptly stamped on his mouth with his horny heel. O'Hara bit viciously at the thing, but his teeth could make no impression upon its leathery under-surface, and before he could shout again he found himself gagged with a piece of wood, which was bound in its place by a couple of withes. Despair seized him then, and for a moment or two he lay still, with the manhood knocked fairly out of him by a crushing consciousness of impotence, while the gabble of squeak, and whistle, and grunt, still hushed cautiously, broke out more discordantly than ever.

The withes about his limbs bound O'Hara so cripplingly that only his neck was free to move, but presently, craning it upward, he caught sight of his persecutors for the first time. They formed a squalid group of little, half-starved, wizened creatures, not much larger than most European children of fourteen, but with brutal faces that seemed to bear the weight of whole centuries of care and of animal self-indulgence. They were naked, save for their foul loin-clouts; they were abominably dirty, and their skins were smothered in leprous-looking ringworm; they had not an eyelash or an eyebrow among them, for the hairs had been plucked out by the root, but their scalps were covered by frowsy growths, gathered into loathsome chignons on the napes of their necks. Every man was armed with one or more spears, and from the waist of each a long knife depended, sheathed in a wooden scabbard hung with tufts of hair. One of them—the man whose face O'Hara had caught a glimpse of above his shoulder—flourished his sheathed knife insistently in his captive's face with grotesque gesticulations, and O'Hara shuddered every time that the disgusting tassels that bedecked the scabbard swept his cheek. The fading daylight was very dim now, enabling O'Hara to see only the *form* of the things by which he was surrounded: *colour* had ceased to have any meaning in those gloomy forest aisles. The grinning savage prancing and gibbering around him, and brandishing that sheathed weapon with its revolting trophies, puzzled him. If he meant murder, why did he not draw his blade? In the depth of his misery the inconsequence of this war-dance furnished O'Hara with an additional torture.

Presently two of the Mûruts came suddenly within his field of vision bearing a long green pole. This they proceeded to thrust between O'Hara's flesh and the withes that were entwined about him, and when this had been accomplished, the whole party set their shoulders under the extremities of the pole and lifted their prisoner clear from the ground. Then they bore him off at a sort of jog-trot.

The thongs, tightened fearfully by the pressure thus put upon them, pinched and bruised him pitilessly; his head, lacking all support, hung down in an attitude of dislocation, waggling this way and that at every jolt; the blood surged into his brain, causing a horrible vertigo, and seeming to thrust his eyes almost out of their sockets; he thought that he could feel his limbs swelling above the biting grip of the withes, and an irresistible nausea seized him. Maddening cramps tied knots in his every muscle, and had his journey been of long duration Timothy O'Hara would never have reached its end alive. Very soon, however, the decreased pace, and the shrill whistling sounds which came from the noses of his Mûrut bearers, told him that the party was ascending a hill—for these strange folk do not pant like ordinary people, and the uncanny noise was familiar to O'Hara from many a toilsome march in the company of native porters. Presently, too, between the straining legs of the leading files O'Hara caught a flying glimpse of distant fire, and that, he knew, betokened the neighbourhood of a village.

A few minutes later, just as he thought that he was about to lose consciousness, the village was reached—a long, narrow hut, raised on piles, and with a door at either end, from the thresholds of which crazy ladder-ways led to the ground. Up the nearest of these rude staircases the Mûruts struggled with their burden, banging his head roughly against each untrimmed rung, and threw it down on the bamboo flooring with a chorus of grunts. For a moment there was silence, while the entire community gathered round the white man, staring at him eagerly with a kind of ferocious curiosity. Then with one accord all the men, women, and children present set up a diabolical chorus of whoopings and yellings. They seemed to give themselves over to a veritable insanity of noise. Some, squatting on their heels, supporting the weight of their bodies on arms thrust well behind them, tilted their chins to the roof and howled like maniacs. Others, standing erect, opened their mouths to their full extent, and emitted a series of shrill, blood-curdling bellows. Others, again, shut their eyes, threw their arms aloft, and concentrating every available atom of energy in the effort, screamed till their voices broke. The ear-piercing din sounded as though all the devils in hell had of a sudden broken loose. Heard from afar, the savage triumph, the diabolical delight that found in it their fitting expression, might well have made the blood run cold in the veins of the bravest; but heard close at hand by the solitary white man whose capture had evoked that hideous outcry, and who knew himself to be utterly at the mercy of these fiends, it was almost enough to unship his reason. O'Hara told me that from that moment he forgot the pain which his bonds occasioned him, forgot even his desire for escape, and was filled with a tremendous longing to be put out of his agony—to be set free by death from this unspeakable inferno. His mind, he said, was working with surprising activity, and ' as though it belonged to somebody else '. In a series of flashes he began to recall all that he had ever heard of the manners and customs of the Mûruts, of the strange uses to which they put their prisoners, and all the while he was possessed by a kind of restlessness that made him eager for them to do *something*—no matter of how awful a character—that would put a period to his unendurable suspense.

Meanwhile the Mûruts were enjoying themselves thoroughly. Large earthenware jars, each sufficiently large to drown a baby with comfort, were already standing round the enclosed veranda which formed the common-room of the village, on to which each family cubicle opened, and to these jars the Mûruts—men, women, and children— repeatedly addressed themselves, squatting by them, and sucking up through long bamboo tubes the abominable liquor which filled them. Each toper, as he quitted the jar, fell to howling with redoubled energy, and as more and more of the fiery stuff was consumed, their cries became more savage, more inarticulate, and more diabolical.

Half a dozen men, however, were apparently busy in the performance of some task on a spot just behind O'Hara's head, for though they frequently paid visits of ceremony to the liquor-jars, they always staggered back to the same part of the room when their draughts were ended, and there fell to hacking and hammering at wood with renewed energy. O'Hara was convinced that they were employed in constructing some infernal instrument of torture; and the impossibility of ascertaining its nature was maddening, and set his imagination picturing every abominable contrivance for the infliction of anguish of which he had ever heard or read. And all the while the hideous orgies for which his capture was the pretext were waxing more fast and furious.

Suddenly the hidden group behind him set up a shrill catcall, and at the sound every Mûrut in sight leaped to his or her feet, and danced frantically with hideous outcry and maniacal laughter. A moment later a rattan rope whined as it was pulled over the main beam of the roof with something heavy at its end, and as the slack of the cord was made fast to the wall-post opposite him, O'Hara was aware of some large object, suspended in mid-air, swinging out into the middle of the room immediately above him. This, as he craned his neck up at it, struggling to see it more clearly in the uncertain torchlight, was presently revealed as a big cage, an uneven square in shape, the bars of which were some six inches apart, saving on one side where a wide gap was left. He had barely time to make this discovery when a mob of Mûrut men and women rushed at him, cut the bonds that bound him, and mauling him mercilessly, lifted him up, and literally threw him into the opening formed by the gap. The cage rocked crazily, while the Mûruts yelled their delight, and two of their number proceeded hastily to patch up the gap with cross-pieces of wood. Then the whole crowd drew away a little, though the hubbub never slackened, and O'Hara set his teeth to smother the groans which the pain of the removed bonds nearly wrung from him. For the time fear and all other emotions were forgotten in the acuteness of the agony which he endured, for as the blood began to flow freely once more, every inch of his body seemed to have been transformed into so many raging teeth. His extremities felt soft and flabby—cold, too, like jellies—but O'Hara was by nature a very strong man, and at the time of his capture he had been in the pink of condition. In an incredibly short while, therefore, the pain subsided, and he began to regain the use of his cramped limbs.

He was first made aware of his recovered activity by the alacrity with which he bounded into the centre of the cage in obedience to a sharp prick in the back. He tried to rise to his feet, and his head came into stunning contact with the roof; then, in a crouching attitude, he turned in the direction whence the attack had reached him. What he saw filled him with horror. The leader of the Mûruts who had captured him, his eyes bloodshot with drink, was staggering about in front of him with grotesque posturings, waving his knife in one hand and its wooden sheath in the other. It was the former evidently that had administered that painful prod to O'Hara's back, but it was the latter which claimed the white man's attention even in that moment of whirling emotions, for from its base depended a long shaggy wisp of sodden yellow hair—the golden fleece of which O'Hara and Bateman were in search. In a flash the savage saw that his victim had recognised the trophy to which he had already been at some pains to direct his attention, and the assembled Mûruts gave unmistakable tokens that they all grasped the picturesqueness of the situation. They yelled and howled and bayed more frantically than ever; some of them rolled upon the floor, their limbs and faces contorted by paroxysms of savage merriment, while others staggered about, smiting their fellows on their bare shoulders, squeaking like bats, and clicking like demoralised clockwork. A second prod with a sharp point made O'Hara shy across his narrow cage like a fly-bitten horse, and before he could recover his balance a score of delicately handled weapons inflicted light wounds all over his face and hands. As each knife touched him its owner threw up his head and repeated some formula in a shrill sing-song, no word of which was intelligible to O'Hara save only the name of Kina-Balu—the great mountain which dominates North Borneo, and is believed by the natives to be the eternal resting-place of the spirits which have quitted the life of earth.

Then for the first time, O'Hara understood what was happening to him. He had often heard of the ceremony known to the wild Mûruts as a *bângun*, which has for its object the maintenance of communication between the living and the dead. He had even seen a pig hung up, as he was now hanging, while the tamer Mûruts prodded it to death very carefully and slowly, charging it the while with messages for the spirits of the departed, and he remembered how the abominable cruelty of the proceeding had turned him sick, and had set him longing to interfere with native religious customs in defiance of the prudent Government which he served. Now he was himself to be done to death by inches, just as the pig had died, and he knew that men had spoken truly when they had explained to him that the unfortunate quadruped was only substituted for a nobler victim as a concession to European prejudice, to the great discontent of the tame Mûruts.

These thoughts rushed through his mind with the speed of lightning, and all the while it seemed to him that every particle of his mental forces was concentrated upon a single object—the task of defending himself against a crowd of persecutors. Crouching in the centre of the cage snarling like a cat, with his eyes bursting from their sockets, his every limb braced for a leap in any direction, his hands scrabbling at the air to ward off the stabs, he faced from side to side, his breath coming in quick, noisy pants. Every second one or another of the points that assailed him made him turn about with a cry of rage, and immediately his exposed back was prodded by every Mûrut within reach. Suddenly he heard his own voice raised in awful curses and blasphemies, and the familiar tones of his mother-tongue smote him with surprise. He had little consciousness of pain as pain, only the necessity of warding off the points of his enemies presented itself to him as something that must be accomplished at all costs, and each separate failure enraged him. He bounded about his cage with an energy and an agility that astonished him, and the rocking of his prison seemed to keep time with the lilting of his thumping heartbeats. More than once he fell, and his face and scalp were prodded terribly ere he could regain his feet; often he warded off a thrust with his bare hands. But of the wounds which he thus received he was hardly conscious; his mind was in a species of delirium of rage, and all the time he was torn with a fury of indignation because he, a white man, was being treated in this dishonouring fashion by a pack of despicable Mûruts. But he received no serious injury; for the Mûruts, who, like the 'modern major-general', were 'teeming with a lot of news' for their dead relations, were anxious to keep the life in him as long as might be, and, in spite of their intoxication, prodded him with shrewdness and caution. How long it all lasted O'Hara never knew with certainty; but it was the exhaustion caused by loss of breath, and by the wild leaping of that bursting heart of his, that caused him presently to sink on the floor of his cage in a swoon.

Then the Mûruts, finding that he did not answer to their stabs, drew off and gathered eagerly around the liquor-jars. The killing would come soon after the dawn—as soon, in fact, as their overnight orgies made possible—when the prisoner would be set to run the gauntlet, and would be hacked to pieces after one final, delicious *bângun*. It was essential, therefore, that enough strength should be left in him to enable him to show good sport, and in the meantime their villainous home-made spirits would bring that measure of happiness which comes to the Mûrut from being suffered, for a little space, to forget the fact of his own repulsive existence. Accordingly, with noisy hospitality, each man tried to make his neighbours drink to greater excess than himself, and all proved willing victims. With hoots and squeals of laughter, little children were torn from their mothers' breasts and given to suck at the bamboo pipes, their ensuing intoxication being watched with huge merriment by men and women alike. The shouts raised by the revellers became more and more shaky, less and less articulate; over and over again the groups around the jars broke up, while their members crawled away, to lie about in death-like stupors, from which they roused themselves only to vomit and drink anew.

Long before this stage of the proceedings had been reached O'Hara had recovered his senses, but prudence bade him lie as still as a mouse. Once or twice a drunken Mûrut lurched on to his feet and made a pass or two at him, and now and again he was prodded painfully, but, putting forth all the self-control at his command, he gave no sign of life. At last every Mûrut in the place was sunken in abominable torpor, excepting only the chief, from whose knife-scabbard hung the tuft which had once ornamented the chin of the explorer. His little red eyes were fixed in a drunken glare upon O'Hara, and the latter watched them with a fascination of dread through his half-closed lids. Over and over again the Mûrut crawled to the nearest liquor-jar, and sucked up the dregs with a horrible sibilant gurgling, and at times he even staggered to his feet, muttering and mumbling over his tiny, busy chin, waving his weapon uncertainly, ere he subsided in a limp heap upon the floor. On each occasion he gave more evident tokens of drowsiness, and at last his blinking eyes were covered by their lashless lids.

At the same moment a gentle gnawing sound, which had been attracting O'Hara's attention for some minutes, though he had not dared to move by so much as a finger's breadth to discover its cause, ceased abruptly. Then the faintest ghost of a whisper came to his ears from below his cage, and moving with the greatest caution, and peering down through the uncertain light, he saw that a hole had been made by sawing away two of the laths which formed the flooring. In the black hole immediately beneath him the faces of two of his own Dyaks were framed, and even as he looked one of them hoisted himself into the hut, and began deftly to remove the bars of the cage, moving as noiselessly as a shadow. The whole thing was done so silently, and O'Hara's own mind was so racked by the emotions which his recent experiences had held for him, that he was at first persuaded that what he saw, or rather fancied he saw, was merely the figment conjured up for his torture by a delirium which possessed him. He felt that if he suffered himself to believe in this mocking delusion even for an instant the disappointment of discovering its utter unreality would drive him mad. He was already spent with misery, physical and mental; he was consciously holding himself in leash to prevent the commission of some inane extravagance; he was seized with an unreasoning desire to scream. He fought with himself—a self that was unfamiliar to him, although its identity was never in doubt—as he might have fought with a stranger; he told himself that his senses were playing cruel pranks upon him, and that nothing should induce him to be deceived by them; and all the while hope, mad, wild, hysterical hope, was surging up in his heart, shaking him like an aspen, wringing unaccustomed tears from his eyes, and tearing his breast with noiseless sobs.

As he lay inert, and utterly wretched, unable to bear up manfully under this new wanton torture of the mind, the ghost of the second Dyak clambered skilfully out of the darkness below the hut-floor and joined his fellow, who had already made a wide gap in the side of the cage. Then the two of them seized O'Hara, and with the same strange absence of sound, lifted him bodily out of the prison, and through the hole in the flooring on to the earth below. Their grip upon his lacerated flesh hurt him acutely; but the very pain was welcome, for did it not prove the reality of his deliverers? What he experienced of relief and gratitude O'Hara could never tell us, for all he remembers is that, gone suddenly weak and plaintive as a child, he clung to the little Dyaks, sobbing broken-heartedly, and weeping on their shoulders without restraint or decency, in an utter abandon of self-pity. Also he recalls dimly that centuries later he found himself standing in Bateman's camp, with his people gathering about him, and that of a sudden he was made aware that he was mother-naked. After that, so he avers, all is a blank.

The closing incidents of the story were related to me by Bateman one evening when I chanced to forgather with him in an up-country outpost in Borneo. We had been talking far into the night, and our *solitude à deux* and the lateness of the hour combined to thaw his usual taciturnity, and to unlock his shy confidence. Therefore I was put in possession of a secret which until then, I believe, had been closely kept.

" It was an awful night," he said, " that upon which poor O'Hara was missing. The Dyaks had gone out in couples all over the place to try to pick up his trail; but I remained in the camp, for though there was a little moon, it was too dark for a white man's eyes to be of any good. What with the inactivity and my fears for O'Hara I was as ' jumpy ' as you make it; and as the Dyaks began to drop in, two at a time, each couple bringing their tale of failure, I worked myself up into such a state of depression and misery that I thought I must be going mad. Just about three o'clock in the morning the last brace of Dyaks turned up, and I was all of a shake when I saw that they had poor O'Hara with them. He broke loose from them and stumbled into the centre of the camp, stark naked, and pecked almost to bits by those infernal Mûrut knives; but the wounds were not over-deep, and the blood was caking over most of them. He was an awful sight, and I was for tending his hurts without delay; but he pushed me roughly aside, and I saw that his eyes were blazing with madness. He stood there in the midst of us all, throwing his arms above his head, cursing in English and in the vernacular, and gesticulating wildly. The Dyaks edged away from him, and I could see that his condition funked them mortally. I tried again and again to speak to him and calm him, but he would not listen to a word I said, and for full five minutes he stood there raving and ranting, now and again pacing frenziedly from side to side, pouring out a torrent of invective mixed with muddled orders. One of the Dyaks brought him a pair of trousers, and after looking at them as though he had never seen such things before, he put them on, and stood for a second or two staring wildly round him. Then he made a bee-line for a rifle, loaded it, and slung a bandolier across his naked shoulders, and before I could stay him he was marching out of the camp with the whole crowd of Dyaks at his heels.

" I could only follow. I had no fancy for being left alone in that wilderness, more especially just then, and one of the Dyaks told me that he was leading them back to the Mûrut village. You see I only speak Malay, and as O'Hara had been talking Dyak I had not been able to follow his ravings. Whatever lingo he jabbered, however, it was as plain as a pikestaff that the fellow was mad as a hatter;

but I had to stop explaining this to him, for he threatened to shoot me, and the Dyaks would not listen. They clearly thought that he was possessed by a devil, and they would have gone to hell at his bidding while their fear of him was upon them.

" And his madness made him cunning too, for he stalked the Mûrut den awfully neatly, and just as the dawn was breaking we found ourselves posted in the jungle within a few yards of the two doors, which were the only means of entrance or exit for the poor devils in the hut.

" Then O'Hara leaped out of his hiding-place and began yelling like the maniac he was, and in an instant the whole of that long hut was humming like a disturbed beehive. Three or four squalid creatures showed themselves at the doorway nearest O'Hara, and he greeted them with half the contents of his magazine, and shrieked with laughter as they toppled on to the ground, rolling over and over in their death-agony. There was such a wailing and crying set up by the other inhabitants of the hut as you never heard in all your life—it was just Despair made vocal—the sort of outcry that a huge menagerie of wild animals might make when they saw flames lapping at their very cages, and above it all I could hear O'Hara's demoniac laughter ringing with savage delight, and the war-whoops of those little devils of Dyaks, whose blood was fairly up now. The trapped wretches in the hut made a stampede for the farther door: we could hear them scuffling and fighting with one another for the foremost places. They thought that safety lay in that direction; but the Dyaks were ready for them, and the bullets from their Winchesters drove clean through three and four of the squirming creatures at a time, and in a moment that doorway too, and the ground about the ladder foot, were a shambles.

" After that for a space there was a kind of awful lull within the hut, though without O'Hara and his Dyaks capered and yelled. Then the noise which our folk were making was drowned by a series of the most heart-breaking shrieks you ever heard or dreamed of, and immediately a second rush was made simultaneously at each door. The early morning light was getting stronger now, and I remember noting how incongruously peaceful and serene it seemed. Part of the hut near our end had caught fire somehow, and there was a lot of smoke which hung low about the doorway. Through this I saw the crowd of Mûruts struggle in that final rush, and my blood went cold when I understood what they were doing. Every man had a woman or a child held tightly in his arms—held in front of him as a buckler—and it was from these poor devils that those awful screams were coming. I jumped in front of the Dyaks and yelled to them in Malay to hold their fire; but O'Hara thrust me aside, and shooed the Dyaks on with shouts and curses and peals of laughter, slapping his palm on his gun-stock, and capering with delight and excitement. The Dyaks took no sort of heed of me, and the volleys met the Mûruts like a wall of lead.

" I had slipped and fallen when O'Hara pushed me, and as I clambered on to my feet again I saw the mob of savages fall together and crumple up, for all the world as paper crumples when burned suddenly. Most of them fell back into the dark interior of the hut, writhing in convulsions above the litter of dead; but one or two pitched forward headlong to the ground, and I saw a little brown baby, which had escaped unharmed, crawling about over the corpses, and sqeaking like a wounded rabbit. I ran forward to save it, but a Dyak was too quick for me, and before I could get near it he had thrown himself upon it, and . . . ugh !

" The Mûruts began cutting their way through the floor-ing then, and trying to bolt into the jungle. One or two of them got away, I think, and this threw O'Hara into such a passion of fury that I half expected to see him kill some of the Dyaks. He tore round to the side of the hut, and I saw him brain one Mûrut as he made a rush from under the low floor. One end of the building was in roaring flames by this time, and half a dozen of the Dyaks had gone in at the other end and were bolting the wretched creatures from their hiding-places, just as ferrets bolt rabbits from their burrows while O'Hara and the other Dyaks waited for them outside. They hardly missed one of them, sparing neither age nor sex, though I ran from one to the other like a mad-man, trying to prevent them. It was awful, . . . awful, and I was fairly blubbering with the horror of it, and with the consciousness of my own impotence. I was regularly broken up by it, and I remember at the last sitting down upon a log, burying my face in my hands, and crying like a child.

" The thing seemed to be over by then: there was no more bolting, and the Dyaks were beginning to clear out of the hut as the flames gained ground and made the place too hot for them. But, at the last, there came a terrific yell from the very heart of the fire, and a single Mûrut leaped out of the smoke. He was stark naked, for his loin-clout had been burned to tinder; he was blackened by the smoke, and his long hair was afire and waving behind him. His mouth was wide, and the cries that came from it went through and through my head, running up and up the scale till they hit upon a note whose shrillness agonised you. Surrounded by the flames, he looked like a devil in the heart of the pit. In one scorched arm he brandished a long knife, the blade of which was red with the glare of the flames, and in the other was the sheath, blazing at one end, and decked at the other by a great tuft of yellow hair that was smouldering damply.

" As soon as he saw him O'Hara raised a terrible cry and threw himself at him. The two men grappled and fell, the knife and scabbard escaping from the Mûrut's grasp and pitching straight into the heart of the fire. The struggle lasted for nearly a minute, O'Hara and his enemy rolling over and over one another, breathing heavily, but making no other sound. Then something happened—I don't know clearly what—but the Mûrut's head dropped, and O'Hara rose up from his dead body, moving very stiffly. He stood for a minute or so, looking round him in a dazed fashion, until at last his eyes caught mine. Then he staggered towards me, reeling like a tipsy man.

" ' Mother of Heaven!' he said thickly, ' what have I done? What *have* I done?'

" He stared round him at the little brown corpses, doubled up in dislocated and contorted attitudes, and his eyes were troubled.

" ' God forgive me !' he muttered. ' God forgive me !'

" Then he spun about on his heel, his hands outstretched above his head, his fingers clutching at the air, a thin foam forming on his lips, and before I could reach him he had toppled over in a limp heap upon the ground.

" I had an awful business getting O'Hara down country. He was as mad as a March hare for three weeks. But the Dyaks worked like bricks—albeit I could not bear the sight of them—and the currents of the rivers were in our favour when we reached navigable water. I know that O'Hara was mad that morning—no white man could have acted as he did unless he had been insane—and he always swears that he has no recollection of anything that occurred after the

Dyaks rescued him. I hope it may be so, but I am not certain. He is a changed man anyway, as nervous and 'jumpy' as you make it, and I know that he is always brooding over that up-country trip of ours."

"Yes" I assented, "and he is constantly telling the first part of the story to every chance soul he meets."

"Exactly," said Bateman. "That is what makes me doubt the completeness of his oblivion concerning what followed. You see his sufferings at the hands of the Mûruts supply the only conceivable excuse for his share in that morning's butchery, '*et qui s'excuse s'accuse*.' What do you think?"

[January 1903

7

SALAMANCA

Edward Hutton

The sun was just rising over the boundless plain, full of dust, where the little cities are so hard to find, when I set out on my journey for Salamanca, that lies scarcely fifty miles away from Medina del Campo, a little wretched village that lends its name to the junction of the lines from Salamanca and Segovia. In spite of the monotony of the landscape the view was very beautiful under the level light of the sun, that gave to that limitless desert an infinite wideness and immensity that were hidden at midday. A great old tower of brick, rosy in the sunrise, stood on a little hill behind the station ; far, far away I descried the faint outlines of blue mountains, and nearer, but still far away, a cloud of dust rose where a herd of swine moved from one hill to another. So I watched day dawn upon that silent golden world.

The coach in which I travelled, divided by low wooden barriers into five compartments, was full of men and women, who continually passed in and out at the innumerable little stations at which we stopped. A strange, a delightful company ; for all, without exception, were in some indefinable way beautiful. I know not how it was, but in every face, and especially in the old, I found a certain distinction as it were, a raciness, that was more than a mere absence of vulgarity. They were simple people, who had not lost touch with the eternal things : day and night still ruled their lives, the sun for them was a kind of god, the rain a sweet mercy from heaven ; and for them, too, the seasons were even yet a pageant, and autumn was for sowing and summer for reaping. It is impossible for me to compare them with an English crowd of third-class passengers—they were not a crowd, they were just men and women. Not one of them had ever seen that which we call a city, not one of them had even been able to forget what we have perhaps lost for ever, not one of them had suffered the tyranny of the machine or the newspaper, or seen the sky covered by anything but clouds. And so they were beautiful, it may be, because they were quite natural people, whom it would have been impossible to imagine in the distress of our trumpery cities. Nor were they without a certain gentleness of manners : though I was a foreigner—and foreigners are rare in third-class carriages in Spain, and more especially on the road to Salamanca—I must confess that it was I who stared. And yet every now and then I would catch the last glimpse of a smile fading from a girl's face, or from the eyes of an old man, at my strange appearance, my horrible tight clothes, my English hat, my absurd and hideous collar and hard shirt.

So the time passed, as slowly we crept across that immense plain, while the summer sun rose out of the east in his greatness and strength, scattering his burning gold over the dust that, without a single green blade or shrub or shady tree, stretched away for ever over the low hills and shallow thirsty valleys. It was a long journey ; and when at last I saw the tower of the cathedral, and the great and ancient city rising out of the plain, I was very ready for the walk that it seems necessary to take from the station to the city almost everywhere in Spain.

It was along a road six inches deep in dust that I came at last to the ruined ancient gates of Salamanca. How rosy everything was, and indeed the city is the colour of a Gloire de Dijon just before it drops its first petal. Over all that vast melancholy country she seems to look with an inscrutable smile. Around her are the desolate places. She is the rose of the desert. She lies upon two hillsides, and fills the valley between. Her streets are narrow and steep, with many turnings ; and the traffic is for the most part just the continual passing to and fro of many mules and asses. When a cart passes by, or, more rarely still, a carriage, the noise is deafening, echoing again and again between the tall houses in those narrow streets paved with rough stones. Pass through this city so beautiful and so desolate, past the cathedral, the Colegio Viejo, the university, the Casa de las Conchas, the Convent of Santo Domingo, down at last to the old Roman bridge that still strides over the Tormes ; everywhere you will find her smiling that inscrutable smile—at sunrise, at noon, or at sunset—over the barren miles of dust that, it might seem, will one day overwhelm her like a forgotten sphinx, an unremembered idol.

It is thus in summer she stands, a tawny inscrutable statue upon her hills, dead or asleep or dreaming I know not, who have loved her in the long languorous days because she is all of rose and gold. And in spring, when the desert lays at her feet all his treasures—infinite fields of waving corn, green and scarlet with poppies and golden— all day long I have heard the wind come to her over the priceless fields, and seen his white footsteps tumultuous as on the sea, and I have listened with the desert that has blossomed for her, that has brought her his gifts, waiting for the word that the wind should bring from her till the flowers have died under the sun, and the corn is reaped, and the wind has passed on his way, and all I heard was the word of eternal patience and of indestructible silence—Hush. . . .

Well, it is to the cathedrals that the traveller first goes, having seen their great cupolas, it may be, far and far away over the desert. And indeed from afar they are beautiful, on the one side or on the other; but in any closer view it is really only the older Romanesque building, quite dismantled now, that is not disappointing—the newer pretentious Gothic church being full of ineffectual work, overloaded with ornament and late decoration. They stand side by side, the smaller and older building indeed priceless, though not built of precious stone, supporting, as it were, the newer church. That old golden house, through whose walls the sunshine has filtered for eight hundred years till it seems to be built of stone that the sun has stained with its life and made precious, is a building for the most part of the twelfth century, the first Mass being said here in the year 1100. Cruciform in its design, it originally consisted of nave and aisles, with five bays, three eastern apses and a dome or lantern over the crossing —a thing very lovely and original, if we consider it carefully, lifted into the sky on pillars, between which the sunlight falls as among the carved lines of the windows, where the shadows are so cool and the wind sings to itself in the long hot days.

'Fortis Salamantia', an old Spanish writer calls the church, summing up for us in the phrase really the chief characteristics of the place, its strength consisting not only in the solidity of its stones but in a certain indestructible spirit also, that informs it even today when it is dismantled, It is as though you had wandered by chance into some monastic church, where everything passes quietly and with a certain precision and order, in which you might seek in vain for the enthusiasm of a great congregation, the immense emotion of the world. And for those, indeed, to whom stone is of all things the most beautiful in architecture—the surface, precious as it were with the bloom of the centuries, and beautiful too, since it holds still something of the simplicity of the hills—the ' old ' cathedral will remain how much more lovely than the ' new ', where everywhere you may trace the ambitious thoughts, the insincere laborious workmanship of the Renaissance, in which natural things have so little part, it might seem, anxious as men at that time seem to have been, here in Spain at least, to bring all things under their feet.

Time, that most subtle artist, has made the old church beautiful with all his infinite thoughts, laying upon pillar and gateway the gold and the light of his sunsets, the flowers that he has gathered in all the springs. And, indeed, he is a master whom a true architect, a true painter, will always in due measure trust. It might seem that it is only for those who are not simple enough, or not patient enough, that he can do nothing : something of that want of simplicity, of humility, is to be found, I think, in all the later buildings of Spain, where the architect has so carved everything with tracery and ornament that the utmost time can do is to destroy bit by bit, piece by piece, the dainty lace-work, the restless ornament, making a little space of plain stone on which he may contrive to leave the beauty of his passing.

As you return from the ruined cloisters and certain late

chapels, among which is one where the Mozarabic ritual is still used six times in a year, you enter the new cathedral by a door at the top of a flight of steps in the south aisle. It is as though you had suddenly stepped from the woods into an eighteenth-century garden full of topiary work. A certain broad Gothic manner informs the church, it is true, and yet spoiled as just that, to any sensitive eye, it may be, by reason of the complexity of everything, its futile labour, its immense ambition, the absence of simplicity. From outside we may see how unfortunate the church really was in its birth, how restless it is in its impotence for anything but rhetoric, towering into the sky a magnificent failure, covered with decorations, content with its own grandiose immensity ; happiest at night under the stars that are powerless to discern its insincerity, its real vulgarity ; most miserable when the sun in its fierce impartial way strips it before the world, laying bare to the desert and the hills every gesticulating crocket and scroll, every shouting pinnacle and fantastic empty niche.

Not far away you find the university founded by Alfonso, King of León. It is a spare, rather sad world that little old college now broods over. For here, where once all the world was proud to send its sons, is now a school devoted, it might seem, to a system of almost primary education and to theology. Children, as of old, for nothing seems to change in old Spain, sparely fill the benches that should hold undergraduates. Never have I seen a ruin so terrible. One of the oldest universities in the world (though Oxford takes precedence of it by a decree of the Council of Constance in 1414), in old days its students were more than ten thousand in number ; its professors, its learning, had a great reputation not only in Spain but throughout Europe. Among its famous sons were saints like St Dominic and St Ignatius Loyola, and poets like Fray Luis of León and Calderón de la Barca. Today it numbers some four hundred pupils.

A letter of Peter Martyr gives a vivid picture of the literary enthusiasm of the place in the fifteenth century; for it seems the throng was so great to hear his introductory lecture on some Satire of Juvenal that every avenue to the hall was blocked by the crowd, and the professor who later called Salamanca the ' New Athens ', was borne into his lecture-room on the shoulders of the students. In 1594 a member of the Council of the Inquisition, Juan de Zuñiga, as Royal Commissioner, reorganised the schools, founding a faculty of mathematics such as no other university in Europe could boast; and indeed the works of Copernicus were used as textbooks. Yet Diego de Torres, writing in the first half of the eighteenth century, says that he had been five years at Salamanca before he discovered, quite by chance, that there was such a thing as a science of mathematics! Today, as you pass under the little gateway that faces the façade of the cathedral, coming into the great cloister with its beautiful but ruined gallery, out of which you pass into the classrooms so meagre and bare, the tragedy that has fallen upon Spain seems to find expression very pathetically in the fate of this college once so splendid. And indeed we are in the home of the ' poor bachelor ', a student who for the sake of learning is willing to be hungry, to content himself with very few of the material comforts of life.

The more fortunate among these undergraduates live on three or four pesetas a day but it would seem they are rare; the many find lodging with the burgesses of Salamanca who receive them *a pupilo* as they say, for which they pay a peseta or a peseta and a half a day. The straitness of their surroundings, the modesty of these homes, may better be imagined than described. But there are students even poorer who come to Salamanca, the veritable brothers of Don Cherubini, who pay for their lodging, their food, and the necessities of life—those things which seem to be so few in Spain—not more than ten pesetas a month and I have been told of those who live for five. They come at the beginning of term, bringing with them their beds and certain necessary provisions, such as a basket of *garbanzos* and some dried fish, certain little Spanish sausages, *chorizos*, and, it may be, a little home-grown wine. But for the most part they drink water, that *agua fresca* which is so precious in Spain that it is sold in the streets.

How strange, how impossible Salamanca might seem to anyone coming from Oxford or Cambridge ! How splendid is the courage that is willing to suffer such poverty for the sake of learning ! Poor splendid bachelor, you are one of the heroes that Spain keeps ever in an abject world. In your strong heart I will believe lies the future of Spain. You are of the ancient race which at Lepanto neither slept nor quenched its thirst till it had accomplished its desire. And yet, is it learning you get, after all, in exchange for your privations ? I know not. Yet if all I was told may pass for truth, even that pearl for which you have sacrificed everything is denied you : the old great learning lost, the new dreams of science, of philosophy, passed over in silence, while the great tradition is gone for ever, save that you in your poverty have preserved what you could in your heart. But as you journey homewards over the great vague roads, they are yours, the immense beautiful dreams that are left in your heart : while, O fortunate, there remains still the earth your only bed, the sky your blue curtain, it is still easy to love, to sing, to pray, to believe, and to trust in God.

Among the rest there may still be seen at Salamanca certain figures almost English in their neatness : they are the students of the Irish College. Housed as it is in one of the loveliest palaces in a city of palaces, that Irish College is, I think, just a survival, very valuable as just that it may be, yet still something that is a little fantastic when one remembers that in Ireland herself better learning may be had without difficulty ; and, if we ignore for a moment the influence of so old, so venerable a place as this sweet fallen city, a larger view of the world, a stronger sense of life. And yet I for one would not have that Irish College suppressed for the world. It is still a witness, when all have forgotten, to the greatness of Spain, and I will believe that, in spite of every misfortune, they are fortunate who live in so old, so beautiful a city. Yet it is true there are misfortunes. Before I left Salamanca for good, I wished to possess a book, an edition of Homer, a book of Virgil, a play of Sophocles, whose title should bear the imprint of the University—as who should say, at Salamanca at the University Press was this book printed ; but this was not to be. In vain I searched every bookshop, every counter ; no edition of the classics, no edition even of Fray Luis' poems has, within living memory, been printed for the University ; and, if you will believe me, all that the booksellers of Salamanca seemed to possess were certain foreign novels and the little cheap reprints, ' Biblioteca Universal ', printed at Madrid.

It was at the University that I saw the manuscript of the poems of Fray Luis of León, whose ashes are in the little chapel in the cloister. Born at Belmonte de Cuenca in 1529, Fray Luis entered the Augustinian Order when he was eighteen years old, and in 1560 became Professor of Theology at Salamanca. But I wish only to recall here his encounter with León de Castro, who, in those days, held the Greek chair in the University, and with whom Fray Luis was not friends. During some public discussion Fray Luis, it seems, threatened the Greek professor with the Inquisition, and with the public burning of his treatise on Isaiah, which, for what we know, may have been a villainous production. However, de Castro anticipated him, denounced him as a Jew to the Dominicans, and since he had, poet as he was, translated the Song of Songs into the Castilian tongue—a grave offence it might seem —he was arrested in March 1572, and imprisoned here in Salamanca for four years or more. In spite of his enemies, however, he was acquitted at last on 7th December 1576, and on his return to the University, where the chair of Theology had been kept for him, he began his first lecture in these words : '' Señores, as we were saying the other day. . . .'' It was so in old Spain that they ruled the world.

It was, however, a greater matter that in 1482 was being debated in the hall of the great Dominican Convent of San Estéban. The University professors, ecclesiastics for the most part, to whom the matter had been referred by the king, had pronounced against the proposed voyage of Don Cristobal Colon as a thing " vain, impracticable, and resting on grounds too weak to merit the support of the Government ". It was this pronouncement that the Dominicans, with the Archbishop of Seville, Diego de Deza, at their head, were debating. Deza, later the successor of Torquemada as head of the Inquisition, in those days certainly was one of the most liberal and intelligent men in Spain. He and his Dominicans, to their undying glory, were too enlightened to acquiesce in the sentence of the professors. They offered Don Cristobal their hospitality and their friendship, and not only cordially embraced his idea but obtained for him a promise from the Catholic kings that at the conclusion of the war they would find 'both time and inclination to treat with him'.

That old great convent, restored though it be for the most part, might seem to hold even yet some remembrance of that splendid presence, some deathless grace or greatness from those days so long ago. As I wandered through its passages, up its immense staircases, through numberless empty and deserted cells, out at last to the poor forsaken garden, where on a little hill a great lonely crucifix, black in the sunset, blesses the desert, it was of him, the great adventurer, I spoke with the old Friar who accompanied me. "His genius was so great that although I have never seen the sea, when I remember him and his dreams I seem to understand everything : the promise of the sunset, the immensity of the ocean, the vision that must be true." The old Friar, with his long white beard swept over his shoulders by the wind, seemed in the twilight to be speaking as much to himself as to me.

Far, far away over the desert the bells of Salamanca recalled to the world the birth of Christ. But he was thinking of other things. In his eyes was the light of the great enthusiasm, his old worn hand trembled as he stretched it out over that sad and beautiful world. "I have heard that he could discern the nearness of land in a piece of floating seaweed or in the flight of a bird, or in the strength of the wind ; when one speaks of him cities, clouds, and mountains disappear, and only what is formed by the spirit remains. Like the greatest saints, he seemed ever to be listening to a voice silent for other men."

Then he was silent. Out of the desert night was coming. When at last we turned and made our way slowly back to the convent it was quite dark.

[April 1906

8

UNDER THE HAMMER AND SICKLE

Eric Linklater

I S.S. *ДЧАРОВ*

There were three of us in Pahlevi : Radcliffe and myself
and Mrs Rodney, who had come through Persia with a
shooting-stick and a tireless demand for hot baths. Pahlevi
is on the southern shore of the Caspian Sea, and for the
moment our business was to go to Baku in the territory
of the U.S.S.R. On the map and from a distance it had
looked a trifling journey of about two hundred miles, but
at Pahlevi we came into sea-mist and a fog of regulations
and a cloudy babel of tongues. We spoke French and a
little German and enough Persian to ask for shaving-water ;
but the matter of passports and police exeats and customs
needed Russian, or more Persian than a dozen household
terms would encompass.

This was our difficulty before dinner, a shadow over
the caviare and fried sturgeon, the chicken and spinach
and Persian oranges. But the shadow shortened as the
evening passed, and eventually disappeared under the boots
of a little moth-eaten kind of fellow who introduced himself
as a Russian *émigré* of the old régime, now a man of affairs
and acquainted with the *douane*, capable and willing to

take all our troubles on to his own narrow shoulders. His name was something like Haemorrhage, and once, he said, he had been a rich man. We nodded sympathetically and filled his glass.

Everything would be quite all right, he said. He knew the Police and the Customs. He knew everybody, and everybody would assist in making our journey pleasant and expeditious.

What was the *Udarob* like, this ship which was to take us to Russia? *Magnifique!* he replied. She was lying at the quay now, and in the morning she would take on her passengers and exquisite foods to tempt their idle palates on the silky calm of the inland sea. Ah, *magnifique!* And the Russian railways? They too, it seemed, were *magnifique.* Our spirits rose, and we called for another bottle of wine. In wagon-lit and in restaurant-car everything was ordered with perfect cleanliness, and splendour tempered only by surprising cheapness.

We clapped M. Haemorrhage on his dingy shoulder and drank his health for his good news.

" My name is Humoreske," he corrected us diffidently.

" *C'est égal,*" we assured him, and went to bed happy.

In the morning he led us importantly from police station to customs sheds, and to noisy money-changers, where with the mysterious aid of bobbins on a wire frame the tomans of Persia were exchanged for Soviet roubles. Eventually we looked through a tall wooden paling and saw the *Udarob*, a pile of luggage, mail-bags, and a dozen or two passengers waiting with indifferent patience. Four porters, hairy men in dark smocks and long boots, demanded extortionate sums for a minimum of service. M. Humoreske regretted his inability to pacify them. They bellowed with greedy wrath and extended enormous avid hands. M.

Humoreske seemed anxious to go. He accepted our remuneration and left us with inconspicuous speed, while the porters squabbled ferociously over the last of our Persian money.

The boat seemed small for the number of passengers, but we had been assured of cabins, and went up the gangway confidently. It was unpleasant to find all the cabins opening off a central saloon, but travellers' choice, like beggars', is sometimes limited, and we sniffed the stale air with dutiful philosophy.

The stewardess, a middle-aged peasant with a handkerchief round her head, was incomprehensibly explanatory in Russian, but with nods and becks made it clear that the lady's cabin was here and the men's there. Mrs Rodney looked through the door of hers. It was very small, completely airless, and already occupied by a melancholy-looking Turk and a stout Frenchwoman, whose fingers glittered with splendid rings as she stooped comfortably to take off her boots.

"Take my things out of there immediately. I insist on having a cabin to myself," said Mrs Rodney, and scorning the seats in the saloon, sat resolutely on her shooting-stick to await a more happy disposal. The stewardess was puzzled. Misunderstanding, she showed Radcliffe and myself to our room. In it were two Circassian girls, one plump and painted, the other like a dishevelled and dissipated Madonna. It looked embarrassing, and our Puritan inhibitions took us by the elbow and led us out again. The stewardess was now puzzled enough to be unhappy; and Mrs Rodney sat on her shooting-stick and coldly demanded that the captain should be summoned immediately.

When the ship pulled out we, with all our baggage, sat

aloofly on a hatch, insular even under the Hammer and Sickle. The flag of the Soviet floated overhead, and packed in stuffy cabins men and women—Russians, Persians, Georgians, and Turks—accepted its red protection. We decided to sleep on deck. Our berths, once disowned, had quickly been claimed by others; but we had bedding-rolls, and the weather was mild. A night under the Caspian stars might not be unpleasant.

By and by a bell rang for dinner, and we returned to the saloon. At the head of the table was a Belgian official in Persian service with his wife; next to him there was a little dark-skinned man wearing a Soviet badge—an enamel flag lettered C.C.C.P.—and a remarkably pretty girl; the Madonna—her hair framed lankly the long oval of her face—and her luscious friend; the brown-faced melancholy Turk from Mrs Rodney's cabin, and a bald, oldish Persian; several nondescript Russians and a vivacious fair-haired girl; the fat aquiline Frenchwoman with the rings; and ourselves.

A shuffling grey-moustached steward carried in an enormous soup-tureen and set it laboriously in the centre of the table. On each side of it a plate was piled with vast ragged slices of bread. There was communal passing of soup plates and ladling of thick meaty broth, and the meal started with a clatter of spoons and babble of talk. The Russian girls were cheerful and noisy, and their voices were rich with laughter, but the two Circassians ate silently, their heads bent low over their plates. They bit hungrily into their bread, and put it back on the table with little circular stains of red on it from their painted lips.

When the soup was finished the steward brought two flat dishes of sturgeon. That, too, was divided, plates were cleaned, and the meal was over. We thought of M.

Haemorrhage, and regretted his second bottle of wine.

Morning came white and windless as we awoke in our blankets on the boat-deck. Slowly the sun climbed a colourless sky, but never showed himself clearly, hiding all day behind a thin curtain of mist. The sea was calm and expressionless, a glazy bottle-green, opaque, and looking deadly deep. Faint far-away hills seemed to keep pace with us, so alike were they and so slow was our speed, for, in spite of the *Udarob* being a mail-boat, she had taken in tow a lighter filled with a week's sturgeon fishing, and the black hulk hung heavily on our tail.

Each meal was like the first supper, communal bowls of soup and massive wedges of new bread. The Russians grew more talkative, the girls more mirthful; the melody of their laughter roused even the listless weary Madonna. We exchanged polite phrases with the Frenchwoman, who was going to Paris by way of Moscow, and we enlisted the aid of the whole table when we tried to ask the steward for beer. The pretty dark-haired girl with the Soviet official was the first to take our meaning. " *Peeva!* " she shrilled delightedly to the bewildered steward. " *Peeva! Peeva!* " shouted the company in chorus, laughing happily, and the steward shambled away amiably gesticulating. We did our best to bow all round the table. This at last was *magnifique*.

The melancholy Turk and his Persian friend did not come down to lunch. They were standing by the shore-ward rail, looking unhappily at the hazy outline of land.

" We don't seem to have gone far," Radcliffe remarked.

" No," said the Persian a little tremulously. " It is difficult with this boat. She is so old, and they are frightened of the engines. My friend here has just been talking to the driver." He pointed to a large quartermaster standing woodenly at the wheel.

"He told me that they have gone down now to see how much she is leaking," said the Turk. "They dare not go out of sight of land in case she sinks."

We looked again at the quartermaster; he had the solemn air of a constitutional jester, and we felt relieved.

There was another diversion in the afternoon. A small bear-cub escaped from its home in the fo'c'sle and, pursued by the ships' boys, padded clumsily aft. It climbed a ladder, and disappeared through the open door of the captain's cabin. Unhesitatingly the boys followed it, tumbling over each other into the sacred stateroom, and finally retrieving the bear from the captain's bunk. With a cord round its neck the cub sat unhappily on the deck, shyly hanging its overgrown head and considering the spectators out of sidelong eyes.

Attracted by the sound of the chase a boy in knicker-bockers—a hitherto unnoticed passenger—appeared with a kind of attenuated and half-grown beagle, a fierce little dog, which immediately attacked the bear. The cub was unwilling either to fight or play, but clipped the dog neatly on its ear; infuriated, the pseudo-beagle bit savagely, and the bear fled in ungainly frog-hops, whining pitifully. It was caught and taken back to the fo'c'sle, where the baiting continued.

About this time the stewardess came out to sun herself in a yellow dress, brightly flowered. All morning she had been busily working on deck polishing brass. The crew took life easily, sleeping or talking, and one serious-looking seaman spent half the day on the boat-deck reading a work of apparently devotional literature. But the stewardess polished brass and carried soapy water incessantly, and forward an ancient cook could be seen slowly and interminably cutting meat and baking bread.

The colour of the sea changed gradually from bottle-green to a hueless grey, and a wet sunset smudged the haze with half-hearted dyes. We should have reached Baku early in the afternoon, but the fishlighter in tow had delayed us, and now it did not matter when we arrived, for Soviet regulations do not permit passengers to be landed after sundown. Night fell and brought a cold wind with it. The black shape of the sturgeon hulk relentlessly pursued us through the dusk. Northwards a crescent of light faintly broke the darkness. This was Baku ; and in an hour's time we anchored to wait for dawn and permission to land.

II BAKU

A smell of oil blew out on gusts of cold wind from the dingy grey town that clung to the side of a mean little hill. An officer of the Soviet Political Police in a long drab greatcoat and green cap stood at the head of the gangway. At the inner end of the wooden pier porters, customs officials, and droshky drivers battled with calculated anger over our baggage. We drove through dingy untended streets to a hotel. The houses were colourless and shabby, with broken windows and gaping patches on the walls where plaster or cement had rotted and fallen away. Baku, the Caspian gate to Soviet Russia, is a dismal portal.

But the hotel was more cheering. Mrs Rodney was given a room with a genuine European bath and crowed happily, and in a little while we went down to a breakfast that consisted mainly of nobly heaped dishes of fresh caviare. We meant to go on to Batum, across the Caucasus, by train that evening, and after walking for an hour or two by cold roughly cobbled streets and through desolate public gardens, we again gave ourselves, body and soul, to the flesh-pots. For both soul and body need sustenance in Baku, the one for the harsh winds and the other for the drab town and the sight of white-faced, hurrying, miserable-looking citizens. There are big well-made men to be seen, and the soldiers in their long greatcoats are like massive moving statues, but there is a bleak look in their faces ; there are few women, and no children play about the streets.

"Happy comrades," said Radcliffe thoughtfully, and hurried us back to lunch. We looked at the menu. "Caviare ! " he said decidedly. "Bortsch ! " cried Mrs Rodney ecstatically. "Sucking-pig," I replied. The waiter inclined his head and produced a wine-list. In the inspired manner of the Virgilian lots—for they were all Georgian wines, and we did not know one from another—Radcliffe pointed a finger at a name which looked like a series of pothooks and treble clefs, and we waited expectantly. In time and order they came, caviare, crimson bowls of bortsch, with thick seasoned cream, succulent pig of ethereal flavour, and a pleasing golden wine—a gastronomic parade that would flatter an empire, so that we began to think kindly of the Soviet and its brotherly ways.

"I told you that it wouldn't be so bad as people said," declared Mrs Rodney. "This is the best coffee I've tasted since we left Baghdad."

We drove to the station happily, thinking of our Pahlevi *émigré's* description of the magnificent Russian trains. The station was very crowded with green-capped policemen, railway officials by the score, and hundreds of citizens. They stood in patient queues at the ticket-offices, or sat with Oriental stillness on their bundles and boxes. Our guide—a Russian who spoke some French—disappeared for half an hour and returned smiling. We picked up our rugs and prepared to follow. "There are no places on this evening's train," he said. "It is unfortunate, but you will be able to go by another train tomorrow."

Our happiness vanished. Baku for one day was not too bad, but Baku for two days was unthinkable, for we were proud then, though our spirits were humbled before we left Russia. However, there was nothing to do but reserve soft seats for the morrow—First, Second, and Third have been abolished with all class distinctions, but there is still a financial barrier between Soft Seats and Hard Seats—and inform the Police, who are interested in all such details, that we should be staying a little longer than we had anticipated.

Our interpreter led me to the local headquarters of the Soviet Political Police. A green-capped official, whose remarkably handsome features were slighly obscured by three days' growth of beard, continued to read his newspaper while the interpreter explained our unfortunate position. After a minute or two the interpreter whispered that perhaps it would be better to wait a little. We waited. Then I suggested that he should try again; and this time Green Cap condescended so far as to jerk an informatory thumb at the room opposite. We were approaching it when the door opened and a superior clean-shaven Green Cap came out and began a muffled conversation with Green Cap Number One. Again we waited. I ventured to interrupt, and both stared coldly at me for half a minute before continuing their exchange of official secrets.

A slight commotion outside at last distracted them, and through the open door we saw an old woman and a hatless good-looking girl arguing with the sentry on duty. Green Cap Number Two shouted an order, and the girl was pushed into his room; the old woman called something to him, laughing, and Green Cap followed the girl, shutting his door behind him. I nudged the interpreter, who stated our humble case again and more acceptably, so that we were told to go upstairs and consult the proper authority there. I was shown into a room where two more Green Caps sat silently examining papers, and to one of them I gave our passports. He reached for a large volume, apparently containing instructions, and I sat and waited while he began to read carefully through it. By-and-by I heard a clicking noise behind me, and turning round I saw the other policeman fondly spinning the chamber of his revolver. Six cartridges lay on the table. He cleaned them with his pocket-handkerchief, and carefully reloaded. A cold little breeze seemed to stir in the short hair at the back of my neck, and a gentle dew of apprehension broke on the palms of my hands. So this is Russia, I thought. The policeman closed his revolver decisively, and rose noisily to his feet.

The other one, who had patiently been reading his book of regulations, began to talk in indifferent French. It seemed that we could remain for another night in Baku—it would have been difficult to refuse us permission—but should we stay for more than twenty-four hours it would be necessary to report our presence once again. I thanked him, and looked nervously round for the one with the revolver. But he had gone. Perhaps even in the U.S.S.R. they do not shoot sitting birds.

They dine late in Russia, and at ten o'clock we began to eat in a gradually filling restaurant. To our surprise, the Belgian customs official and his wife who had been fellow-passengers from Persia in the *Udarob* were sitting at the next table. They had been going to Moscow, but they too had been unable to find seats, and were condemned to wait five days for another train. We shuddered, and thought with secret thanksgiving of our own departure on the morrow.

Slowly the tables filled with their nightly customers. Russians in dark blouses, with unshaven cheeks and ludicrously manicured hands (it is fashionable to leave the little finger-nail long in the Chinese manner), crowded the restaurant. Except for a few foreigners there was not a decently dressed man in the place, and the few women there were painted so as to produce a mere cosmetic impression of human features. Here was the proletariat taking its ease at last, pouring rich Bortsch down its hairy throat, while the constant popping of corks was like a comradely echo of long-ago machine-guns in the streets of Moscow. By midnight the scene was getting noisy, for more and more men and a few more women came in from the streets, rankly scented women and rough-clad men. Half of them were prematurely bald, and the other half thatched with long unruly hair.

In the morning we heard vague sounds from a curtained room, and looking in saw a faro game in progress with fairly heavy stakes on the board. Round the tables, haggard and red-eyed, sat many whom we recognised as having been among the previous night's diners. By and by they came into the restaurant and breakfasted on bread and wine and caviare. Then they went back to the faro table, and settled down to another session of impassive gambling. It might have been bricklaying for all the interest they showed in their cards.

Like emigrants we and the Belgians clustered together,

our imprisonment now shared by a large hearty Frenchman
who had served as an interpreter with the British forces
during the war, and who retained as a legacy of that great
comradeship an impressive use of "Quite!" and "Awfully", and that demoded encomium "Perfectly good".
He had lost a perfectly good suitcase, it seemed, and had
been charged a prodigious number of perfectly good francs
for reporting the loss to a rotten kind of R.T.O. "Awfully
bad luck, wasn't it?"

"Quite!" we answered, and sympathetically redirected
the conversation to Arras and older memories.

Soon it grew time to expect our guide with the promised
tickets, and we gathered all our luggage in readiness. The
minutes passed and no guide arrived. The hotel staff
showed us their watches, and indicated when the train
would go. We nodded impatiently, and went out to look
for the missing Russian. By the pavement were two
droshky drivers who shared the secret of our intended
departure, and who, with loud explanatory cries, showed
us more watches, and made it desperately clear that we
were about to miss our train, for without the Russian
guide (who had our passports) we were helpless. We went
inside again and thought the long thoughts which fill the
evenings of Siberian prisoners.

At last the Russian came. "There were no seats to
be obtained on this train," he said.

"But we had reserved seats," we reminded him.

He stammered a little, and groped for his broken bits
of French. "But later they were all required *pour des
gens sovietiques*," he explained.

"I knew all along that that is what would happen,"
said Mrs Rodney, and sat down on a shooting-stick planted
so firmly that it seemed an English oak rooted there on

alien soil.

" Will there be seats tomorrow ? " asked Radcliffe.

" Not tomorrow, I think," said the guide.

" The day after ? "

" They say that they cannot promise you seats for any day."

" I told you they were all liars," remarked Mrs Rodney illogically, while we began to consider the prospect of long months spent in Baku, waiting for a Soft Seat on a train that would never arrive.

" What about going back to Persia ? " said a doubting heart.

" You cannot," replied a sinister-seeming German who had joined our counsels. " Your visas are made out for transit from Baku to Batum, and so you cannot go from Baku anywhere except to Batum. You must wait." He paused. " I am not surprised that there is trouble made for English people in Russia. It is the fault of your Foreign Secretary, is it not ? "

For a fortnight we had seen no newspapers, and an awful doubt crept into our minds that meanwhile Sir Austen [Chamberlain] had been writing notes to the Soviet on black-edged ultimatum paper. With a hollow laugh the German left us.

" There is a slow train which goes as far as Tiflis," ventured the guide. " Perhaps you may find seats on that."

" When does it leave ? " we asked in chorus.

" About midnight ; but perhaps it will be late."

There was no certainty that we would find seats at Tiflis any more readily than at Baku, but Tiflis was halfway and more across the Caucasus, a capital city with a reputation for beauty ; and to stay at Baku was like staying with beggars at the back door of a great house. We decided to go to Tiflis.

III THE CAUCASUS

A Russian railway carriage is like a cabin on a small ship, a slender well of space between narrow bunks at night and abominable confinement by day. The Tiflis train lay moored at a dark platform, and cautiously we sidled down the black tunnel of a corridor to our cabin. In one of the lower berths a Soviet official lay fully dressed ; he was young and white-faced, with thick lips and wide-open gloomy eyes, and on his blouse he wore the Soviet medal for bravery. A little later he pulled off his long boots of soft black leather, unbuckled his revolver, and put it beneath his pillow. He ate a crust of bread and prepared to sleep.

About three o'clock in the morning the train—which should have left at midnight—pulled out of the station, and labouring through the last hours of darkness at last came to a bare plain, white in the morning and stretching to the distant snowy wall of the Caucasus. All day we rode slowly, parallel with the great jagged range, across long flat fields here and there flooded so deeply that the water was level with the track. At intervals of an hour or two the train stopped at little wayside stations where all the passengers hurried down to buy bread and pieces of cooked meat, oranges, and glasses of tea. The only excitement came in the afternoon, with a jarring sound as of brakes suddenly applied, and when the train came to an uneasy standstill we found a foolish buffalo dead and tangled among the wheels of one of the coaches. It was pulled out and left for the crows, and we continued our bloody path to Tiflis.

It was evening when we arrived, and, knowing three words of Russian, prepared to interrogate, argue with, and ultimately persuade Russian railway officials who knew no English. It was easy to find out that a train left for Batum in two or three hours' time. It was easy to indicate that we wanted to go by that train. And then there came a check. A council of workers assembled to discuss the question of arranging accommodation for us, and a long debate ensued, full of interest for the participants. At last it was decided that there was no room for us, and heads were shaken decisively at our renewed request for tickets. Producing a watch and raising our eyebrows to dizzy heights of interrogation we endeavoured to find out when there would be a train able to take us. Regretfully, so it seemed, they gesticulated the impossibility of giving us any assurance. We began to grow desperate, for our funds were incapable of supporting us indefinitely in idleness in the capital of Georgia.

And then Radcliffe rose to heights of dramatic art. He addressed the Workers' Council in English, French, and Hindustani, and they, though all uncomprehending, were impressed by the passion of his words. He pointed longingly to the west, he showed one empty pocket and the other holding only a few poor coins ; the hearts of the workers were clearly touched. This was the crucial moment. He pulled out a notebook and pencil, and in a few lines drew a steamer leaving a lonely quay. " Batum ! " he said, again looking westwards ; and pointing despairingly to the ground beneath him, " Tiflis ! " he said. He stretched longing hands to the distant town, and again drew a picture, a house on the far side of an angry sea.

"Our home," he said simply and quite incomprehensibly.

We stood silent as slowly the debate began again. There were plainly two parties in the council by this time, and it seemed that our party was winning. Finally a red-faced man like a butcher smacked a clenched fist into an enormous hand and decided in our favour. He led the way to a ticket-office, and after saluting the council we followed gratefully.

Another night in the train took us into a great open valley, into vineyards and rich meadows rolling down to a river from huge wooded heights, while in the distance snowy peaks scarred with their dazzling spears the blue expanse of a cloudless sky. This was Georgia, a gracious country nobly inhabited, for at the little stations enormous broad-built men, like giants in their hairy boorkas and astrakhan caps, strode magnificently or stood and laughed in open mirth with handsome, rosy-faced girls. All the way to the sea were wooded mountains and green meadows, flowers and orchards and rivers, and every league, it seemed, taller men and more handsome girls. Batum came at last, on a green point curving slowly out into the Black Sea, and, as happy as schoolboys on holiday, we climbed down to the sunny platform.

The only flaw in our happiness was that we were hungry, for we had been compelled to economise even on wayside bread and meat. But a hotel was not far away, a bank where we could draw more money, and a droshky ready to take us to both. Our surviving roubles were just sufficient to pay for transport to the hotel. There the first person we saw was the melancholy Turk who had been our fellow-voyager on the Caspian Sea, and who had succeeded in leaving Baku a day before us.

He looked more melancholy than ever. "The ship was

gone," he said. " There will not be another one for ten or perhaps twelve days."

We stared at him, and the sun seemed to go behind a cloud. " Oh, nonsense," we said half-heartedly.

" It is true," said the Turk.

" Well, I'm hungry," said Mrs Rodney impatiently, " and ship or no ship I want something to eat."

" There is no food here today," said the Turk.

" What ! " said Mrs Rodney awfully.

" It is Easter, and everybody is drunk," said the dismal Turk.

We had forgotten the Russian Easter, which lags a week behind our own, and the Turk's information was correct.

Two servants of some sort appeared and carried our suitcases upstairs, staggering from side to side. Laughing happily, they brought a second bed into the room which Radcliffe and I were to share, and gazed blankly at Mrs Rodney's immediate order for a bath.

" Bath ? " she demanded. " *Bain ?* Hot water ? *Hammam ?* "

" There is no bath," said the Turk, who had followed for company's sake.

The elder of the servants asked for our passports—in Russia a passport is immediately handed to the hotel-keeper, who communicates with the police—and, grinning at the photographs, they carried them away.

In a little while we went down to investigate the matter of food. The boots and his friend—whom later we came to know as George—were sitting at the foot of the stairs.

" Passports ? ' said the boots.

" You've got our passports," we answered.

He held up two, counted them, and pointing to Radcliffe, repeated " Passport ? "

"I gave you my passport," said Radcliffe angrily.

"He has lost it," said Mrs Rodney. "I knew he would. It was ridiculous to give it to a drunken creature like that."

The boots only shook his head dumbly, and George took up the tale, repeating "Passport?" in a high-pitched voice.

"Better leave them till they're sober," I suggested, but Racliffe said no, and felt in the boots's pockets to see if he could find the passport for himself. It was not there. Then he searched George, and George being ticklish began to laugh. George had a squint and a magnificent moustache, and when he laughed his eyes and the tips of his moustache all converged to a central point on his nose. It was an attractive laugh, but it disappeared when Radcliffe pulled a passport from his trouser pocket. George's chin dropped, and he looked at the missing document with the amazement of a child watching the flags of all the nations drawn inexplicably out of a conjuror's mouth.

The boots laughed hoarsely. "Passport!" he said. "Ho, ho, ho!"

George's spirits returned, and he giggled, "Hee, hee, hee! Passport!" This was excellent fun. "Hee, hee!" he said.

"Ho, ho, ho!" replied the boots.

Both laughed uproariously. "Passport!" they said at intervals, and dug each other in the ribs. It was a champion jest, a proper joke for a Georgian Easter, and they took their fill of it.

But we were hungry, and borrowing some roubles from the miserable Turk we set out to look for food in this town which was enjoying itself too much to worry about trade.

IV AN ENGLISH SHIP

George was a kind of chambermaid. The morning after our arrival we saw him on the dirty veranda outside our room—there was a view of dingy roofs on one of which a yellow cat lay dying—looking pale and ill. With one hand he pressed his aching head and cupped in the other lay two white tablets at which he gazed suspiciously. He had just taken Mrs Rodney her morning tea, and she, properly diagnosing his condition as the natural sequel of a Russian Easter, had given him aspirin. Doubtfully he placed the tablets on his tongue, and with a shuddering effort swallowed them.

There was a dim air of pain about all the hotel staff that morning; and the waiters, burly men in Russian blouses, considered the breakfast they dilatorily served with sour distaste. And then we went to look for a ship.

The harbour was beautiful, a deep blue bay lying below wooded hills, while to the north a chain of snowy mountains reached, ragged and gigantic, far into the sea. Along the water-front were tables at which the workers of Batum sat and drank their coffee. And in an Italian shipping office there was a man who confirmed the patient Turk's information that there would be no ship to Constantinople for another ten days. We thought of our letters of credit, once so fat and confident, and now shrinking to meagre old age; we thought of our leave, how ' time flyeth and slippeth marvellously away ', and all three of us we blanched.

" But there are oil-tankers and cargo ships; perhaps one of them will take you," said the shipping agent. " If you go to the Soviet Shipping Company's office they will tell you there. They speak English," he added reassuringly.

The personnel of the Soviet Shipping Company appeared

charming. There was Mr Rakovsky, who had been an officer in the old army, and had survived the dawn of revolution to become a water-clerk at a hundred and fifty roubles a month; there was Mr Balin, a sailor with a sailor's cap stuck resolutely on the side of his head and an air of happy truculence; and Mr Levinsky, who was pale and had a humid eye. They gathered round us, and summoning a fat man with a shaven bullet-head and an unpronounceable name to assist, they gave us advice and encouragement.

It was quite likely, they said, that the captain of one of the oil-tankers would take us to Constantinople, or perhaps to Alexandria. There was a German ship leaving the following day, and an Italian one the day after. And there was Captain Fletcher, an Englishman, whose ship was now discharging and in a few days would go on to Novorossiisk and Odessa to load cement and wheat—a voyage round the Black Sea might not be unpleasant. But they would inquire of all these ships whether it would be possible to give us a passage.

Our spirits rose past Fair and Set Fair, and being in the neighbourhood of Very Dry we invited Mr Rakovsky to dine with us that night. He came and told us stories of the war on the Austrian front; how the Russian infantry advanced fourteen or fifteen deep, only the leading two or three ranks being armed, so that those who followed had to wait for men in front to fall wounded or dead before they got rifles and could fight for themselves. He told us, very cheerfully, of the communal houses which have superseded private property, and spoke with apparent gratitude of the eighteen square yards of floor space to which every adult worker under the Soviet is entitled. He told us of his wife who had been making Easter pies and entertaining her neighbours—out of his salary of a hundred and fifty roubles a month—and of her attendance at medical classes in her spare time. He spoke charmingly, as a survivor of the old order, of the new régime, and he made it seem a very gallant adventure, so that we forgot broken houses and dirty streets, and forgave the youthful crudities of Soviet rule.

But life, like Marjorie Daw, has continual ups and downs, and after dining with Young Russia on top of the see-saw, we spent the following morning with disappointment in the depths. George had recovered from his Easter potations, and was no longer amenable to discipline. We rang and shouted for tea.

" *Si chas*," said George, and went blithely on his way.

' *Si chas* ' is the Russian for ' Anon, anon, sir ', and its promise of immediacy is never made except to be obliterated by the encroaching tides of postponement. In a calendar of minutes *Si chas* would be the Greek *Kalends*.

We rang for shaving water.

" *Si chas*," said George, and returned to crack another joke with Hubert, his fellow-chambermaid.

We summoned Hubert, and very determinedly said " *Chai !* " holding three fingers erect beneath his nose, indicating by word and action that three glasses of tea should be brought.

" *Si chas*," said Hubert, and wandered dreamily away.

We knew before we left the hotel what would await us at the quay. The German captain would be unable to take us. The morning was foggy, and the cobbled streets were slippery with rain. It was inevitable that greyness should dominate that day, and inevitably it did.

The German captain was not prepared to take the risk of adding passengers to a cargo of benzine. We suggested that what risk there was was really ours, but the captain, it seemed, had been quite definite. We could not interview him personally, for his ship now lay out in the harbour, and, unfortunately, the Russians said, permission to go aboard could not be granted. It was contrary to regulations.

And the Italian? we asked.

Mr Balin shrugged his shoulders. " I have seen him too," he said, " and he does not like passengers ; and besides, it is not easy to land people in Constantinople from a cargo ship or an oil ship. I do not think he will take you."

Could we not see him ourselves ? we asked. It was difficult, said Mr Balin, to know just where to find him. It would be better to leave everything to himself and Mr Levinsky.

" I don't trust that man," said Mrs Rodney decisively as we walked round the harbour.

We walked as far as the *Don*, Captain Fletcher's ship, an Arcos vessel trading between the Black Sea, home ports, and the Baltic. At the foot of the gangway stood a Russian sentry—every ship in the harbour was similarly guarded— and a lean red-faced man in stained blue uniform.

" Is the Captain aboard ? " asked Radcliffe.

" No," said the lean red man, " he went ashore an hour ago. But what d'you want ? I'm the Chief Officer here."

" We thought we would like a talk with the Captain," said Radcliffe a little vaguely.

" If it's tobacco you want, try mine," replied the chief. " I know what it is to be in a town like this, where you can't get anything fit to smoke. And the beer's rotten, too. But 'ave you tried that wine of theirs ? You get a bottle with sixty-six on it ; that's the best, and it's not half bad."

We took the Chief Officer—his name was Merrick—

into our confidence, and told him of our plight and the hopes falsely raised by our Russian friends.

" Don't you trust 'em," said Mr Merrick. " I know Russia, and I know the Russians. He's all right "—he indicated the sentry, a cheerful-looking peasant in ill-fitting uniform—" and all the ordinary people are all right. But the officials ! " And Mr Merrick spat, as though his opinion could be safely represented only by an asterisk. " Go and see the captain of that Italian ship yourselves. He'll take you all right if you pay him, but if the others get at him first, why, they'll probably put him off it."

" That's exactly what I feel myself," said Mrs Rodney. " I distrusted those people from the start, and I still distrust them."

" But what's their idea ? " I objected. " Why should they want to keep us here ? "

" Got shares in the hotel perhaps," suggested Radcliffe gloomily.

" You never know," said Mr Merrick. " That's what I always say about Russia." He looked warily over his shoulder at the empty quay, and repeated darkly, " *You never know !* "

Again there seemed a lurking suggestion of Siberia in the air as we went to search, and search in vain, for the Italian captain. On his ship a steward said he was ashore, and in the office they told us he had gone back to his ship. And, as we played hide-and-seek in this way, the thought came again that perhaps Sir Austen Chamberlain had been writing tactless notes to the Soviet.

By morning the German tanker had gone, and the Italian lay out in the harbour ready to go. But while we sat and drank our coffee on the quay, discussing the advisability of learning Russian to aid us in our prospective internment, Mr Rakovsky came towards us smiling happily. " I have good news for you," he said. " An English ship is coming in either tonight or tomorrow morning, and will be sailing again in forty-eight hours. An English captain will be sure to take you."

Marjorie Daw's heels left the ground again, and we soared deliciously into thoughts of freedom. There is more than romance in that phrase " an English ship "— there is solid comfort in it. In England you are in Kent or Northumberland or Devonshire ; you are local, or even parochial. But in an English ship abroad you are in England itself, which, for all that pessimists may say, is a very blessed thing.

We went through the town to a long shingle beach that afternoon and joyfully played ducks and drakes on the Black Sea. The routine visit to the harbour on the following morning was crowned by the magnificent spectacle of a Red Ensign hanging modestly over the stern of a black but comely tanker. We had grown cunning by that time, and divided our forces. Radcliffe went to the shipping office ; Mrs Rodney was sent to drink coffee a little farther down the quay, with orders to halt anybody who looked like an English shipmaster ; and I took a droshky and drove round to the ship.

The driver, with the native courtesy and camaraderie of Russia, offered his cigarettes and struck a match for me, and then lashed his horses to a sudden gallop. Swaying and jolting, we roared through the cobbled streets with a sound of shouting and smitten iron, but at the end of a superb progress I drew blank at the ship, for the captain had gone ashore. Returning to the office, I found neither him nor Radcliffe, and rain had driven Mrs Rodney from the quay.

While I was considering what to do, a bootblack, whose stance was nearby, called something in incomprehensible Russian, and pointed round the corner. I followed the line of his finger, and came to a little wine-shop. Sprawling on the counter, a bottle in one hand and his pipe in the other, was Radcliffe. With unerring precision he filled brim-full three glasses, and the three glasses passed into the hands of Mr Balin, Captain Fletcher of the *Don*, and Captain Archer of the *Tamarisk*, the tanker which had just arrived. It was a hearty scene. The sides of the small dark tavern were lined with shelves on which stood rows and rows of bottles; long lines of tall bottles and companies of squat bottles, old bottles and clean new bottles; bottles with curious Georgian labels, and sinister bottles without any labels at all; bottles of wine, beer, cognac, and vodka. It was difficult to believe that in such an atmosphere as this any request could be refused, any hope fail to fructify.

Radcliffe introduced me to Captain Archer. The Captain pushed his hat farther back from his broad red forehead, and said, " Now, what the devil made you come to Russia ? You've come from India, your friend says, and you're going home. Well, then, is this the sort of way home that any sane man would choose ? "

It is always a difficult matter to defend one's sanity, and Captain Fletcher, recognising the delicacy of the situation, tried to turn the conversation to easier paths. But Captain Archer was one of the bull-dog breed. " I've got to know something about you before you come aboard my ship," he said. " Tell me why you came to Russia."

" Curiosity," answered Radcliffe, " idle curiosity."

" Then you're a Nosey Parker," said the Captain triumphantly. " That's what you are. A Nosey Parker ! "

"Have some more wine, Captain," said Mr Balin tactfully.

Mr Balin's seafaring cap was recklessly on the side of his head, and there was a twinkling light in his blue eyes. He was enjoying himself as a Russian should in a wine-shop. He was helpful, too, and made laborious jokes at which Radcliffe and I laughed heartily.

"There's a lady with you as well," said the Captain. "Now, what's she doing in Russia? Russia's not the sort of place for a lady to come to."

"Oh, Captain!" said Mr Balin.

"That's all right, Balin. You know me and I know you. But I don't know these people. Now just you tell me why the lady came to Russia."

"Curiosity," said Radcliffe again.

"Women are like that," Captain Fletcher remarked knowingly.

"And they make things difficult on a ship," added Captain Archer.

"Very difficult," corroborated Captain Fletcher.

"Never take a woman on a ship. That's my rule," said Captain Archer.

"It's my rule too," replied Captain Fletcher.

This was deep calling to deep, and we sat in stricken silence while the master mariners condemned the ways of woman at sea and swore that the ocean should be kept free of her and all her whims and vapours.

"Once, when I was young, I took my wife a voyage with me," said Captain Archer.

"Ah," said Captain Fletcher non-committally.

"Now if it hadn't been for this Mrs Rodney I might have taken you two," Captain Archer continued, "but she complicates things. And besides, what's she doing in Russia? That's what I can't get over. Mind you, I'm not inquisitive, but I like to get to the bottom of things. What's this Mrs Rodney doing in Russia?"

"Having a holiday," I answered forlornly.

"Where's her husband?" asked Captain Archer sternly.

"In India," Radcliffe replied.

"Ah!" said Captain Fletcher.

"Let us have another bottle of wine," said Mr Balin helpfully, and handed round the platter of brown bread, radishes, and cheese which properly accompanies morning drinking in Russia.

Like the wine in the glasses hope ebbed and flowed. Captain Archer's difficulties were one by one countered and overcome, and again, like importunate ghosts, came indefatigably to the attack. Captain Fletcher was on our side, and yet could not overcome his sympathetic prejudices against women at sea. Mr Balin laughed and made cumbrous jokes, and Radcliffe paid resolutely for more wine.

At last sentiment seemed to win. "I'd like to help you," said Captain Archer. "Honestly I would. I don't want to leave fellow-countrymen stranded, if I can do anything to assist them."

"Especially when one of them is a lady," added Mr Balin.

"H'm," said Captain Archer. "Well, it's time to be going, and I'll think things over and see what can be done."

We went out into the street and down to the harbour. The Red Ensign still hung limply over the stern of the *Tamarisk*, a dingier red than the fiery face of her captain.

"I'll help you if I can," he said, "but all the same I'd like to know—to really know—what you're doing in

Russia ? "

Radcliffe swallowed visibly, and replied, "Holiday-making, travelling, rubber-necking, seeing the world."

" Nosey Parkers," said Captain Archer, and walked away indignantly.

V MAY DAY IN RUSSIA

We returned from our inconclusive morning's work to find Mrs Rodney writing letters. Sublimely indifferent to the depressing view from her window—the yellow cat still lay a-dying on the flat red roof—she was interweaving colourful descriptions of Russian scenery with rattling denunciation of Russia's policemen.

" We are going to the theatre tonight," she said, after listening to the tale of our endeavours with philosophic detachment. " I met Mr Rakovsky, who said it would be good, and the seats are only a rouble."

A stock company, having come to the end of the Caucasian season, was giving selections from its repertory as a farewell performance, and there was a pleasing air of intimacy between actors and audience. The star turn was a woman, a comedienne, a singer, a dramatic artiste with an astonishing range of expression. She tore passion to rags, she sang folk-songs with a kind of wild emotion and despairing sympathy, she dropped tumultuously into low comedy. And the house rose to her. They shouted for their favourite songs, and she, with a favourite's impatience, snapped her fingers and consented to sing them. Now it was something with a tremendous revolutionary lilt in it, a song of broken barricades and triumphant insurgence, now something of lewd winking and innuendo that speared a way for rollicking laughter. She had Marie Lloyd's trick of hanging the end of a story on a wink, and pointing a moral with a *moue*. She was a Marie Lloyd of the steppes, a sansculotte Bernhardt of the streets. And the audience loved her.

It is a little alarming to find how adventitious words are to the simpler forms of humour, to discover that the scribe is a mere appendage to the tumbler, and how miserably the librettist trudges in the proud wake of the clown. Words fill an empty space—like progressive citizens adventuring into new suburbs—but they are not really necessary. The performance concluded with a sketch of the familiar errant-husband-plus-exasperated-wife type, a crude thing in which a bearded Cossack, gorgeously in his cups, hid behind a tree while his wife, at the door of their cabin, told us what she would do to him when he came home. Not a word did we understand, but the pantomime, stripped of verbal explanation and aided only by onomatopoetic noises, was extravagantly funny. The woman alternately wept and invented fresh vengeances, and the Cossack behind his tree blanched and groaned and spoilt his groaning with a hiccup. Common stuff, but done with a riotously full spirit, and without the words —which were probably cheaper than the story—it was purely and irresistibly a piece of that hilarious mockery with which man, in his wiser moments, knows how to treat his shortcomings and his minor tragedies. The sketch finished with a reconciliatory duet and a dance of sheer abandon to the joy of stamping feet and whirling limbs.

Closer acquaintance with mockery came the following morning. Captain Archer was red and stern and reserved in his manner. He had thought things over very carefully, he said, and the difficulties in the way of taking passengers from Russia were too many and too grave for him to overcome. Port authorities could make things very unpleasant for a shipmaster who failed to observe their wishes.

"Does that mean that the people here have told you not to take us?" asked Radcliffe bluntly.

"It means that I might have my ship delayed if your passports were found to be irregular," said the Captain, and blew his nose in some embarrassment.

"But our passports are perfectly in order," indignantly exclaimed Mrs Rodney.

"And it's difficult for a merchant ship to land passengers at Constantinople. It's difficult to land passengers from Russia anywhere except at a home port. I should have to sign you on as members of the crew, and then take you to a British consul to sign you off wherever I landed you. They don't like people who come from Russia anywhere on the Continent, and I might have trouble. Trouble would mean delay, and delay means money, especially with an oil boat; and then I'd get more trouble from my owners. Honestly I'd like to help you, but it can't be done."

So there was an end of that; and the next day, sitting on the water-front with a cup of Turkish coffee and the glass of water which invariably accompanies it, I watched the *Tamarisk* slide quietly out of the harbour, moving westwards to open sea. The Red Ensign over her stern shook itself for freedom after having hung in draggled obscurity for two whole days in Russia, and an hour of sunlight lit up the great snow mountains to the north. It was a pretty sight, but a prettier would have been Batum disappearing behind the broad white wake of the outgoing ship.

By and by a ragged youth, drifting aimlessly along the

quay, sat down beside me. After a minute of speculative silence he said, " *Sprechen Sie deutsch?* "

I shook my head.

" *Alors, vous parlez français ?* "

" No," I replied, to save trouble and the embarrassment which always followed a pretence to fluency.

" But I speak English too," he countered eagerly. " I am a student. I was a student at Leningrad and then at Moscow. I studied Oriental languages and art. But now I can study no more." He shook his head and stared glumly at the sea. His coat was in tatters, and the soles of his boots were tied to evasive uppers with string.

I asked him why he could no longer study.

"'I wanted to go away, to go to Persia and India, and see those places. But they would not let me. And then I said I would go to Tiflis, to the university there, and they let me come away from Moscow. But now I do not want to study any more."

" What are you going to do, then ? " I said.

He looked over his shoulder, but no one was behind him. He looked up and down the quay, and no one was within a hundred yards. And then, " I am trying to escape," he whispered fiercely.

" To escape from—— ? "

" From Russia ! But all the ships are guarded, and every road is guarded."

That was perfectly true. A sentry was posted on every ship in the harbour, and a mile out of the town picquets watched the approach to the Turkish frontier under the frowning encouragement of hill-top forts.

" There are thousands of young men trying to escape from Russia," said the student with miserable satisfaction.

A day or two later I met Mr Merrick, that suspicious

man, the mate of the Arcos ship—which was still unloading—and told him about my student.

" 'E was probably a spy," said Mr Merrick encouragingly, " set to watch you and try to make you talk. That's the sort of thing they do in Russia. First they've got the Political Police, those fellows that wear the green caps. Then they've got spies on the Police—everybody knows about them. And then they've got other spies spying on the spies, but nobody knows who they are. They don't even know each other. I've got my suspicions about one or two people in this very town, though." Mr Merrick closed one eye slowly and significantly.

" I know Russia," he said with grim pride, and told of certain things he had seen in Leningrad during the early days of revolution ; of street murders, seemingly un-provoked and certainly unpunished ; of sudden anonymous threats and their ghastly fulfilment ; of desperate escapes, and of a midnight battle fought by moonlight on the ice.

That day, as it happened, the streets of Batum were dressed in red, for the morrow was May Day. Red flags hung from every window, and a scarlet flush filled the mean little streets, darkly reflected in cracked window-panes and in the stagnant gutters. May Day fell on a Sunday, and from Friday night to Tuesday morning the workers held holiday, drinking, singing, and adventuring in charabancs. The parade of soldiers and workmen was impressive to some degree, but the spectators seemed animated more by idle curiosity than by enthusiasm. The troops filled three sides of a square, and untidy processions with banners crowded behind them. The soldiers chatted amiably and smoked cigarettes, while the workers sang occasional choruses. At the appointed time an officer of high rank, attended by one orderly, rode up on an ungroomed horse. The parade put out its cigarettes, and came leisurely to attention. In the centre of the square there was a small raised platform on which a large ginger-coloured dog had been sleeping. Roused by the sound of several hundred pairs of heels coming together, it sprang up and barked. Then, in the way of dogs, it sat down again and began to bite its loins for fleas.

The General rode round the square and put some question to each side in turn, a question which was answered by a deep-voiced rumbling " Har ! " He dismounted and strode to the platform. The dog jumped down. The general read aloud some message of May Day, some manifesto of brotherhood or vindication of the Hammer and Sickle. (Later we were told that the announcement to the troops included reports of a twenty-four hours' general strike in Britain and a sweeping Cantonese-Communist victory in China.) The General remounted his horse, and the dog returned to the platform to roll contentedly on its back. Recruits affirmed in unison their allegiance to the Soviet, and the workers sang a cheerless song. Policemen moved a company of spectators to make room for the fire brigade in brass helmets ; their tardy arrival was greeted with another song, and then the parade dissolved into its component parts, and the dog lay down to sleep again.

Slowly time passed. The regular passenger steamer which serves the Black Sea ports was nearly due now, and we waited patiently. The hotel was saddened by the sight of George, the chambermaid, suffering from a raging toothache. His superb moustache no longer swept proudly upwards but sadly drooped, one side distorted by a swollen cheek. His squint was fixed in the introspective misery of pain, and he took orders with such dumb helplessness that one never had the slightest expectation of their being executed. Hubert, his confrère, stuck his tongue in his cheek to simulate an enormous gumboil, and laughed at him heartlessly. But George was past the sting of ridicule. Even the mockery of being offered a lump of sugar failed to move him. Even our Flit gun ceased to interest him.

The Flit gun belonged to Mrs Rodney, and was popular throughout the hotel. Being warned before leaving India that parasitic life abounded in the beds, curtains, walls, and public vehicles of Persia and Russia, she had had the forethought to buy a metal spray and a tin of insecticide called Flit. With Flit we had come scatheless through Persia and across the Caucasus without a scar. Now in Batum the common house-fly is an intolerable plague. In black battalions it swarms on foodstuffs and window-panes, on walls, and on the offal in the gutters. Our bedrooms were noisy hives, and the restaurant by day was a buzzing cloud. First we cleared the bedrooms. Thousands of flies, massed in dense formations, fell before the deadly spray. Then we settled the stragglers. High fliers were picked off with masterly lefts and rights, and cheepers were beaten out of their corners to be driven to the same ineluctable doom.

At breakfast-time on our second morning in Batum we attacked the restaurant. In the windows we enfiladed long lines of flies, and on stale bread we massacred their vast reserves. The Flit gun slew its thousands, while the waiters stood by and applauded. At first they were open-mouthed with astonishment; then interested; and finally rapturous. They borrowed the gun and set out to slay flies on their own. They stalked fugitives and stood on chairs to reach high roosters. They brought the cook up from the kitchen to see their prowess, and they blew venturesome sprays against the wondering faces pressed to the windows from outside. The Flit gun became an institution and in the end it saved our reputation, for on leaving we found ourselves without enough Russian money for tips ; and Mrs Rodney, calmly and masterfully, sold the gun to the syndicate of waiters for ten roubles.

Our ship arrived, and the hour of her departure was published. The melancholy Turk, who had followed us all these days growing visibly older and more dejected, laughed aloud for relief and offered us innumerable cups of coffee. We paid five roubles each for a certificate that we were free from infectious diseases—apparently the mere possession of five roubles was sufficient evidence, for we saw no doctor—and bought, for seven roubles apiece, police permission to leave the town. We packed and waited. And then we had to unpack, for the ship decided to lie in Batum for one more night.

In the morning we filled a droshky with our luggage and another with ourselves, and drove, for the last time, to the quay. The entire staff of the hotel stood on the pavement waving good-bye. George, still holding tightly to a bottle of aspirin (a parting gift), wept a little—his toothache inclined him to tears—but Hubert laughed enormously, while the waiters proudly held aloft their new fly gun.

A last trial awaited us. The customs shed, where officials went through our baggage like a cyclone hitting a jerry-built model town, was some hundreds of yards from the ship, and between us we had thirteen separate pieces of luggage. There were porters in plenty, but the price they demanded, one rouble per package, was about eleven roubles in excess of our remaining resources. We said, not proudly but quite decidedly, that we could carry our luggage without assistance. Mrs Rodney went aboard, and

Radcliffe followed carrying two suitcases. Surrounded by wrathful growling porters, I stood and guarded the remainder.

Radcliffe took his burden aboard, and set out to return for more. But scarcely had he left the ship than a loud shout stopped him. A burly surly-looking Green Cap at the head of the gangway bellowed something incomprehensible, and angrily beckoned Radcliffe to come aboard again.

Radcliffe shouted, "What for?"

Green Cap roared a third time.

"*Pourquoi?*" shouted Radcliffe. "Kiswaste, you jungly?"

Green Cap came clumsily down the gangway and along the quay. Radcliffe took out his passport, showed the police exeat, and said, "Is that what you want?"

Green Cap shook his head, and Radcliffe, his patience exhausted, turned to go. The policeman immediately seized him by the arm, swung him round, and threateningly drew his revolver half out of its holster. Radcliffe expostulated, and the policeman called to three more Green Caps in the vicinity. They surrounded Radcliffe, and a spirited conversation began in an ill-fitting mixture of broken French and German. He had infringed the laws of Russia by doing a porter's work and carrying his own luggage aboard.

"*Es ist verboten,*" they told him, "*aux voyageurs d'apporter les bagages—aus, nach den Schiff. Il y a des ouvriers qui font cela.*" And they marched him back to the customs shed, called four porters, and pointed to our remaining baggage. The porters carried it off, and we followed in silence. Once aboard we offered them our remaining Russian money, one rouble eighty kopecks. The storm broke immediately. But we had no more money, and Green Cap scratched his head in bewilderment. The Chief Steward approached, and Green Cap turned to him, volubly, explosively, and convincingly, for the steward pulled out his pocket-book and gave the policeman a ten-rouble note. Green Cap went ashore, and the steward explained in Italianate English that he was happy to be of assistance to us ; the policeman had told him that we wanted to borrow money to discharge our just debts, and the ten roubles would accordingly go down in our bill at an equitable rate of exchange. Were we travelling Saloon or Second Class?

" Second," we said dejectedly ; and watched Batum and Russia—Holy Russia—slowly fade and sink beneath the broad white fantail of the steamer's wake.

[September 1927

9

AFOOT ON THE ARCTIC HIGHWAY

Matt Marshall
('Tramp-Royal')

In 1920, by the Treaty of Dorpat, Finland acquired the Lapp district of Petsamo, a narrow corridor of land running northward between Russian and Norwegian territory to the shores of the Arctic Ocean. And in 1931 there was completed there the great Rovaniemi-Petsamo highway—begun in 1916 by the Imperial Russian Government, but later held up by the Revolution—which has the distinction of being the only motor road in the world to run from civilisation to the shores of the Polar Sea.

Starting from the town of Rovaniemi, eight kilometres south of the Arctic Circle, this unique highway, after cleaving its way through virgin forests and over barren mountains, ends at Liinahamari on Petsamo Fiord, some three hundred and thirty miles north of the Circle.

This was the road that lay before me, and which I was about to journey afoot.

Six weeks previously I had set out from Viborg in the extreme south of Finland and tramped all the way up through the Land of the Thousand Lakes to where I was now: Rovaniemi in Lapland; so that if and when I arrived at Liinahamari I should have walked Finland from end to end.

Burdened with a full pack on my back, and a smaller pack, also full, at my side, and wearing a heavy winter overcoat, I crossed the high bridge over the log-laden Kemijoki River, passed along under the shadow of Ounasvaara Hill, which people climb at midsummer to view the Midnight Sun, and so, crossing again the river on another bridge, attained the road where it soars to enter the inevitable *metsä*: the forest that, like a mighty battle host tossing its spears and banners in the breeze, awaits one's exit from every Finnish village, town, and city; the forest that walls in every path and road; the forest through which I had been journeying for weeks; the forest of melancholy spruce, graceful bird, odoriferous pine; the unending, all-enduring, all-conquering forest that is Finland.

Taking a farewell look back at Rovaniemi, last notable outpost of civilisation, I turned and fared with the road between the imprisoning greenwood walls.

Just short of the red post marking the eighth kilometre from Rovaniemi I came upon a white post bearing a notice-board which announced in Finnish, Swedish, German, and English that here the imaginary line of the Arctic Circle crossed the road; thus:

NAPAPIIRI
POLCIRKEL
POLARKREIS
POLAR CIRCLE

It gave me a thrill. To think that I had walked, actually walked, thus far! To think that from now on I should be journeying in the Arctic regions! To think that here in the midst of the unpeopled Northland, hemmed in by primeval forests, standing alone, afar from men, on this solitary. . . . But before I could finish the thought six big touring cars and two buses dumped their human freight on the road beside me, and I was almost trodden underfoot in the rush to see who should be first to be photographed standing astride the Polar Circle.

In disgust I resumed my way, still thrilled nevertheless. Let Kodaks click, let conducted tourists swarm, I was at last where I had long striven to be. I was at last footing *Jäämeren Tietä*—the Ice Sea Road—the Arctic Highway.

Broad and straight between its parallel walls of crowded pine and spruce, it ran ahead in uninterrupted perspective.

Although the July sun shone bright and warm, yet a keen wind blowing steadily from the north made me thankful for my winter overcoat.

At long intervals apart I encountered crofts: red-painted log cabins standing in the midst of forest clearings, where backwoodsmen toiled stripped to the waist.

The road, considering the high latitude, was amazingly busy. Cars passed frequently, as did carts and cyclists. Twice a caravan of gipsy vans came jingling along, bearing a load of the cleanest, best-dressed gipsies I had ever seen. While the women wore voluminous skirts and had coloured bandeaux round their heads, the men sported full-sleeved shirts of linen so snowy white as to dazzle the eye. Indeed, it was only by the typical dusky complexions, and the equally typical soliciting of cigarettes and pennies, that I knew them for gipsies. Compared with the mongrel British variety, they were princes and princesses, the aristocratic Romanies one reads about but rarely meets.

That night—if night be the correct name for what was as bright as a midsummer's day—I thankfully downed packs within a workmen's hut near where a bridge was being built.

The workmen had gone home, and only a wooden pin held the door in place, so I made no bones about making the hut my quarters for the night. With shavings and wood-chips I kindled a fire outside and cooked supper, which I carried inside and ate behind the shut door; for I did not wish to have passers-by know of my presence there. Then I contrived a bed of empty cement sacks and retired early, congratulating myself on having for once eluded the mosquitoes, whose nocturnal attentions had made so many of my nights sheer purgatory.

At six in the morning I rose and cleaned up the hut, then set about breakfast. But in the middle of the meal, as I sat in my shirt-sleeves and bare feet with a mug of tea in one hand and a sandwich in the other, the door burst open and in walked the ganger. So astonished was he at finding me there so completely at home that he could utter not a single syllable of protest or anything else. He could only gulp and gesticulate, hopelessly incompetent to deal with my unprecedented presence there. Nor did I help him. Smiling apologetically, but saying not a word, I finished breakfast and hurriedly packed. Then civilly wishing him " *Hyrästi*," I made my exit—to the amazement of the men who had meanwhile arrived and who almost dropped their tools as I stepped unheralded and unexplained among them.

All day I pursued the forest road, feeling like a perambulating comet. For while my head was completely enveloped in a nimbus of dancing mosquitoes, behind it trailed a long tail of more of these pests, whining their hymn of hate.

' There are rest-houses owned by the Government every twenty to twenty-five kilometres along the Petsamo road.

A night's lodging costs ten marks, a cold meal eight marks, and a hot meal fifteen marks.'

So said a German-English handbook which I had bought in Rovaniemi. But although I had kept an anxious lookout for these hostelries ever since hitting the Arctic Highway, so far I had not seen any place that even looked like an inn, Government-owned or otherwise. Nay, I could scarcely believe such places existed. They sounded too good to be true. Tenpence for a night's lodging, eightpence for a cold meal, one and threepence for a hot meal—it was highly improbable, I reasoned, that here in the Arctic regions could be inns (only half a day's walk apart, too) which could exist on so cheap a tariff. Nevertheless, being a Scotsman, I kept on keeping an anxious look-out for these improbable impossibilities.

The rare houses I passed were all alike: log cabins painted red, with the framework of the windows picked out in white. The still rarer hamlets, also, consisted of from two to six of these cabins, widely scattered. And look as I would I failed to discern about any house the slightest clue to its being an inn. The *majatalo* sign was conspicuous by its absence. I badly needed an inn, too. My provisions were all but consumed.

Hunger sharpening my powers of observation, I began to notice that some of the houses had flagstaffs in front of them. And since flagstaffs suggest flags and flags suggest Government, I deduced, my dear Watson, that those houses thus distinguished must be Government houses— Government rest-houses!

As luck would have it, I reached this brilliant conclusion on a stretch of road destitute of houses. It was growing late, besides, and a heavy rain was beginning to fall. Quickening my pace, however, I rapidly demolished the kilometres separating me from the next house, which to my joy had a flagstaff in front of it.

Entering by the back door without knocking—for experience had taught me that knocking at a Finnish house was a waste of time—I found myself in the spacious *pirtti*, or living-room, ankle-deep in birch leaves. Two men wearing open-necked khaki shirts and Russian boots sat by the table poring over a large map. Government surveyors, obviously. And where else, I asked myself, would Government employees lodge if not in a Government rest-house?

But alas, it was no Government rest-house. In answer to my inquiry in broken Finnish, one of the men explained that it was a private house, but that the place I sought lay two kilometres farther along the road. He even drew a sketch of it, requesting me to note particularly the flagstaff and post-boxes by which it was distinguished.

Greatly heartened, I sped off through the heavy rain. Sure enough, at the end of the second kilometre stood the house the man had sketched, but without the flagstaff and with only one post-box outside: a plain wooden receptacle for letters such as most houses along the road had. Still, I entered and asked of the man of the house if that was the *majatalo*. It was not, he answered. Two kilometres farther along. . . .

Rushing from the house, I once more sped off through the rain. Sure enough, at the end of the second kilometre stood another house, likewise without flagstaff and with only one post-box. Nevertheless, I entered. Inside were two women, mother and daughter. They must have just finished taking a bath—the *sauna* or hot-vapour bath beloved by Finns—for they were both bare naked. But I did not mind that. I asked them if that was the *majatalo*, feeling sure it was not. Nor did feeling err. The *majatalo*, explained the daughter, coming out on to the rain-swept porch regardless of her nudity, lay just two kilometres farther along. . . .

A third time I sped off through the rain. A third time a house stood, sure enough, at the end of the second kilometre; this time a house with flagstaff and two yellow-painted metal post-boxes outside. The rest-house at last!

Well, maybe it was. Anyway, I did not rest in it. Knock after knock on the locked door failed to rouse anybody within, always supposing there was anybody within. For the house looked and sounded empty. The only noises stirring in its otherwise silent interior were those of the rain battering on the shingled roof and the echoes of my repeated knocks. So I desisted in disgust, and spent the night trying to rest on the log floor of the empty cowshed.

The following afternoon I arrived at Sodankylä village, 130 kilometres north of Rovaniemi.

Before coming to it, however, a few miles to the southward, where beyond the hamlet of Aska a branch road strikes off eastward to lonely Lake Ora, I encountered my first beasts of the forest.

Since leaving Viborg, you must know, the hundreds of miles of woodlands bordering the road had oppressed me with their utter lifelessness. Deader woods would be difficult to imagine. Silent, except for birdsong and the occasional tinkle of a cattle-bell, not a rabbit, not even a squirrel, enlivened their lonely aisles. One single little lizard and a solitary black snake were all I had seen of wild life. It was unnatural, uncanny, positively unnerving. But in my bones I felt that the lifeless woods were watching me and waiting, waiting with the tireless patience of the wild for the moment most favourable for them to move, when they would open and let out a beast, a creature born of silence and loneliness and brooding gloom, to set upon me and bear me off to its lair in the forest depths, there to subject me at its leisure to a lingering death of fiendishly devised agonies and torments.

Here beyond Aska it seemed as though that moment were now come.

Between the hemming woods I walked, thinking only of reaching Sodankylä. So accustomed had I grown to the ever-accompanying forest that I paid it scarcely a glance. I was dimly aware of its being ancient pinewood, open and clear of under-brush, floored with white and mauve reindeer moss and strewn with what looked like the tusks and rib bones of mammoths, but which was deadfall: great gnarled and twisted limbs and boughs, predominantly grey in colour, blanched here and there by years of sun and rain to the whiteness of bleached bone. But greyness, let me repeat, predominated; a gravestone greyness. This sombre colour clothed dying and dead trees like a pall, its ashen hue changing in the sun to the grisly silver of a leper's skin. And in the lifeless forest not a breath of wind stirred.

Crack! Somewhere in the woods ahead a brittle branch snapped, trodden upon by something. The report sounded in the deathly quiet like a pistol-shot. Walking on, I kept my eyes fixed on the place where the something was. Then from the grey background of the woods an indefinable grey mass detached itself and took form, and there glided on to the road a big grey beast with branching antlers, lifting high its splay feet and moving without sound or apparent effort.

It turned its frontlet in my direction, took a long look, tossed its wild head, and came loping towards me.

Now, I knew there were elk in Lapland, as I knew there

were bears and wolves and reindeer. But I somehow associated reindeer with the open tundra and not with the forest. I pictured reindeer as travelling together in large herds attended by Lapps, and not roving singly unattended. I also pictured them as being brown beasts and not grey, tame and not wild, ungainly and not graceful. This, then, I concluded, must be an elk. I had read, too, that elk have occasionally been known to attack men, chopping them to death with their great hoofs. So you can imagine me, burdened as I was with two heavy packs and armed only with a short stick, feeling shaky about the knees as this horned monster came loping towards me.

Its absolute fearlessness quickened my heartbeats. With unslackened pace, however, I walked to meet it, fully convinced that, since it belonged to the deer kind, it would presently wheel in fright and leap away. But the beast did neither. It only halted and gazed straight at me, refusing to budge an inch. I waved my stick. But it only tossed its head, and I was forced to come to a halt.

Barely three yards separated us. The brute's nearness thrilled me. I could plainly see the thick grey 'velvet' silvering its antlers like a coating of hoar-frost. The width between the uppermost tips, which were flattened as though beaten out on an anvil, seemed enormous. I took fearful note, also, of how the nethermost tips, which swept right down and outward in front of the beast's big eyes, were even more flattened, being of the same size and shape and sharpness as a butcher's cleaver.

Raising my stick, I brandished it in the brute's face, yelling like mad. The beast swerved and plunged past me. I turned—to find myself confronted by a second grey beast which, unbeknown to me, had been standing close at my back. The other's mate, presumably. Again flourishing my stick and yelling, I succeeded in putting it to flight. But neither it nor the other fled far. I seemed to attract them like a magnet. For a couple of kilometres they stuck to me; now at my heels, now plunging past to gallop ahead and await my coming, when they would stand, one on either side of the road, eyeing me till I was gone on, whereupon they would both fall in behind, padding silently in the soft sand.

Luckily, at the end of the second kilometre a motor-car came along hooting its horn, and the two animals left my trail and took to the woods, their grey bodies and almost white legs merging immediately with the grey of the standing timber and the white of the deadfall and lichen, so that they disappeared like dreams, completely melting from sight long before they were out of view.

A twice-daily service of passenger mail-buses runs throughout the summer months between Rovaniemi and Petsamo, and Sodankylä is the first bus-stop of importance on the northward journey.

This village, which has a population of about eight hundred, consists mostly of a long street of red-painted log houses. There is a good hotel—Hotelli Polaris—and one or two inns, besides provision stores, refreshment kiosks, a chemist's, a school, a huge church, a sawmill, and a post-office with telephone and telegraph.

On palings opposite the Polaris are hung assorted antlers, bearskins, skulls, and claws, each ticketed with a price-tab made of wood, which find ready buyers among visitors. For a few marks a motorist can purchase an impressive pair of antlers, which it is the custom to fasten between the headlights of one's car when returning south. Or, if trophies of the chase do not appeal, there is always the little Lapp girl dressed in red-and-blue native costume. You cannot miss her. Indeed, she will not let anybody miss her. And on the tray she carries you will find a wide choice of souvenirs in the form of ornamental sheath-knives, paper-cutters, candlesticks, &c., hand-made of reindeer bone by Lapps. And you will then wonder no more at the phenomenon of the Midnight Sun. For if all the specimens of genuine Lapp-work which fill the souvenir shops of Finland are genuine specimens of Lapp-work, then those sunny summer nights must be a godsend to the poor overworked Lapps. The number of barrels of midnight oil saved must be uncountable.

I stayed the night and the following day and night in Sodankylä. All the time public buses and private cars never ceased to arrive and depart. The weather remained bright and warm; the Arctic sun flooded the land with a golden light lovelier than that of Andalusia. There was no nightfall, no twilight, nothing but gorgeous daylight. The tonic air, pungent with pine, clear as crystal, made the heart glow and the pulses quicken.

Most of the time I spent roaming the pinewoods surrounding the village. I cut down a sapling, straight and strong and taller than myself, and made of it a staff, which I hid in the heather beside the first kilometre-post on the forest road. And on the morning of my departure, when with packs provisioned and feet fit again I passed that way, I cast aside my short stick, possessed myself of the staff, and felt adequately armed against any grey beast with hoofs and antlers.

At the tenth kilometre the bordering pines fell away to reveal the log village of Sattanen and a glimpse of the River Kitinen that had been secretly paralleling the road all the way from Sodankylä. But after that it was the silent woods again and the lonely road and the plaguing mosquitoes and flies and the sweltering heat and the monotony of continual heel-and-toe, till at noon I downed packs on the forest verge and lighted a fire and drummed-up,

I ate the meal as wide-awake as a sparrow pecking at a crust. The silence and loneliness of the grey groves, which were floored with bleached deadfall and snowy lichen like those beyond Aska where the two beasts had materialised, strung me to a high pitch of alertness. Staff within reach, knife loose in its sheath, axe ready to grasp, I kept turning my head and cocking my ears all ways. A pile of antlers lay dumped by the roadside, proof positive that this was big-game country. I would not be caught napping again, I vowed. Preparedness. . . .

From round a bend in the road came a bellowing as of beasts. The still groves trembled; the highway shook to an oncoming rumble like the approach of thundering hoofs. Affrighted, I leapt to my feet. Staff in one hand, axe in the other, I awaited the rush of stampeding herds.

Round the bend swung two heavy motor-lorries hooting their horns and crowded with navvies. Pulling up opposite my fire they backed in, one on either side of me. The men, armed with picks and shovels, scrambled down and began loosening the sand of the roadside bank and shovelling it into the lorries. In sadness I packed up my gear and silently stole away. The wild Arctic had certainly scored that time.

The afternoon's march carried me northward past Petkula—which consists of a Government rest-house and little else—along a desolate road misty with mosquitoes; and night saw me encamped on the river bank a few kilometres south of the lonely ferry-inn of Peurasuvanto.

Had I known of this inn I should certainly have slept there. I had come forty-six kilometres, and was dog-tired and nigh bitten to death; but sleep and rest were denied me. Half the time I sat with my head in the smoke of the fire, cursing the mosquitoes. At times I tried enveloping myself completely in blanket and groundsheet, but this proved too suffocating to be safe. Had it been a dark, silent night, things would have been different. It was bright day, however, with the blue sky blazing overhead and the forest full of the thrush's song. Only a dead man could have slept through such a noisy, unnatural night.

In the morning I pursued the river road to Peurasuvanto, where I stood cursing the inn for a time, then got the ferryboy to paddle me across the river in his canoe.

On the far bank a wilderness road awaited me. All day the forest hedged me in. The heat was fierce and the flies were terrific. I counted no less than seven different kinds of these pests. There were midges, tiny houseflies, ordinary houseflies, mosquitoes, beastly yellow flies, big black gadflies, and dragon-flies. They fought about me in whining clouds and trailed behind me like coiling smoke. Although I wore gauntlets and had my ankles bound with clouts and wore a puggaree made from the tail of a spare shirt, yet I suffered agonies. The backs of my ears, my neck, my forehead, and my eyelids were caked with blood and black with swatted carcases. And though the mosquitoes stung hard, the big black gadflies stung harder. Their vicious jabs were like electric needles plunged into the nerve-centres. Unlike the mosquitoes, moreover, the gadflies expertly evaded death. I could kill only about one in every ten.

At twenty kilometres from Peurasuvanto ferry-inn I came to a Government rest-house: a lonely lodge in the wilderness complete with flagstaff and yellow post-box and bearing the name Lohijoki, meaning Salmon River.

For days now I had been encountering these hostelries. They were no myths, I had to admit. They occurred regularly every twenty kilometres or so. But as yet I had not put up at any. Nor did I call in at this Lohijoki one, having dined *al fresco* shortly before. I passed on, determined, however, to put up for the night at the next rest-house, twenty kilometres farther on at a place called Vuotso.

In the golden evening I reached this. It stood on the fringe of pine barrens, its ruddy log buildings plain to see against a background of dark spruce forest. From twin flagstaffs two flags fluttered gaily in the breeze.

In front of it waited a big yellow mail-bus on the point of departure. From the main building tourists were issuing after a quick meal. More tourists were making purchases at a little kiosk and inspecting the antlers, bear skulls, and claws displayed for sale. On the house-porch a family of Lapps in native blue-and-red costume struck a barbaric note. Mosquitoes and gadflies worked overtime. Two men dressed like ship's officers mingled with the crowd; and when the passengers were all aboard, one of these manned the elevating gear of a Customs boom that barred the highway, and the bus roared away up the long spruce avenue to a dwindling chorus of farewells.

From the Finnish mistress of the hostelry, who spoke fluent German, I learnt that I could be accommodated for the week-end, the tariff being tenpence for a night's lodging, eightpence for a cold meal, and one and threepence for a hot meal, just as the handbook said. These charges were fixed, too. On the wall of the public bedroom—a big clean chamber this, furnished with three beds and the usual fixtures—a printed *taksalista* told in detail exactly how much each item should cost. In every rest-house a similar pricelist is prominently displayed, so that overcharging is impossible.

Hot or cold, the meals were appetising and filling, consisting principally of *smörgasbord*—that is, a variety of side-dishes of delicatessen; while of milk and buttermilk there were positively gallons. A plateful of black and white bread and several coffee-cakes and a six-cup pot of coffee comprised breakfast; and you could order a meal at any time.

The people of the house, including the two Customs officials and the Lapp handyman, were very friendly. The women-folk cooked all the time, the officials smoked all the time, and the Lapp—who changed into native dress only when parties of foreign tourists arrived—laughed and cracked jokes all the time. Small-made, with unusually long arms and a comical face, he was a born clown. His quick-change act invariably doubled him, and us, up with merriment. His tiny wife and little girls, on the contrary, never laughed and seldom smiled. They were creatures apart, mysterious and silent as the Polar night.

Vuotso was plagued by mosquitoes and gadflies. These made life a misery. They were fiercest in the afternoon and evening, the morning being comparatively free from them. During the night they obscured the sunbeams streaming in through the windows in which mosquito frames had been fitted, and their ceaseless whining made sleep impossible. Before allowing me to retire, the man of the house sprayed my room with insecticide, and bade me skip nimbly in and shut the door. Even so, it took me a good quarter of an hour to kill the mosquitoes that had skipped nimbly in along with me.

On the advice of the Customs men I bought at the little kiosk a fivepenny bottle of *Puhdasta pikiöljyä* (pure resin oil): brown frothy stuff which, when applied to the face and hands, repels mosquitoes by its pungent, tarry smell. It causes the skin to smart at first and has to be applied lavishly, but is certainly effective, although its power begins to wane after an hour or so. I had seen backwoodsmen and navvies with a bottle of the stuff tied to their belts, but had mistaken it for a wee bottle of beer!

Throughout the week-end the weather remained sunny and uncomfortably warm. On Sunday afternoon the mistress of the house told me that if I cared for a swim I should find an ideal spot for bathing at a bend of the river nearby.

Naked boys were splashing about in the water here, and a man lay talking to them on the bank. I undressed and went in without a costume, knowing that these Finns would see nothing unusual in that. And I had not been bathing long when two buxom young women appeared. After watching the boys and me for a couple of minutes, they began to undress on the bank in full view of all of us. They divested themselves of every stitch of clothing except a scanty pair of linen pants, and came leaping down to join me. They wanted a swimming lesson, they said.

A day's lonely march along forest-bordered highway brought me to Laanila.

This little place lies off the road on a sparsely wooded hillside. Two large log-houses and several smaller ones compose it, and the nearer of the former is an inn and Government rest-house combined.

The floor of the lobby of this was strewn with rawhide rucksacks and deerskin sleeping robes, whose owners, in number about a score, were finishing supper in the great kitchen as I entered.

They were a husky lot, tanned and weatherbeaten and

dressed in rough, toil-stained backwoods garb. On my appearance they stopped laughing and joking while a tall young fellow, guessing that I was a foreigner, approached and asked what I wanted. He was more refined in manner and bearing than the others, and it came as no surprise when I found he could talk English. With his help I fixed things up with one of the serving-girls, and was presently seated at a bench eating heartily of a meal of new rye bread, cheese, fried meat, raw-looking fish, German sausage, and milk and porridge.

While I ate, my refined friend explained his presence there. He was a Helsingfors journalist, he said, sent by his paper to get a story about Laanila. Sixty years back the district had been the scene of a gold rush, and now gold had been discovered again; not in any spectacular quantity, but to an extent sufficient to cause excitement. The diggings were just down the hill from the house, and these men at supper were gold-diggers.

" Regular 'forty-niners, too, some of them," I remarked, regarding them with new interest. " They might be characters in a story by Bret Harte or Jack London."

" Yes, it is the Klondike over again. Where we are now is even higher up the world than the Yukon. Arctic gold, with a vengeance."

Business calling him away, I struck up an acquaintance-ship with a picturesque old sourdough, who showed me over the diggings.

At the foot of the hill a stream—a tributary of the Ivalojoki—had been diverted into an excavated channel, and in the bedrock thus exposed the gold was found. No easy planning here, but arduous, backbreaking toil with pick and crowbar and shovel was necessary before even the pay-dirt could be collected. What I took to be rock-crushing plant, and a system of sluice-boxes, completed the picture, which depressed rather than inspired, and disappointed by its utter lack of anything appertaining to the romantic.

East and west of Laanila, stated my guide, the precious metal was likewise being sought; and the sweeping gesture with which he accompanied the statement said plainer than he: " There's gold in them there hills, pardner—*gold !* "

Back at the inn, seated on the porch steps, he confided to me—with the aid of my vest-pocket Finnish-English dictionary—that his account in the Bank of Finland was mounting rapidly. His two partners and he had struck it rich. Going into the house, he returned carrying a tin mug fitted with a wooden lid. This rattled when he shook it. It contained the day's yield. He told me to hold out my hand, and emptied on to the palm about half a dozen nuggets. I examined them with interest. They were little shapeless pieces of soft yellow metal that might have been the fillings from an old set of false teeth. Gold undoubtedly. But a handful of peanuts would have thrilled me more. I returned them without regret.

Later, on my mentioning that I was a Scotsman, the old sourdough grew strangely excited. Pointing to himself he cried, " *Nimi*, *nimi*—Maclean, Maclean " and began dancing round me, his face beaming. I did not understand him, however. Though I knew that *nimi* was Finnish for ' name ' and that Maclean was—well, Maclean, I could not believe that that was *his* name. For he was a full-blooded Finn, a snub-nosed Tavastlander, and knew not a single word of English. Still, I asked him to write the name down. And he did as plain as print—' Maclean '.

Just then, to his regret and mine, his partners called him away, and the mystery remained unsolved, for I did not see him again. But is it too much to fancy that the old boy was descended from some Scottish soldier of fortune, a far-wandered Dugald Dalgetty who fought under the great Gustavus Adolphus in the seventeenth century when Finland belonged to Sweden, and who married and settled in Finland?

From Laanila the highway soars to cross the shoulder of a barren mountain-top. For kilometres ahead the eye can follow the ribbon of road with its single line of telegraph poles as it mounts the long slopes almost to the summit. For miles around, far away below, lies spread a mighty panorama of hills and lakes and forestland. As the traveller ascends he sees the tall timber thin out and cease, its place taken by dwarf-birches, gnarled and twisted and contorted, which continue to shrink and diminish with increasing altitude until they are no bigger than heather clumps. Then they disappear altogether, and only the heathy hilltop remains beneath the sky.

In places, lines of woven fencing shield the road against encroaching snow. But on that burning July day there was no snow. Far, far away on the face of a remote hill I caught sight of two patches of white, but that was all. It was hard to realise I was nearly two hundred miles within the Arctic Circle. I was sweating profusely. A gang of navvies on the road worked stripped to the waist. I saw a lizard sunning itself on a rock. Not a cloud sullied the high blue dome overhead, whence the intolerable sun beat upon the mountains. I felt I was in Spain again, climbing sierras.

Where the road attains its highest point a cart-track, flanked by post-box and signboard, branches off to the ultimate summit. The track is one kilometre long and leads to a small hut built right on the top of the mountain (Kaunispää). If you watch closely you discern there the figure of a man, dwarfed by distance to the size of a pin-head, continually moving about and looking to all points of the compass like the genius of the great lone land surveying his domain. If you can read Finnish you learn from the signboard that he is a wildfire watcher. He is stationed there to keep a lookout for forest fires and spread the alarm by telephone.

Thereafter the highway drops to the tree-line again, descending a wooded valley to enter highland pinewoods and wind by hillfoot and lakeside to the crofter settlement of Törmänen, and thence, alongside a broad river flowing through green lowlands, to Ivalo.

At Ivalo, which is a tidy little busy village of red-painted log-houses with a comfortable inn and a first-class hotel, the Arctic Highway forks. The north-west branch leads to the village of Inari on the shores of the great Inari lake, whence it is possible to proceed by motor-boat to Kirkenes in Norway, and from there sail by Arctic coaster round to Liinahamari; while the main, or north-east, branch continues abreast of the lakeside into the ceded corridor of Petsamo, hugging the Norwegian frontier most of the way to Liinahamari, where the Highway ends.

The tourist season being at its height, I had to put up with a shake-down in the writing-room of the inn at Ivalo. But the mosquitoes could not get at me there, so I was content.

Next morning I hit the highway betimes. For the first five kilometres it traversed low green riverlands, but after that coniferous jungles walled it in; and I walked on timorously with knife and staff ready to use against anything antlered that might suddenly appear.

That the woods harboured brutes in considerable numbers was evident from the many hoof-prints marking the soft sand of the road. Nor did I for long proceed unaccosted. Out from the grey forest a grey beast suddenly glided. It stood eyeing me a moment, then made to approach. But, brandishing my staff and shouting, I caused it to turn aside, and it glided back whence it had come.

So began a series of nerve-racking encounters that was to continue all day. The country simply teemed with these animals. Every hundred yards or so I caught sight of them, either standing picturesquely posed among lakeside lilies, or wading and plunging through creaming shallows, or moving like ghosts in the woods parallel with the road, or crossing the highway behind and ahead of me. They sprang out on me, charged down on me, galloped past me, trailed me. Strangely enough, though, they showed no inclination to molest me. I felt that they bore me no grudge for my intrusion into their wilderness. On the contrary, they seemed to welcome my presence. And although my fear of them waned somewhat, yet familiarity with their great splay hoofs and wide-spreading, many-branched antlers did in no wise breed contempt. I was for ever on the alert.

Beyond the lonely rest-house of Könkäänjärvi, near which I dined on milk and sandwiches at midday, the country grew wild in the extreme. Rough, shaggy jungles of pine and fir sloped steeply from the road verges. The highway twisted and twined and coiled and dipped and rose like a scenic railway. The woods were as untamed and virgin as Eden. Huge rocks and boulders mottled with plush-like lichen stood among them, and here and there a turf-roofed lean-to, solidly built to defy blizzard and hurricane, but long vacated, spoke mutely of nomadic Lapps. And always the road soared upward to a divide. Always the grey beasts of the forest came and went.

Occasionally I encountered a family of them, the young with antlers just beginning to sprout. Once I happened upon a very young beast with no antlers at all, stretched dead by the roadside with its belly eaten away, and near it two big grey dogs lying gorged and licking their chops. One of these half rose, as I passed, but lay down again, and I fell to wondering what breed of dog they were. Lapp hunting dogs, maybe.

All the afternoon as I toiled up between the piney jungles I was followed by a big buck with an enormous spread of horns. Nothing that I could do dissuaded him from trailing me. By the frequency with which he stopped and snuffed my footprints and galloped downwind to snuff my scent, he seemed to relish me immensely. Sometimes he would charge past at so close range that I had to leap aside to escape his antler tips. I could tell him from the others by the length of his white beard and by a certain malformed tine sticking out above his right ear.

At last I could suffer him no longer. I faced him with staff whirling and axe poised, yelling and cursing. But the brute stood up to me, tossing his head and pawing the ground. I lunged at him. The staff caught in his horns. He sent it flying far up the road—and swung round and coolly trotted after it.

Then two things happened simultaneously. A big grey shaggy-maned dog, similar to the two I had seen beside the dead deer, emerged from the woods to stand in the middle of the road regarding me, and a motor-lorry passed packed with a load of trousered girls all standing up and clinging to one another. (Surely a remarkable thing, this, to meet in the Arctic regions?)

As the driver caught sight of the big grey dog he shouted

" Susie!" His mate shouted " Susie!" All the girls shouted " Susie!" And Susie, who had probably never been so be-Susied in its life, turned tail and disappeared, while the lorry hurtled on.

Alone once more, I retrieved my staff and proceeded up the road. At the top an old roadman armed with a rake was making passes at my big buck, who refused to be scared off. Between us, however, we managed to put the animal to flight, and I offered the man a cigarette and stood awhile, glad of his company.

" *Hirvi ?* " I remarked, at a loss for something to say, nodding after the departing buck. " An elk ?"

But to my surprise the roadman shook his head and corrected me, saying, " *Poro.*"

I nearly collapsed with relief. It was a reindeer!

" Not an elk ?"

" Not an elk. *Poro,*" explained the roadman. " Elk few and far away. Reindeer and bear here, and *sudet,* but no elk."

" *Sudet ?* What is *sudet* ? " I asked. My meagre vocabulary of Finnish contained no such word.

" *Sudet ?* " echoed the roadman, puzzled to explain. " *Sudet—sudet. Susie!* "

" By heaven," I cried at that, diving for my Finnish-English pocket dictionary and excitedly thumbing the leaves. " I've heard that word before! *Suora—Surru—Susi.* That must be it. *Susi,* a wolf; *sudet,* wolves."

Can you credit it? While the beasts which I had imagined to be man-mauling elks were merely moss-munching reindeer, the brutes I had supposed to be domesticated dogs were actually wild and woolly timber-wolves!

I felt like kicking myself. Yet my inability to tell one

beast from another put me in good company. In Finland's national epic, the *Kalevala*, a chestnut horse is in one place called a blue elk, and in another place an elk is called a—camel.

Mustola, Nellim, Virtaniemi, Nautsi, Höyhenjärvi, Pitkäjärvi, Salmijärvi, Kuvernöörinkoski, Haukilampi, Yläluostari—how the names of the little red lodges in the wilderness come back to me as I con the map and trace my route along the Arctic Highway to its ultimate end by the Polar Sea.

They seem now like the milestones of a dream odyssey, those lonely cabins that harboured me. In that mirage of the mind that we call memory they come and go, recede and advance, beckon and call, in an iridescent mist of rose and purple and blue and gold, even as they shimmered through the opaline haze of the Arctic summer noons and the magical wonderlight of the day-bright midnights.

Along that forested way atop the world, where the earth flattens towards the Pole, I journeyed entranced. There was peace there, and calm, and beauty, and quietude unparalleled. No wind ever blew, no rain fell. Always the great sky flamed with ethereal fire that never waned. The solitary hills, the still lakes, the blossoming tundra, and the flourishing woods basked beneath a sun that neither rose nor set but only circled and shone, day and night, night and day.

Mustola is a far fetch from Ivalo. After learning from the roadman about the wolves, I let out a reef in my legs and burned the wind northward, with the big buck reindeer hot on my trail. But I did not make Mustola that night. I camped by a lakeshore in a derelict log cabin, whose door I had to barricade against the buck who kept trying to force his way in. In the morning, however, he was nowhere to be seen, so I made my escape and soon reached the rest-house, where I breakfasted.

At noon I arrived at a lake with occupied cabins on the shore and a busy sawmill. This was Nellim. I dined here and bought provisions in the general store, then sauntered along to Virtaniemi, which I reached at tea-time.

Virtaniemi is situated where the Paatsjoki River flows out of Lake Inari. It is an angler's paradise. For trout, gwyniad, and grayling fishing it is *the* place in Lapland. The only house is the log hotel belonging to the Finnish Tourist Association. Here, at high cost, I put up for the night, and had for company a German and an Englishman who talked of nothing but fish, fish, fish.

All next day I was traversing a straight stretch of road through the midst of a forest of tiny, stunted Christmas trees. Each time I rested and lay on my back there would hover directly overhead in the mauve-tinted sky a big black bird, beaked and taloned like an eagle, whose cold eyes glared fiercely down into mine. At one place a con-siderable tract of woodland had been ravaged by wildfire, and the charred stumps and blackened timbers presented a most melancholy sight. Then in the evening the booming of rapids smote my ear, and I was in Nautsi.

This place, consisting solely of the hostelry and out-houses, stands near the junction of the Paatsjoki and another river. In the yard were bales of reindeer skins and stacks of antlers; also sledges: real Lapp sledges, shaped like a boat, having a single flat board positioned underneath like a keel instead of runners.

The house was managed by a big jolly barefooted woman who cooked me the tastiest meal I had eaten for weeks. Along with the usual jugs of sweet milk and buttermilk, and cheese, and white bread and brown, she served up two plates of meat, a side-dish of sardines and salmon, a dish of chopped boiled eggs, an entire trout, an immense platter containing slim carrots and fat sausages stewed and sliced, and—oh, lord—golden berries smothered in stiff cream, followed by lashings of coffee.

The charge for this was the regulation fifteen marks. The night before in Virtaniemi I was charged twenty-five marks for some soup in a plate, a bit of fish pudding and two potatoes, and ice-cream and coffee. Which goes to show.

Between Nautsi and Höyhenjärvi the road runs neck and neck with the Paatsjoki, which forms the frontier between Finland and Norway. Thick pine-woods, though, hide the river from view most of the way. Then between Höyhen-järvi and Pitkäjärvi a long string of lakes, through which the Paatsjoki flows on its northward journey to the Arctic Ocean, are glimpsed far on the left, laving the bases of the Norwegian hills, while to the right a wild region of lakes and forestland stretches to the Russian frontier, only a short day's walk away.

Beyond Höyhenjärvi rest-house I shared my dinner with a funny little man on tramp. He carried a rawhide ruck-sack and was dressed in a belted blouse and ragged trousers stuffed into Russian boots with upturned toes. His head was protected from mosquitoes by a white cloth affair similar in shape to a Balaclava helmet, and this, together with his big walrus moustache that overhung mouth and chin, made me suspect I had met Bairnsfather's Old Bill in the flesh. But he was a Skoltlapp, he informed me in bits of English and Finnish, on his way from Murmansk in Russia to the Lapp village of Boris-Gleb (Kolttaköngäs) in the extreme north of Lapland. Like the Lapp handyman of Vuotso, he was a born clown. His red face radiated mirth and good nature. I left him lying helpless on his back, laughing uproariously at one of his own jokes.

From pine-clad highlands alive with reindeer I descended to a dark lakeshore, and thence, by way of a craggy glen opening on a wide strath, I came to Pitkäjärvi rest-house in the late evening.

Aloft along the hillsides above the long water of Pitkä-järvi (which name, indeed, means Long Lake) the highway carried me next day. Then for dusty miles I was plodding across a wide hill-encircled moor where croft cattle stood huddled in the smoke of mosquito-fires which considerate crofters had lit. Over in the Norwegian hills a smoke-pall showed the whereabouts of wilder fires ravaging the forests. And night and another rest-house awaited me at the far side of the moor, where the red cabins of Salmijärvi village flamed in the glow of the unsinking sun.

The dormitory of the rest-house was a large chamber like a loft, furnished parlour style. Varicoloured mats covered the floor, and there were armchairs and a bookcase and reading-lamp. Five immaculate little cots stood along one wall, but I was the only guest and had the place to myself. Two triangular attic windows lighted the room, and through one of these the level rays of the sun streamed in all night, making sleep impossible.

I welcomed morning, therefore, and took the road gleefully. For the end of my journey lay almost within view. I was footing the last lap of my hyperborean hike. Soon there would be no more road to take. To think that an easy two days' march was all that separated me from Liinahamari on the rim of the world by the Polar Sea!

From Salmijärvi the highway leapt the narrows of Salmi lake on a wooden bridge, and thereafter for many kilometres wound amid birch woods in whose sunlit aisles ferns and buttercups and divers grasses and meadow plants flourished in astonishing luxuriance. By way of a long glen —half-way up which was Kuvernöörinkoski rest-house, where I stopped for dinner—the road then climbed to rock-littered heights overlooking a wide, wild heath encompassed by Arctic hills. And on the far eastern extremity of this heath, which took the whole afternoon and evening to traverse, the rest-house by Haukilampi lake sheltered me that night.

Next day was my last day on the road.

At noon I lunched at the Finnish Tourist Association hotel near the most northerly monastery in the world: that of Yläluostari, founded by the saintly Russian adventurer, Trifon, in the time of Ivan the Terrible.

In mid-afternoon, after crossing a moor where peat-cutters were skewering pancake-shaped peats on pointed stakes driven into the ground, I had coffee at the refreshment kiosk adjacent to the picturesque Russian church of Alaluostari, the belfry of which is an octagonal, bandstand-like erection hung with a peal of bells, standing apart on a wayside knoll high above the sunken Petsamo River.

At tea-time, a few kilometres farther on, houses appeared, and I found myself in the busy village of Parkkina. Here I smelt the tang of brine, heard seagulls cry, and beheld with excitement the wide waters—Arctic waters—of Petsamo Fiord stretching between sheer black rocky hills northward to the sea—the Polar Sea—which lay beyond sight round a bend in the straits.

I quickened my pace. Following the road alongside the pungent beaches for five kilometres I arrived at a cross-roads. One branch continued along the shore to the village of Trifona; the other, which I took, climbed up beside thundering river-falls to skirt a placid lake nestling among craggy, snow-crested, heart-chilling hills, and so over a wild pass and down by another lake to where a big cosmopolitan hotel stood above a hill-sheltered haven of the sea. This was Liinahamari.

Here the Arctic Highway peters out. Down along the fiord shore below the hotel it runs, passing a house or two and a steamship pier, then round the bay to come to a dead and smelly end in the yard of a fish-meal factory.

But so inglorious a finish revolted me. I refused to accept as reward for weeks of toilsome travel a fishy smell. Besides, I wished to look upon the Arctic Ocean, which at Liinahamari is shut off from view by mountainous headlands. Next day, therefore, I ascended into the intervening hills by a footpath that starts where the highway ends and climbs amid tarns and bouldery wastes to the paramount summit: that of Siebruoaivi, 900 feet high.

Posts painted red, white, and blue guided me to the cairn on the crest. The prospect here was reward enough. All around, haunt only of reindeer, heaved a desolate world of black, absolutely bare, rocky hills, cracked and riven and fissured, and here and there veined with unmelted snow. In the south glittered long arms of wandering waters. To the west receded the craggy bluffs of the Norwegian shore, their seaward sides mantled in white. To the east, beyond the mouth of Petsamo Fiord, stretched the interminable reaches of the Murman Coast. And in the north, full in front, extending to the far horizon, calm and level as a lagoon, shining and glassy, in colour like sapphires, but striated with lanes of emerald hue, was spread the lone immensity of the Polar Sea.

[September 1936

10

FOOD FOR THE GODS

Nicholas Wollaston

I disliked him as soon as I got into the train. Apart from his two servants he was the only other person in the compartment. He sat at one end with his feet tucked up underneath him on the seat and his lower lip curled over like a Gothic gargoyle. Opposite him, at the other end of the compartment, was a pile of tin boxes full of files and documents. Between him and the boxes, his two servants ran a shuttle service, feeding him with files which he checked and ticked and handed back. As a study of how not to exert oneself, outside the scope of one's work, he was perfect. He held up a finished ale and it was taken from him and another put into his hands. When he wanted the window shut, the light switched on or the fan switched off, he gave a curt command to one of the servants even though the window and the switch were at his side. And when he wanted tea a servant, Thermos in hand, stood by while he drank it, waiting to refill the cup; then he belched and turned to the next file.

He was a civil servant, the sort of Indian bureaucrat who turns officialdom into officiousness; the personification of self-importance, the epitome of ill-manners. He must have been very important, a departmental chief on tour; for at every station some cringing subordinate would come into the carriage, and after three or four sharp instructions and twice as many nervous ' Yes sirs ' would be dismissed. I disliked him all afternoon—until about half-past five.

At that time, soon after leaving Rajamundry, the train rumbled slowly on to the Godavari bridge. The official jumped up and ran to open the carriage door for a better view. He was transfigured.

" I never cross the great Godavari without stopping work to look at it. Come and see."

I was still reeling under the revelation that such an odious creature could become a human being.

" This is the second largest bridge in India and the Godavari is our second greatest river." He spoke exquisite English. " A few miles down there is the dam built by Sir Arthur Cotton in 1852. Magnificent, of course; but if I had my way we should build a bigger one, bigger even than your Boulder Dam. You are not American? Oh! well then you have no idea. Why, the Godavari just would not fit into England! And up there, where it breaks out of the Deccan plateau through the Eastern Ghats, the scenery is enchanting. Like the lochs of Scotland, but three times more beautiful—even than Loch Lomond. I have been to Scotland, so I know." I was recovering. " A hundred miles upstream from here is the Rama temple at Bhadrachalam; that is where Lord Rama crossed the Godavari on his way to Ceylon to bring back his wife, Sita; she had been kidnapped by the King of Ceylon. It is a very holy place and a wonderful temple. You should see it. It was built in the middle of the seventeenth century by a fanatic tax-collector who embezzled six hundred thousand rupees to pay for it; he filled it with treasures and dedicated it to Rama. Such a pity that modern civil servants are equally corrupt but not half so inspired. When the King of Golconda heard about it, he sent for the tax-collector and cast him into a dungeon. But Rama appeared to him in a dream with a receipt note for the money, and on the same day a mysterious person paid it into the King's treasury. So the man was set free. Nowadays, thousands of pilgrims go to Bhadrachalam from all over India." I asked him how I could get there. " There are motor-boats all the way from Rajamundry; they take two days. But at this time of year, when the water is so low, they usually get stuck in the lower reaches. There is a road thirty miles as far as Devipatnam; you can go there by bus and then you can take the boat on to Bhadrachalam. Excuse me, please."

The train had reached the end of the bridge, and the official, who had already gone back to his seat, was holding his hand out to a servant for the next file. At the next station another nervous subordinate stepped into the carriage. I could not bear it and got out on to the platform. I took the next train back to Rajamundry.

The travellers' bungalow at Devipatnam is not a busy place. It is on the river next to the police station and about half a mile from the village. Villagers eat, sleep and weave mats on the bungalow veranda, and the policemen are usually preoccupied with the smoking of large black cigars. It is the country of the tobacco leaf rather than the *pan* leaf, and all the more attractive for it, if only because it makes for less spitting; a woman walking along a path with a powerful cheroot in her mouth is much more comely than a woman with betel-stained teeth and lips, chewing *pan*.

I realised at once what the official in the train had meant about the likeness to Scotland, for it rained all the twenty-four hours I was there. The landscape resolved into that trinity of Highland weather when the three elements of land and sky and water become unrecognisably mixed in a pervading greyness which passes for the order of the day.

The police sergeant and two constables came to see me. "We are Christians by caste," he said. "I am a Baptist and these two are Lutherans. We are the only Christians here, but we are very brave. Last year there was a great flood and Devipatnam was under water for many days. It was the will of God, for there is terrible Sin here. We had a boat and we rescued hundreds of people, but nobody thanked us. Oh, sir, there is terrible Sin!" And he stared at me with a look such as made me wither. But in the remoter parts of India a white skin is still beyond reproach, and the policeman brought me dishes of curry and rice, bowls of sour buttermilk and sweetmeats from the bazaar.

"Only because you are a Christian, sir. We should never do it for a Hindu."

Next morning a motor-launch came past and the policemen hailed it. It came to the bank and I was put aboard.

Sometimes, in fine country, I get a feeling of helplessness, a sort of passive happiness. I take no interest in its details, ask no names, seek to learn nothing about it, but I just lie back and soak it up. Knowledge seems to be irrelevant, almost irreverent, in the face of such beauty. That was what happened to me on the Godavari. The motor-boat took me through forests pouring steeply down into the river and over plains stretching far away across the world to distant shadowy hills, but after two days I knew no more about the country than when I started, save what it looked like. The ravine through the Ghats was impressive, but the country higher up was more beautiful; there were wide sandy banks with little villages on green plateaus beyond, and an occasional palm-tree leaning up against the sky. To me it was all unknown and I did not want to know it; it was too great and wonderful to tackle.

The launch stopped for the night at Kunavaram and I slept on the corrugated-iron roof. After supper, the coxswain took me for a walk through the bazaar—a row of glaring, hissing pressure lamps, hanging each in its own cloud of dazzled insects, dimly lighting a few faces in the stalls behind and a Communist flag drooping in the sky above.

On the second afternoon we reached Bhadrachalam. The travellers' bungalow was already occupied, so I walked through the village with a coolie beside me carrying my bag, looking for somewhere to stay. There were plenty of pilgrims' lodging-houses, but most of them were for Hindus only, and somebody suggested the Tobacco Company. The manager was away for the day and everybody else had taken a holiday, but the supervisor, a tiny bent old man called Mr Chandan, came to my rescue and said he would put me up for the night. He also promised to take me to the temple where he worships every evening. He led me to his house and sat me on a chair on the veranda. There was a string of dried mango leaves over the door and a pattern of white lines drawn with lime on the ground in front; the corners of the pattern were decorated with flowers stuck into small lumps of cowdung. Mr Chandan explained that every morning the ground was washed with water mixed with dung and the pattern redrawn. Then he told me his life story.

He was a Brahmin and had been a wealthy landowner near Rajamundry. But he had fallen into bad company and become a drunkard, a liar and a gambler. He had sold his land to pay off his debts and taken a job with the Tobacco

Company in Rajamundry, where he had continued to squander his earnings. His only child had died and his wife and parents had lived a life of misery on account of the troubles he brought to their door. Then one day two years ago, when his back had become bent almost double with debauchery and the burden of his sins, he had seen the light of God and had resolved to mend his ways. He had applied to his boss for a transfer and for two days he performed *pujas* (offerings) in a Rama temple. On the third day a letter arrived to say that a man with just his qualifications was wanted at the office at Bhadrachalam, Rama's own town. As he stepped aboard the launch to take him up the Godavari he vowed never to sniff the smell of alcohol again.

" Already, thank Rama, my stoop is better and it will be quite gone in another year's time. If all the bloody world were going to the dogs, I should not tell a lie to save it. I work and worship, play with my little dog and water my garden, and now I am respected by both the villagers and by the pilgrims who come to the temple, and also by myself. Lord Rama answers all my prayers, and in my spare time I write his name in a special little book; six hundred times a day is my aim, but usually of course I write it at least a thousand times. As I write, I think of the images of Rama and Sita and Rama's brother, Lakshman, in the temple."

And so Mr Chandan and his wife and I walked through the village by torchlight to the temple, taking with us a basket of flower-garlands which the good Mrs Chandan had made for the gods. We walked slowly on account of Mr Chandan's back, and he muttered prayers to Rama all the way. At the temple gate I left my shoes in a corner of the street and Mr Chandan knelt to touch the threshold with his forehead. Indeed, if he had not told me that his chronic

spinal curve was the result of his whilom sins, I should have
blamed his constant bowings and stoopings in the temple.
Under the gateway he disconcerted me by stopping to turn
round in his footsteps, holding his hands high above his
head and mumbling " Rama, Rama, Rama " as he revolved.
It was the first of the many occasions that evening when I
tried hard to smother my surprise and pretend that such
ritual was all part of my daily life. Through the gate we
walked, and up a flight of steps lined with priests and
beggars huddling in the darkness against the walls. Under
a four-poster *mandapam* (pavilion) a man was reading aloud
from holy scriptures to a few squatting figures. At the top
we went through another gate into a large courtyard containing the principal shrine and surrounded by twenty-four
lesser shrines. At one end was a tall *gopuram* (gate-tower)
and a vast pillar flagstaff with bells at the top.

Round and round the shrine we walked, Mr Chandan
talking and praying, shuffling and bowing. Every now and
then he would step across to the door of a side shrine to lay
his hands on it and gently touch it with his forehead, or
prostrate himself upon the threshold. His wife hovered a
few paces ahead or behind, touching her head on walls and
doors, kneeling to touch it on some sacred slab and hanging
garlands from her basket in auspicious places. Half the
main shrine was open-sided, and in it sat a small group of
Brahmins singing lustily, one of them clapping a rhythm
with his hands. The other half contained the throne-room
of the three idols, the holy of holies, and their bedroom.
Underneath the big *gopuram* a band was playing—trumpets,
clarinets and a drum. Occasionally a bell rang.

Round and round we walked, Mr Chandan ceaselessly
muttering invocations to Rama and information to me.
Even when he stooped to touch his forehead on some

particularly holy spot his talk continued, and once or twice I thought that I had lost him in the darkness, only to find him lying flat on the ground beside me, still chattering. After half an hour we tried to get into the central shrine to offer our *pujas* and have our garlands placed round the idols' necks; but there was a queue of devotees at the door and Mr Chandan said that we should wait until later. Instead we went to another shrine dedicated to the goddess Kali, the Terrible.

We stood in a line at the door of the cell together with about a dozen other pilgrims. Mr Chandan was nearest to the door, and I took a place somewhere in the middle. Everybody prayed aloud, but some of the pilgrims were obviously as unversed in the ritual as I, and they had to be given whispered instructions from the more regular temple-goers. The priest, a handsome man with a hook nose, long hair and a beard, came out of the shrine with a bowl of water and a spoon. He looked like something between a traditional saint and a traditional devil; I should have been no less surprised to see a halo over his head than a pair of horns sprouting from it. He wore only a *dhoti* and his cotton Brahminic thread over his shoulder, and he recited incessant prayers to Kali. The goddess looked Terrible indeed; she was painted black and scarlet with white eyes, and she wore a tattered grey dress. At her feet was a collection of saucers and pots, a brass bell, bits of cloth and a small oil-lamp; it was the sort of mess that fashionable ladies describe as their dressing-table.

We held out our hands and the priest poured into them a spoonful or two of water, or more if he thought we looked worth it. We all washed our hands, some drank a little and dabbed the rest on their heads or the backs of their necks. The priest went back into the shrine and came out again with a plate of flowers and leaves. He gave each of us a handful, and when he reached the end of the line he stopped to pray. Then he came back, holding out the plate for us to return the flowers with a few pieces of money. I fumbled blindly in my pocket and pulled out the first coin, an anna. Cheap, I thought, and so apparently did he; for he hesitated for a moment before passing on to the next man, to see if I would increase my stake. Back in the cell, he placed the plate of flowers and money in front of Kali and knelt beside her. His praying, which had been going on throughout the performance, increased in volume and vehemence, and rose in pitch to a wild chant. Twice he picked up the bell and rang it loud and long, and finally he took the plate and waved it round the Terrible head, put it down at her feet and dropped the money into a brass pot. Then he came out a third time, still chanting, with a saucer of bright crimson powder. He asked the name of each devotee and repeated a prayer for them, dabbing a spot of the powder with his finger on their foreheads. I was terrified, expecting to be branded with a gaudy splash between my eyebrows. To spend an anna on a Terrible goddess was all very well, but to be daubed with a crimson stamp by her priest was too much, and I looked round to see how I might escape into the darkness. Then I heard Mr Chandan call out my name and I knew that I was doomed. But either my name proved too difficult for the priest, or else my one anna had not been sufficient to lift me from pagan anonymity; for after reciting the prayer in front of me he moved on to my neighbour.

Mrs Chandan, who had been lurking in the darkness and had been offered none of the holy benefits, came forward with a garland of yellow flowers which the priest took and hung round Kali's neck. Then he lit a pair of incense tapers at the goddess's feet and knelt again to pray. The ceremony was over, and the devotees, bowing and kneeling towards the shrine, scattered into the night. Mr Chandan stepped forward and sat down on the floor in front of the door with his eyes shut; then he got up, clasped his hands in a final prayer and led me away.

There had been a complete absence of solemnity, and for anybody who had never before witnessed such a ceremony there were moments, particularly when the priest picked up the bell and rang it wildly as he chanted, that were almost ludicrous. I had to look up to the sky, to the trees over the temple roofs and the stars above for a reminder that I was still awake.

After a few more walks round the temple courtyard we went into the main shrine. There was an ante-room with a door at the back into the sanctuary. The three idols, black with silver eyes and mouths, silk robes and jewelled head-dresses, sat on a table. In front of them stood three smaller replicas, less fabulously arrayed. On a table near the door there was a collection of smaller images, and round the room, on shelves and on the floor, were plates of oranges and boiled rice, flowers, cakes and coconuts. The place was thick with the scent of flowers and incense.

The gods were attended by three or four priests who conducted their business without the prayers and incantations of the Kali priest, and the only noise came from the devotees who all prayed aloud and knelt to touch their foreheads on the floor. The officiant was a fat young man with his head shaved except for a thick pigtail which fell in soft rings on his shoulder. His performance was very similar to that of the Kali priest, but with none of the chanting and less of the flourish. He first appeared with water in a bowl which he ladled into our hands and we drank. Then he came along with a dish of flowers which we gave back to him with a little money. Again I fished in my pocket, and this time I pulled out a silver rupee. I had not the courage to put it back and try for something less extravagant. There was an ecstatic gasp from Mr Chandan. The priest was evidently delighted; he came back with half a coconut, and a garland of flowers which he strung round my neck, a privilege which the other worshippers obviously eyed with envy, but to me was but an expensive embarrassment. I fear that my munificence stole the show; for the priest, who came back again with the water bowl, merely dabbed a wet spoon at the other devotees while for me he filled the half-coconut with the precious liquid and added a handful of sacred flowers. Then he asked me if I would like to see the gods' bedroom, and took me to a little room almost filled by a silver cot hanging on silver chains from the ceiling; there were rich crimson bedclothes and a pair of silver sandals. Mrs Chandan came up with her basket of garlands, all of which the priest took, but from the perfunctory way in which he put them on the images, breaking off loose ends and dropping them on the floor, I had a guilty feeling that my rupee had robbed the cremony of any dignity. Mr Chandan said " Very good, very good! " obviously for my benefit and touched his forehead to the ground. I stood embarrassed and sheepish, with a string of flowers round my neck and half a coconut in my hands. I was glad to get out into the courtyard.

Many people had arrived to witness the ceremony of feeding the gods and putting them to bed, and the temple courtyard was fast turning into a bazaar. Mr Chandan discovered that his manager, Mr Krishnaiah, had returned to Bhadrachalam and was already in the temple, so we hurried back to the shrine to watch him offering his *pujas.* Mr Krishnaiah was evidently a Brahmin of importance and he was treated by the priest with great deference, for which no doubt there was a considerable price to pay. His son-in-law beside him, on the other hand, was given his flowers and water with callous unconcern. After they had finished they came out and Mr Chandan introduced us.

" You are very fortunate," said Mr Krishnaiah, " to be able to see the feast of the gods. Not many Europeans have seen it here, and of course low-caste Hindus are not allowed anywhere near." Little did he know how near to being branded with a sect mark I had been, but it was comforting to be told that at least I was granted the status of touchability. I asked him about the feast and he explained that, although Rama was an incarnation of God, he and his wife and brother had been ordinary mortal beings on earth and therefore had to be treated just as other men and women, with the additional reverence demanded by their divine connections. They had to be bathed and fed, put to bed at night and woken by a bell in the morning.

" For our ancestors," he said, " they used actually to eat the food; but now, because we are so full of sin, they reject it as unworthy and it is distributed to the people."

While we were talking a bell rang, the gods' dinner-gong, and we went round to the open half of the shrine which is used as the dining-room. The chief images are too heavy and cumbersome to be moved from the sanctuary, and the three smaller replicas, clothed in white night-dresses, had been brought out to deputise. They were sitting on a table covered with a rich carpet and three priests were waving flowers, bowls of rice and oranges round their heads. The noise was terrific; a choir was singing in front, chanting the names of God and all his saints and famous devotees. The crowd was joining in, bells were ringing, clappers clapping and the band, which had left the *gopuram*, was marching, almost galloping, round the shrine making as loud a noise as it could contrive. Occasionally somebody struck a gong, and anybody who was not singing was praying aloud. To defy any possible charges of neutrality in the matter I simulated with my lips a vague appearance of devotion, but it is just possible that I mumbled what I could remember of the Apostles' Creed. Mr Krishnaiah told me that the chanters recited the names of God's devotees in the same way as a man visiting a Cabinet Minister goes first to the office-boy, then to the chief clerk and finally to the private secretary before reaching the Minister; former saints are merely stepping-stones, the ' proper channels ' to God.

From the middle of the crowd there came a shout of recognition and somebody called my name. I was quite startled, for I had a horrid feeling of guilt about being in the temple at all; but it was only the coxswain of the motor-boat. He came across and embraced me and asked me how I had come by such a magnificent garland of flowers. I told him that I would gladly sell it for half the price I gave, and that it was only my parsimony that had saved me from a crimson spot between my eyebrows.

After the priests had waved the food in front of the idols' faces for about twenty minutes it became obvious that the gods were not going to be tempted to dine that evening. " Alas, they have lost their appetite again! It happens every night," said Mr Chandan. A curtain was pulled across in front of the table and when it was drawn back the gods had gone to bed. We stepped forward and the fat young priest came out of the sanctuary with a charger of cold boiled rice. The devotees held out their hands and were given according to their deserts, which I suspect were reckoned more by their subscriptions to the priests' benevolent fund than by their nearness to starvation. I was still nursing half a coconut, so I foolishly held it out and it was filled to the brim. I ate my rice, dropping as much as I could onto the floor, and Mr Krishnaiah led me away. Under the gateway I managed surreptitiously to leave my coconut behind a naked brass lady with four arms.

Mr Krishnaiah insisted that I should spend the night at his house, but I think the invitation was a great effort for such an orthodox Brahmin, and was probably inspired more by his determination not to let Mr Chandan be my host than by his own hospitality. I was not allowed to take my meals with the family, and although there was a spare bedroom in his bungalow I was given a bed out on the veranda. I sat alone at the dining-room table which had never before been used; for Mr Krishnaiah and his family ate off leaves in the kitchen, sitting on the floor. Next morning I found the glass and crockery I had used lying in the bathroom and I suspect that they were going to be thrown away, having been contaminated.

The bungalow was built in the western style, but was excruciatingly uncomfortable, being neither western nor eastern. Mr Krishnaiah did his best to entertain me and courteously ignored my clumsy efforts to observe the household rules, although there were some awkward moments when the opinions of an English vagabond conflicted with the stringent tenets of Brahminic infallibility. As a concession, after I had taken off my shoes, I was allowed into the kitchen to see the family idols. They were figures of the hill-god Venkateswara and his wife, and they were drenched with rubies and diamonds. " My wife chose the jewellery; it is worth many hundreds of rupees." But the divine couple were made of thin cardboard—strictly two-dimensional.

Mr Krishnaiah, like Mr Chandan, had only recently become a religious zealot, but with him there had been no dramatic conversion. Unlike the little sinner, who was really a fanatical devotionalist obsessed with dogma and rituals, the manager was more concerned with Yogic philosophy and was determined that his soul should be liberated from the cycle of death and rebirth and end up in God's heaven. Although he performed *pujas* at the temple he admitted that idols were not necessary for able men like him, but were for the unenlightened who could meet God in no other way. He had recently become the disciple of a wandering *guru*, a man of supernatural powers, who had dropped for him a few pearls from his wealth of eternal truths; and now, every morning, Mr Krishnaiah rose at half-past three, took his bath, and from four o'clock to six he prayed and meditated before the images on his kitchen floor. By great exertion he managed to free himself from his body and achieve a detachment from the limits of time and place in which he entered a world of light and beauty that could only be the world of God. At the beginning he had only been able to achieve it for a few minutes, then for half an hour, and now for an hour or two. His only requirement, apart from the will to do it and the ability to devote his entire mind to concentration, was complete silence, although once he had reached his state of bliss no disturbance could recall him. He said that if I had come upon him at such a time and cut him with a knife, no blood would have flowed.

His *guru*, however, had powers a hundred times more exceptional; for he could see Mr Krishnaiah off on the Madras train from Rajamundry and be waiting to meet him at Madras station, walking up and down the platform as the train drew in; and he had been seen in Madras, Bombay and Calcutta—all on the same afternoon. Even greater men had lived for years without any food, and been buried for weeks underground without dying, so great was their control over their bodies. But Mr Krishnaiah was only a beginner. In the night I was awakened by him at his prayers on the kitchen floor, and I was tempted to take a knife to him to prove his point. But the veranda door had been locked.

Next morning I told Mr Krishnaiah that I should like to see the temple by daylight and he sent his son-in-law along with me. We bought a coconut in the bazaar, and at the temple gate we were sold a ticket for the privilege of offering the coconut to Rama. The place was dull and lifeless, like the morning scene backstage in a theatre when only props and painted scenery remain of the previous night's show. It was not improved by the corrugated-iron roofs over some of the shrines, which I had not noticed at night. Indeed, the Bhadrachalam temple is not noted for its architecture or decoration; it is famous only for its historical associations, the pilgrimages and the feast-days when the three gods (the replicas) are carried through the village to be bathed in the Godavari.

We went to the main shrine where the fat young priest broke open our coconut and offered it to the gods. They seemed not to be interested in breakfast and he brought it back to us on a tray, obviously expecting another rupee. I decided to keep my money for the beggars at the gate. We walked round the courtyard a few times and then went out.

That afternoon I took a boat across the river into the State of Hyderabad.

[May 1955

11

VISIT TO CORUMBÁ

Gordon Meyer

We went to the station at Sao Paolo like other travellers, and met a charming military policeman, native of Corumbá. Over coffee he said that Corumbá was rough, even violent. The women, combining with the men, assaulted strangers in the streets ; their technique : to come up, one on each side of you, make the old suggestions, and then. . . . He showed on his arm a long scar. Was it necessary to carry a gun then ? Yes, just like in Sao Paolo.

We bought our tickets for two days later. Fearing customs troubles, I had brought no arms ; my Smith & Wesson ·455 and its big belt could not be hidden either in a suitcase or on my person. For twenty dollars I bought a nice-looking Brazilian ·32 modelled on the Smith & Wesson, with a small cartridge holder on the holster and fifty rounds of long ·32 ammunition. It could be fastened on my belt and did not show. It was small after my ·455, but large in comparison with M's ·22. The trouble with carrying a gun is that, once in trouble, you have to use it.

9 p.m. Half-naked on the bunk in the stainless steel compartment which had to be fought for. Astonishment that I can continue and, worse, conscript another to these

grinding enthusiasms. It could have been done by air, even if not by special arrangement with General W. You can go anywhere by air in Brazil, even to the heart of Mato Grosso: there are eighteen companies and seven hundred and forty-eight properly equipped airports, apart from landing strips.

But the object of the journey is the journey. Not pressurised isolation from the feel of the earth and people. The journey at this juncture produces a yearning for the planet to accelerate in its solar orbit and drive the hemisphere swiftly, deeply into its next winter; drags up anguishing recollections of glacial lakes, and streams running brilliantly through the leaning forests of the far south; brings a reminder that the forthcoming departure is for one of the steamiest concentrations of heat on the earth. And as almost noiselessly the gleaming aluminium begins to roll forward, there is a feeling that we are leaving the area of friendships.

Baurú, 7 a.m. The freshness of country sunrises here is an ambiguous freshness; the cool tropic promise is one of noonday ferocity. A two-hour queue wait for a sleeper for the Baurú-Corumbá stretch. Cockaigne is well behind now.

3 p.m., Aracatubu. Another in a daylong series of modern towns, each with airport and towering buildings white as newlaid eggs. This is part of the difference, then. Everywhere evidence of work well done: sowing, wiring, construction. All night and day this big diesel has been hauling the long string of steel cars across this country said to occupy one sixteenth of the earth. Hour after hour through Brazil's riches of coffee, vines, maize, cattle, beans. Yet until tonight we shall not even have left the state of Sao Paolo.

The Major is small, dressed in civilian clothes, carries an expensive camera. His trunks, seen on Baurú station, are very heavy. " Paper . . . I read a lot ! " His eyes are soft, dark, reflective ; not soldiers' eyes. This too has to lead to something.

Nothing now but this silent fight. Against the solar massacre tactics are immobility, wet handkerchiefs, fruit, resignation. Everything has been stopped by the heat except the train. Even the few small clouds do not move. The red earth in the late afternoon light tinges even cattle and houses. But at last opens up a fantastic panorama which in this continent often announces the proximity of an immense river.

At 7.30 p.m. the train is in the approaches to the Paraná. Brief view of Urubupungá, the new giant dam at the rendezvous of Paraná and Tieté—and the rivers of sweat in which we are all squirming. Here once more the loved river not seen for two years, and at this point nearly two thousand miles from its outlet in the Rio de la Plata. For a moment there comes intensely the feel of this continent, never once experienced in Uruguay.

Slowly the bright bridge girders roll by. From the train-end the Major and I lean out to gaze at its singular personality, the noiseless ferocity of its liquid formations, the races, whirlpools, eddies, convulsions, all analogising the multiple discordant elements lining its ambiguous shores.

The last car rolls off the bridge into Mato Grosso. Those two words, for followers, actual or from their armchairs, of Fawcett, Sasha Siemels and others of that calibre, have inflated the strict linguistic meaning, Great Thicket, the world's biggest understatement, into something possessing the authentic ring of danger, hostility, despair and therefore challenge. The area of the Great Thicket, at over half a million square miles, is therefore six times as large as the United Kingdom; and it is not the largest state in Brazil. Few maps in the world have so many blanks, except those of deserts. It is a map of crowds of rivers that may never be named. There are little wigwam signs on the map for settlements of indigenous peoples, some of whom are not yet tamed. Even today nobody knows how many Indians live inside. It is also a place into which white men disappear as if they had left the earth. In that dim penumbra of creation the great geographical decisions are taken : whether the water flows south to the Plata, or north to the Amazon.

This, the southern part, is more inhabitable, but it is low, swampy, often flooded by sluggish rivers unable to drain themselves properly. And the climate is violent in its heat, humidity, unhealthiness. It attracts men of both extremes.

It is difficult to see. Rapid-fading daylight illuminates an earth that is now vermilion, a vegetation that is emerald. Violence is the common denominator of all colours. Sudden saturation of night and forest perfumes.

At dinner conversation was boosted by the Major's surprise that a European should be interested in the military history of the Major's country a hundred years ago. The Paraguayans invaded Mato Grosso in the war against Brazil, Argentina, Uruguay, and later retreated. The Brazilians undertook the fantastic exploit of trying to get through to the river Paraguay from Río de Janeiro, and became as water does in sand. The Major revealed he had been twenty-five years in the army, but, having refused to support the last revolution, had lost his prospects. Now he was finishing his time. "What will you do?" At this he became evasive in a shy way : "I have several offers from big contractors . . ." and tailed off hopefully.

His conception sees the army as something that should remain faithful to the elected head of state ; which makes him dangerously progressive. Yet there is something else about the Major to be explained ; he has a certain way of looking at people which is not altogether unfamiliar. Well, there is time ; we do not get to Campo Grande, the military headquarters, his destination, until tomorrow morning. It seems a pity he has to leave his family in Río just at Christmas. But that is army life, he says. Still. . . .

Over coffee it comes out. He is writing a novel based on his military life ; he will expose everything.

Campo Grande, 6 a.m. Midsummer's Day. The night's surprise was intense cold—we are almost on latitude 20 degrees south. Dew-soaked clothes and bedclothes. The sun, which will make short work of this, is just appearing. I got up to say good-bye to the Major, now at the farthest point of separation from his loved ones, found him being greeted by a charming young woman and two children gazing up at him with much affection. It could give a novelist certain intriguing possibilities.

The landscape exposed by the humid sunrise trailing along after yesterday's onslaught looks as though suffering from a hangover. The men are much bigger, tougher-looking. Most are recent immigrants : Germans, Japanese, Yugoslavs, Paraguayans, Paolistas and colonists from the southern Brazilian state of Santa Caterina. There is no distinct Mato Grosso type. But Mato Grosso must give them some common denominator.

Rivers of rust. Sierras shorn off, revealing wound-shaped cliffs. A vast landscape assumes the lineaments of the Lost Continent of the novels. High mesetas, saddles, narrow passes, saw-toothed ranges ; rivers darkening to chocolate, rapids turning to milk. Into one of the red gorges the train pours itself.

9.40 a.m. finds the long chain of cars straddling the country station of Camizao between massive escarpments. Surrounding forest musical with bird-cries and songs of mango-selling children. Sweet scents of vegetation. The primeval seduction of South American forests. Huge wing-shadows darken the windows.

Half an hour later : Aquidauna, a brand new station ; spotless tiled bathrooms, superb ices. The cool deceptions of early morning mercilessly exposed. For five endless hours the heat will mount.

"Look at the banks for crocodiles !" But there is a mirror in the compartment. A word or two about the compartment. From the coach's drab chocolate and marzi-pan exterior you would not guess the inner sophistication. The first-class compartments, brand new, contain two com-fortable beds, one above the other but widely separated ; a washbasin, plenty of floor space, a comfortable armchair, electric fan, two windows with *persianas*, ample luggage space, four lights, built-in metal coat-hangers, bells for stewards, who come ; and everything pleasingly finished in light synthetic wood and aluminium. Cost, for some thirty-six hours and well over a thousand miles : 8,250 cruzeiros—twenty-seven shillings.

Noticeable too are the efficient service, spotlessness of bathrooms and lavatories, the unfailing supply of water to showers, the absence of insects. Stewards are uniformed in black trousers, white shirts with epaulets, bow ties. The obverse they reserve for compatriots boarding the train for the next town. A huge farmer sits at a neighbouring table ; his desperate order is ignored. A little imprudently, it might be concluded. Finally, one steward : "You must ask the other steward." An old game. The other does not approach ; not only in football is there combination. The farmer's bulk, as he rises, darkens the coach. But he is told at once by the same steward, " We don't serve anyone standing." The suddenness of the fearless attack seats him. They take his money when tired of torturing him ; in return give him beer, as if it were a sop. Similarly, the man delivering the next case of drinks at a small halt asks for cigarettes. " Nothing under 500 cruzeiros." Now the universality of it becomes apparent.

By 6.30 p.m. the sierra is straight ahead, tall, blue-black with the colour of the coming storm. As the train approaches, it seems impossible that there will be a way through the range looming across the track. But the chocolate and maize mechanical caterpillar writhes through. At this moment the storm, breaking, changes an attitude to life.

Such the long preamble to Corumbá. The affair there started deceptively. There were certain signs ; I did not read them correctly. I was tired, wanted to get to a hotel immediately. There was also information to be discovered concerning the day of the week on which you could cross over into Bolivia. I sensed only a vague feeling of unpleasantness ; even this was disguised by the impact of a new place.

The unpleasantness therefore became invested in the absence of proper roads to and from the station, the swamps of mud ; in petty details. All this was fictitious : many small Paraguayan towns have few or no paved roads, and are charming. I was, in a word, unprepared for what was to happen.

Disappointed at the absence of taxis for the arrival of the

only train of importance during the day, I set off through the red slush.

He came towards the station driving slowly, a big dun-coloured man with a bristly moustache. He sat carelessly at the wheel of his green American taxi, looking about him as if collecting train passengers was subordinate to another motive not clear to me. I got into the back, there was dead silence as he drove towards the train.

Most passengers had been met by private cars, or jeeps in the case of those proceeding straight to *fazendas*. A *fazendero*, who was also a prominent Corumbá lawyer, and his *capataz* were preparing to leave in a blue modern American truck. In our conversation on the train he had told me his establishment was ten hours' drive in a launch down river. Quickly they drove away. I was sorry to see them disappear, and did not know why.

The day was no longer sunny, but heavy. There was a lot of rain to come, but something held it up. A breeze was blowing, but the air was violent, under tension. I boarded the train, re-entered the compartment, manœuvred the heaviest case to the window. The big man had not approached to help ; he lounged against the car, smoking a cigar. I beckoned to him.

As he straightened up, his height, the breadth of his chest and shoulders stopped me looking at anything else for a moment. His neck was a thick column as of a primitive idol ; on it sat his head, like a cannon-ball. He looked indestructible.

Casually he approached, his mind, if there was one in that brute frame, on something else ; and he took the case. It was a big case, at full expansion with the many heavy objects inside, almost a trunk. It weighed about sixty pounds. In one hand he took it, as though it were a lady's handbag, and I said, " My God ! "

The drive through the sodden red earth to the town evoked a lawless wild west community, and that was only because of films I had seen. It was soon clear that Corumbá was not an echo, much less an imitation.

" *Vamos ao Grande Hotel.*" And there was no more speech until we got there.

Typical frontier town hotel. In cane chairs at the top and bottom of the steps serving the entrance, men sat about with beer bottles to their lips. Some had drunk enough. Their unshaven faces were red, and the beer, transmuted into perspiration, saturated their clothes. Two small bootblack boys, each on his equipment box, were playing a game in which each tried to shove a brush along the ground past his opponent's guard, to score a goal between the other's legs. The stares of the men, even of the boys, were not hostile, but unfriendly. I noticed these little details because there was at that moment in the procession of events a sort of suspension, as before a theatre curtain rises. And again I felt the same tension in the air.

The fare I calculated would be 1,500 cruzeiros, and I had 2,000 ready. For the moment I did not pay it, as no one helped with the bags, neither from the hotel nor the big man himself. When I had carried the last to the top of the steps, and returned, I asked, " How much ? "

" Five thousand."

The man said nothing more ; he waited. There was a moment's silence.

" I think you made a mistake."

His boredom looked deliberate. For the first time his dangerous look seemed to be connected with me. He still did not answer. It seemed this was his way of beginning.

" In Sao Paolo even, it would not be more than two

thousand."

At this he straightened up as if the better to be appreciated physically. "This is CORUMBÁ."

On all Guaraní words the accent falls on the final syllable. The word exploded in my face; and everything he did not add was now very clear.

"Just a minute," I said.

I went up the stairs between the files of beer swillers, and into the hotel, where no one had moved. "How much should it be from the station to the hotel?"

They were not interested. I had thought what I had sensed was not hostility, only unfriendly lack of interest. That now seemed hostility. I repeated the question to a youth employed by the hotel. A little uncertainly he said, "Two thousand maximum." And I went outside, and down the steps.

He was waiting there, with the same air of disengagement, which was engagement; like a man who has accepted a duel. There was nothing in all this that was unusual for him.

I took out my two notes. "Five thousand is robbery, and you know it."

"You're an American, and you can pay it."

An invisible vapour mushroomed up between us, and it signified unleashed violence. "I am less an American than you are, and it's got nothing to do with it. Here are two thousand; if you don't like it, we'll go to the police."

Almost at once he was in the driving seat. "Let's go," he said, leaving me immobilised with surprise.

The conversation had not been too easy: one side Spanish, the other Brazilian. It was now about to enter the phases of complication. "Can you come?" I asked M.

We got in, and he drove off fast. Suspecting what he

was going to do, I opened my portfolio which I had never let go of and, keeping it out of his sight, got my hand on the butt of the gun inside it. M sat up rigid. Suddenly he turned off to the right, went half the block, stopped dead.

In the middle of a row of tawdry shops such as you find near a West African go-down was a dark blind oblong, like a big black exclamation mark : an empty doorway. He got out, went inside ; we followed, I kept my portfolio in my left hand.

Outside, by the doorway, in a chair sat a man, very dirty, and drunk. Inside it was bare, save for table and chair, and obscure. At the back, in near-darkness, were two rooms. The doors, each with a crude iron grille at eye level, were open. It was impossible to distinguish anything inside the cells ; they exuded an odour of filth and atrociousness.

A man materialised out of the obscurity. The driver said with cold triumph : " This is the *comisario*."

" You are the *comisario* ? " I was too astonished to hide the astonishment.

" Yes," he said. He wore a filthy light brown cotton suit, was unshaven, and had not a mark of authority on him.

" This is Corumbá police station ? "

" Yes."

" They are foreigners," said the big man, and the word foreigner was an insult. " He says I am a thief and that I want to rob him."

" The *senhora* will explain the matter ; she speaks Portuguese."

M began to explain, and the voice of the drunkard outside came thick and strong : " Lock them both up ! Who do they think they are ? Foreigners."

I looked at the one who was said to be the *comisario*.

" Who is that outside ? "

" That is my assistant."

" Your assistant. . . . Well ? What do we do ? "

" You have to pay. That is law."

" The fare is not five thousand. It is two thousand, maximum ; the hotel told me. They must know."

The one called the *comisario* looked at the big man ; the latter suddenly began to talk. His voice was thick and not with drunkenness. There was a sound in the room of dry sticks being snapped, one after another, as again and again his right fist hit his left palm.

" What is he saying ? "

The one in the filthy cotton suit said : " He says that if you don't pay now, he'll settle it his own way and that he'll make a purée of you." He smiled.

The big man was under a strange control ; his determination stonelike. It was what marked the situation. I was cold with rage and distrust.

" You're the *comisario*. That's right, isn't it ? "

" Yes. I'm the *comisario*."

" And while this man threatens assault, you listen. And do nothing."

An appeal which failed because there was nothing to appeal to.

" You have to pay. It is the law."

" What is the name of this man ? "

The man in the doorway stood up straight, bristling. On the other man's face appeared an oily challenge. " Tarzan," he said. He fastened his eyes to my face as he delivered the message.

In the next moment he wondered whether I had taken it for a joke ; he said, emphasising it : " Tarzan we call him."

If I could get my gun out quickly enough, and the three of you went for me, and if I shot you, then Tarzan, and hit the drunk over the head with the barrel; would anyone in this dump even cross the street?

There was the sound of a heavy scuffle on the pavement, followed by a thud. We saw the woman fall. From the chair a delighted laugh.

She burst into the room, screaming, a shabby woman of about fifty. "Did you see? And a policeman too! Tripped me up!"

She stopped a moment, regarding the impassive faces, but she was the only one who had anything to say.

"Well, why don't you do something about it? You're the police, aren't you?" She became hysterical. The one who let himself be called *comisario* stared with that vague curiosity as of cattle disturbed while feeding. The one called Tarzan remained leaning against the only door out of the place, arms folded, his mind on one thing. He was smouldering, but it was controlled. His flexed arms resembled sections of liana, throttling trees. He was awaiting his moment.

They let the woman rave on. The one called the *comisario* turned. "Well, you must pay him now."

Screaming her opinion, the woman went out. Surprisingly, she went out vertically.

"I want you to call the Transport Commissioner."

"At this hour he can't be found." So he did exist then.

"Why not?"

"He goes home; he has no telephone at home."

"Send a messenger."

"We have no one. You can see him in the morning, but you must pay now. In the morning you can make a claim."

Did I look such a sucker? I looked outside; it was getting dark. The big man had not moved; he was awaiting something he was going to enjoy. He wanted 5,000; I knew what he would do for 50,000. There was a moment of total silence; finally he moved.

"He said I was a thief!" Each word a savage blow.

"I did not. I said his charge was robbery [*un asalto*]; and it is."

The big man left the doorway, came right up to me and said a lot of things very fast.

"What is he saying?"

"He says better you both finish it now in there," said M. The *comisario* waited. M said: "Stop getting so excited. Can't you see that's what they want?"

"I'm being blackmailed."

"And how are we going to get out, if you don't pay?"

I avoided looking at the two rooms at the back. In one of them would go what was left of me. Tarzan was the sort who goes on long after the man is prostrate and motionless; with his feet. He was the type who loves his work; our one common characteristic.

In the other room M, for a different treatment. Not a soul we knew had a notion where we were.

"In the morning you can take the case to the Transport Commissioner."

"Then why is it necessary to pay now?"

Suddenly the big man went wild again; he spoke with violence, jabbing his finger at his car. He was going to charge also for all the time we had been here.

"That certainly I shall not pay; he agreed to come here."

There was a long fruitless discussion about it. Then: "Pay now," said the *comisario*; and with that everyone recognised the crisis.

He looked at her who was probably the most attractive girl he had seen in his life. To the four people in that filthy dark room the unverbalised terms were as clear as sunlight. The question had now been turned completely on its axis, and became : will 5,000 get us out ?

" I'll pay *you*. As depositary."

" No, you must pay him."

The law was the man in the doorway.

" If I pay him, I want a receipt."

Two words they exchanged. " No, he doesn't have to give you a receipt."

"What proof will there be then ? Nothing."

"You have my word for it."

To this I could say nothing ; I was recovering from the shock.

The man on the chair outside was shouting again : " Lock 'em up. Put 'em away ! Who do they think they are ? *Foreigners*, shouting at the authorities."

It was in a cold way that M's anger showed itself. She went outside, looked down at the shapeless thing in the chair tilted against the wall ; each swift sentence, in his own language, was a short burst from a Thompson gun :

" You ! Listen to me. Shut your mouth ! And keep it shut ! Stay where you are. And don't move ; for anything ! "

Motionless, silent, the representative of the law in Corumbá remained in his chair. His colleague stared at something he never saw before. The big man, arms folded still, looked unimpressed. His mind was on one thing only. His skull looked as primitive and pitiless as Bourdelle's ' Hercules '.

I pulled out what he wanted. It was like a knife-thrust,

the viciousness with which he snatched it from me. I went out into the street, took out paper and pencil, peered down at his number-plate, and wrote: MT1—20—57, and I do not know why he did not hit me then. For with him it was not only the note; and we both knew it did not end there.

M was talking quietly to the self-styled *comisario*; her voice sweet and cold. She had seen how it had to be.

"You know. . . ." She paused in a conversational fashion. "I really would think what I was doing, if I were you. You see. . . ." She looked at him with something like sympathy, but it was not. "We can make things *very* difficult. We have close friends in the presidency. . . . Of course, it's your affair. Don't think for a moment I'm threatening, but you know as well as I do that this is not the way to run the police service. . . ."

She came out; it was nearly dark now. Big thunder clouds were piling over the town, coming in from the endless swamp and forest encircling us. In there lived thousands of different kinds of animals; for their own special kind of republic they made their laws, and kept them. A man who understood that did not have to go in fear; he had to take the same elemental precautions.

The representative of the law in Corumbá appeared behind us.

"*Senhora*, I wanted to say. . . ."

"What is your name?"

"Juvenal, *senhora*, Juvenal."

"Well, Juvenal, maybe I shall recommend you."

"Thank you, *senhora*." He did not notice the ambiguity. "I am an educated man. (*Eu tenho muita cultura*. . . .) There are many here without any culture, but I am different. I have a culture."

The first heavy drops fell out of the sky; before we reached the hotel, walking, a solid mass of water was falling.

We went up to the bare room, and locked the flimsy door. I took a shower, dressed. M took a shower. I buckled on the ·32 under a lightweight floppy coat, and we went down.

The eating-room was very large, occupying one side of the hotel. Windows on three sides. One side looked out onto the plaza central. All the windows were open. I chose the most tactical table, but it had one blind side. A few tables were occupied by drinkers. They all stared the same stare we now knew; we were foreigners. Like nearly all the Mato Grosso inhabitants seen so far, they were big men, tough-looking. Only the waiter was small, and anxious for the story.

He had been a victim of Tarzan's attention. He lowered his voice, looking out of the windows. " You must be careful. He is well known. He always does this. If the people protest, he beats them up. The people here are very revengeful; he will certainly try to avenge himself on you. *Very* revengeful, the people ! "

One thing animals are not.

Even a long ·32 seems on the small side at times. Could all six chambers be emptied into him before he got to me ? We went upstairs, locked the door. With a shocking crash the thunder broke over town, river and forest. The lights wavered, went out; came on again, more feebly than before. Total darkness alternated with repeated blazes of lightning. The rain hit the streets with a noise like that of boiling fat. From outside came a cry, the sound of footsteps running. All that night the ferocity fell on the town ; as if re-charging it.

In the morning the stormclouds were drawn back, recoiling like a serpent preparing its offensive. But the air was fresher.

The young waiter with the fearful face and wide unsure grin had been pondering the events of the evening before, and had a suggestion. "But don't say I told you!"

"Is it far to the headquarters?"

"You'll have to take a taxi."

First the fare was ascertained; it was quite modest.

The military headquarters of Corumbá are some way out of town, in the general direction of Bolivia. The drive gave wide views over the curving river Paraguay, the horizons of forest beyond it.

The General was absent. Officer in command, said an efficient courteous orderly, was Lieutenant-Colonel Marques. He was a spare man in his late thirties, a clean-shaven, efficient-looking soldier in his shirt-sleeved uniform. Also extremely courteous.

The office was large. Wide windows offered extensive panoramas of Mato Grosso. Comfortable armchairs. A long sofa against the inner wall; to this the Lieutenant-Colonel gestured, and offered coffee.

He listened attentively from an armchair, and after a very few minutes ordered a telephone call to be made. The phone at the other end was evidently out of order; he sent a jeep. He lit a cigarette which he smoked through a black holder, and before he had finished it an orderly announced someone. Into the room walked a large corpulent man, shirtsleeved, booted, wearing horn-rimmed glasses and a thick moustache.

The Lieutenant-Colonel rose. "This is the Traffic Commissioner and Head of Police." He turned to him. "The *senhora* speaks Portuguese, she will explain the matter to you."

M said : " Last night your men on duty were drunk."

The Traffic Commissioner and Head of Police was unsuccessful in concealing his reaction. He looked at the Lieutenant-Colonel : " The man who was drunk is already under lock and key."

" It has happened to him before, hasn't it ? "

" Yes."

From time to time he stirred uneasily as M related the case.

" The driver has been to see me this morning."

" The one they call Tarzan ? "

" Yes. You know he is called Tarzan ? "

" Yes, we know."

Marques said : " I would ask you to investigate this matter." It was quiet, courteous, and just as if he were on a parade ground. This had not happened to the Traffic Commissioner before.

" Let me have your report as soon as possible, so that we may study it," continued the Lieutenant-Colonel quietly. " And advise us what action you have taken regarding the driver."

The Traffic Commissioner and Head of Police rose, and did not like having to express his apologies.

Marques too got up, and turned first to us. " It is quite possible that this driver, who is known to be a dangerous man, will try to revenge himself. The people here are very revengeful : they don't forget the smallest thing. If anything happens, don't hesitate to telephone me. In fact (he turned to the Commissioner), it might be better for you to take no action against the driver until these people have left Corumbá. How long are you staying ? "

" Until the train leaves for Santa Cruz."

" You are going there by train ? There is a plane."

" By air we shall see nothing."

" I do not envy you."

The Traffic Commissioner left. He had been called ; he was dismissed. Then Marques said: " We regret this. Unfortunately in Corumbá we are a long way from real law and order. The only order here is the army. There are not half a dozen men in the police force. No one likes the work. So the army is constantly being called upon. But I hope you will have no more trouble, and that there will be a train tomorrow or the day after."

I had had misgivings about walking into a military headquarters wearing a concealed gun, but after one thing Marques had said, I was now glad to have it on me on the long walk back to the hotel.

We took a table in that vast inhospitable eating-room, ordered the only thing that can be ordered in Corumbá. The little waiter bent his head over the table. " All this morning he's been sitting in the plaza."

" Tarzan ? "

" Yes, just out there." He flicked an eye at the open window.

" In his car ? "

He became excited. " No, on that bench. They've taken his car away from him." The nervous grin split his face.

So the Traffic Commissioner did not care to wait.

" Can you see him now ? "

He lifted only his eyes. " It seems he's not there. But . . . remember what I told you. Careful ! "

He looked as pleased as a film director at the end of a successful scene.

It appeared that the train would leave two mornings

later. Not the famous ' *tren de la muerte* ', but a recent addition, a diesel rail-car. The Litorina, it is called. Presumably, the car resembled one of the marine snails of that genus. But a comparatively fast snail : it would take twelve hours against the Death Train's three days and two nights for the four hundred-odd miles to Santa Cruz de la Sierra.

The Death Train is much favoured by the *contrabandistas*. It consists of a long string of old freight cars and one or two coaches with wooden seats. Nothing else ; no lights, lavatories, or any other kind of facility. The *contrabandistas* are said to be extremely tough ; the frequent customs inspections, therefore, consist of a rapid bargaining. A price is struck immediately, the train proceeds.

There being few seats and much demand, we took a taxi to the station and bought two tickets.

The luggage had to be deposited the day before the departure, 20 kilos maximum per person. We had to present ourselves at 6 a.m. ; the Litorina would leave at 8. We went back to the hotel in the same taxi ; the total fare was 2,500 cruzeiros.

I engaged a driver for the following morning. He seemed honest, and would charge 1,500 cruzeiros. If Tarzan wanted his revenge at a convenient last moment, he might try something, either in combination with the driver or by himself, in the dark hour of our departure.

M took the nearside seat, I the offside. If we were stopped, it would probably be by another car coming in from the offside ; she was to stick her pistol in the driver's neck, make him drive on ; I was to deal with Tarzan. If we were stopped by someone on foot, it would be easier. We arrived without incident.

The station for the Litorina is a thick slab of concrete

on which has been erected a rough shed, long since peeled of its paint. The roofing is split and broken, and a narrow strip of planks does not really do service as a platform, since it is rotting and falling to pieces.

As instructed, we are here at 6 a.m. The offices are locked. There is a certain amount of bustle and noise from within, but the occupants can evidently do nothing for us. We wait—standing, there is no place to sit—for forty minutes. Finally, at 6.40, the doors are opened, from the outside, we file in ; the cockerels and hens, the hitherto occupants, retired behind some props.

The interior is a kind of warehouse ; in it, islanded, a desk : the office. The baggage has been here, out of the owners' control, since yesterday, by order ; now it will be inspected. Meanwhile, the railcar, bright in its wasp-yellow and green, sleeps on comfortably in a little siding.

M has not found a place in which to have coffee. Without it she cannot allow a day to begin ; nevertheless, the day is proceeding without her. It is a protracted nightmare. By some freakish inversion, the other member of the party of two finds the situation amusing, and in other ways—that is, subtracting the station, the indignities, the farce of travelling in this out of gear country—even lyrical. The sun, for example. It is coming up out of the sierra, or appears to be ; the air is cold, sweet, the forest fresh and washed. No doubt later there will be trials : heat, discomfort, dust, dirt, thirst, lack of hygiene, more petty officialdom. But later is not now.

The method of loading is taking on certain characteristics. It consists of creating an impassable block of passengers on the narrow platform strip, exactly opposite the door of the ' office '. It is successful in creating another challenge to human endeavour : everyone now has to force the cleared baggage through the human barrier. After it is all over, the two-car train quietly rolls in from its siding. Having taken our seats in it, we are driven out by the diesel fumes, nauseated and, some of us, vomiting. It is at this moment that M says: " There's Tarzan."

The cannon-ball head was rolling over the tops of all others in that milling crowd, questing here and there. It disappeared, came into view again, as its owner carried on his search.

At last he came on the platform itself, came up abreast of the rail-car, and I had not the slightest doubt that he would start something. The conditions were ideal: to denounce him we would have to lose the train and our luggage. Just at that moment the snail uttered a tremendous spluttering roar and rolled forward. Through the windows we concluded with our eyes a perfect transaction.

[March 1967

12

THE DAY OF THE *DORDOLEC*

Leslie Gardiner

To Kristoforica in the Munella highlands of the Mirdita district of northern-central Albania is a long road and not at all a continuous road. The part of the route which deserves the name of road follows the twists and ascents of the Mati gorge only as far as the copper-mining towns. Students and a brigade of ex-partisans built it in the late nineteen-forties, blowing tunnels through the limestone rock and creating shelves along the canyon face with explosives the Germans left behind. They built no bridges, not knowing how to, and kept to the northern side of the river channel, which happened to be the difficult side. But they made a road of it, a real highway by Albanian standards, the ' Highway of Light and Power '. It bears a good gravelled surface and the cracks and cavities which appear are kept filled with round polished stones. There are safety posts on the most dangerous hairpin bends, political slogans on poster boards cemented to the rock-verge, Red Stars and hammers-and-sickles graven on the precipice face, clearance heights and heads of Marx and Engels frescoed on the tunnel entrances and canopies of over-hanging rock. There is a carriageway wide enough in some places for a lorry and a donkey to pass each other, if the donkey sidles up against the cliff or slithers round on the other side, kicking stones into space. It is densely trafficked, as Albanian roads go, for it connects the coastal highway with not only the copper towns of Rresheni and Kurbnesh but also the new Josef Stalin hydroelectric scheme in the lower Mati gorge, the fount of Power and Light. Stand at the turning point at the head of the pass and you will sometimes see ten vehicles in as many minutes.

Beyond Rresheni only an Albanian would call it a road. It forks where the river forks and the Kristoforica branch begins to climb beside the cascades of the Fan-vogel which, having poured out from one of the highest snow-water lakes and picked up calcium salts on the way, leaps along in a flurry of cloudy emerald lather. Yet this road—this muletrack for toughened mules—carries its traffic too, by the look of the lorryloads of smooth round stones, tipped at intervals along it. It is alarming to think of the typical powered vehicles of modern Albania lurching over those limestone ruts, floundering at the V-shaped torrent crossings: over-age tractors which served a lifetime on the State farms of Russia and Czechoslovakia before they came to a harsh retirement-job in the steepest, stoniest land of all, and top-heavy, tiny-wheeled, square-nosed trucks with their canvas hoods and loudly vibrating bonnets, the like of which you have seen among the Leylands and Tilling-Stevenses of World War One newsreel clips. You see them still in the Mirdita highlands of Albania, struggling over the merest sketch of a motor-road, or more often stopped in the middle of it with boulders under the wheels and the driver flat on his back underneath the chassis.

This part of the Fan-vogel route dies, as you knew it must, under your feet before it has extricated you from the folded ridges which rise, line upon line, to the snow-water lakes. From that point it is every traveller for himself, by whichever route he chooses. Kristoforica's roots go back at least to the eighth century and there has never been another access-path to the village; but it seems that no two pilgrims, no two mules or donkeys, have ever agreed on a common route out of the gorge, or into the next, or out of that and over the limestone corrugations of what, anywhere else, would be a badlands of sharp hillocks, a geological wilderness of rubble and chopped escarpments and switch-back trails; and what, in Albania, is called a plateau.

We are a long time reaching Kristoforica, but that is the way when you set out for the highland villages. Navigating by clumps of stones which have been dropped, one supposes, from the panniers of donkeys—a guarantee of the Government's pledge to provide lines of communication between every village in the Popular Republic—you find yourself on the knife-edge of a long straight ridge. The road—the mule-path—begins again. A peasant in a red skull-cap tramps towards you and mutters a ' *Tung-jatjeta* ' as he passes. Two or three women appear. They are veiled, trousered and heavy-booted and each of them, by a fringed strap round her forehead, supports the cocoon-shaped bundle of a baby on her back. They make the sign of the cross, turn aside and by way of an awkward detour regain their path after you have gone.

Leading-marks of boulders, splashed with red paint, confirm that your road is at least going *somewhere*. Vegetation appears: prickly pear, drawing nourishment from Heaven-knows-where, laying its flat spiked blades across the track. On one a visitor—he must be a visitor, from the other world, the world of New Albania—has inscribed with his penknife: LET US BUILD SOCIALISM RELYING MAINLY ON OUR OWN EFFORTS.

A tangle of fig branches creeps round some ruins; its roots, too, must have probed dozens of yards through subterranean warrens in search of water. There are bee-hives, painted red blue, strung in a line against the sky. And there stands an outpost of Kristoforica, there on the ribs of the mountain, a drystone dwelling like a squat, rectangular watch-tower, capped with ancient pink pantiles, windowless unless you can call a couple of barred arrow-slits on the upper-floor-level windows.

The tiny peasant fortresses are scattered across the slope of the hill beyond it, all alike but no two together, each seemingly erected with the object of giving its owner as much seclusion and privacy as was consistent with a vague collective security. All that the inhabitants have in com-mon, you would say, is fear of invasion by strangers. Between lowest and highest cottage there may be an altitudinal distance of five hundred feet; from east to west, perhaps a quarter of a mile.

There are of course no shops, no post-office or anything of that kind; nothing resembling an administration, a communal centre or village dust-patch, on which in more civilised spots the elders can congregate and smoke in the shade of a plane tree and talk over old Turkish times. No trees. Culture halls and schools, with which the present régime is dragging its most primitive nationals to within hailing distance of the century of educated man, stop many miles short of Kristoforica. There is even a village church, at the far end, near the goat-track to the Munella summit—which shows you how backward they are. It is a cottage-fortress like the rest, one room up and one down, a stable for donkeys six days a week, distinguished by the small Greek cross on its nail-studded door.

To Kristoforica within the past ten years the Party has

brought both water and power. The fountain, a hollow concrete cube let into a wall of rock, washes the dust off your boots as you emerge from a corridor of limestone and stop to take in the strategical prospect of the bluff down which Kristoforica tumbles. It wears on one side the emblem of Socialist Albania and on the other a plaque explaining how Major Asim Xoxhe met a herioc end during the winter campaign of 1943, defending the limestone-corridor route, which led nowhere, from Fascist beasts and monarchist traitors.

The villagers do not know this Xoxhe; he belongs to a foreign tribe, a southern one by the sound of his name. Fascists and monarchists are titles they cannot understand. They are not clear what was the purpose of the winter campaign. Local opinion, as far as any local has an opinion, regards it as a late phase in the centuries-long battle against the Turk. The struggle for liberation, the struggle to establish the Party, had nothing to do with Kristoforica's perennial struggle for survival. Their men-folk, throughout the turmoil of those years, continued to walk across the mountains to Bicaj, the nearest township, returning with a sack of grain on their shoulders or carrying a sharpened ploughshare, the whole journey taking them one week. They brought back rumours of fighting, of villages burned and rope-bridges cut down—but it was really no news to Kristoforica, only another chapter in the tales old people could tell, part of the pattern of life—as they conceived it—beyond the environs of the Munella. The Bey, it was true, had not yet returned. His palace—twice the size of any peasant's cottage, like two peasants' cottages stuck together in fact, stood abandoned, derelict. His garden, which had taken first share, rather more than half, of a limited water supply, was a jungle of laurel and fern, and the frogs in his marsh had grown to extraordinary size. One day he would return, one day the village would rebuild his house, replant his fields and clear the jungle and the marsh. It had always happened that way; the pattern of events endlessly repeated itself.

The stream which bubbles off the mountain and is the village's *raison d'être* still loses itself in that marsh and in blocked irrigation channels among the Bey's untended cornstrips and row of vines, except for a trickle which works a labyrinthine passage through the fissures of the limestone and collects in a pool two hundred feet below. There the women wash their clothes. They have labelled the fountain ' *Uji Qelbur* '—Stinking Water—and it serves only to provide village boys with cupped handfuls, with which to chase village girls, when the girls have ventured out alone.

If the girls pass by in numbers, as they usually do, the boys slink away in different directions. Every evening the girls sit in a row on the fountain's concrete slab, unveiled and Turkish-trousered and swinging their farm-booted feet, whispering secrets, and no boy comes near them. Kristoforica is one of those highland villages where the women do all the work and run the economy too. Men —you see it in the slinking individuality of the small boys— accept a passive, solitary role. They are good-natured, lack-lustre, shifty and henpecked. They have lost control, if they ever had it. For centuries the young men of Kristoforica have had to emigrate to live. For a lifetime they underwent the trauma of the years in cafés of the Greek ports or kitchens of the Macedonian monasteries, and came home broken and ingratiating to brides who had in the meantime grown as tough and harsh as the land they strained to subdue. In Kristoforica, just where the fountain drips out of its twin copper tubes, where the donkey-track exists by the corridor of the rocks, young brides used to say farewell to emigrating bridegrooms. It is still called the Place of Tears.

With the fountain, the Party presented power. It is represented by a Tannoy-type loudspeaker, wedged in the fork of a pine-branch and slung from the reeling wall-end of the former Bey's house which, having been three-quarters demolished during the war, hides behind its drystone façade as handsome a heap of round, smooth stones as you will see all the way from the Mati gorge.

The loudspeaker brought music, political speeches, proceedings of the Chamber of Deputies and live broadcasts of the show trials in the Courts of People's Justice from far-off Tirana. Only the frogs responded to it. They did their strident utmost every night to drown the foreign-sounding croak and crackle of the Tannoy. The village paid no attention. Some fault developed in the land line, and the loudspeaker fell silent. No one knew why, no one remarked on it, no one reported the defect, no one came up from Tirana to repair it and no one cared.

Early last April, in the season of melting snow, a light rainstorm swept the Munella highlands. It was to be the last for nearly nine months. In June the corn which the peasant women had sown in mud and running ice was appearing here and there in patches of bleached shoots which seemed to have worn themselves out with the effort of striking through ironbound earth. Most of the crop never appeared at all.

By July the south-facing slope of Munella, arid and scrubby in the best of seasons, looked as though a great heath-fire had passed over it. A goat or a sheep died every day. Kids and lambs trembled from malnutrition, as helpless as on the day they were born. At night, when it was cool enough to let the herds out, they staggered as far as the Bey's field, pushed and prodded all the way, and lay down without hope on brown, matted grass and corn which shrivelled on the stalk.

Peasants took on a defeated, withered look, like their crops and livestock. Everyone of course flocked to the fountain for water. The cry of '*Uji Qelbur*' was never heard, because roof-top cisterns had run dry and the rivulet had disappeared into the fissures, never to come out again. Women who lived near the fountain constructed tiny aqueducts in mud, to move a trickle of water among the grain; quarrelled with their neighbours and egged their menfolk on to fight about it. Children spent their time chasing dogs and hens away from the outfall. The fountain never ran dry, but there was never enough water. The rock-hard earth and the limestone outcrops drank it before it reached the plantations.

Kristoforica folk are devout enough, but they have not for some time—some time in the fifteenth century—been on good terms with their saint. Barely a hundred years ago, according to village history, he had to send a plague of boils to remind them of their duty to decorate his shrine and pay his priest. The present-day father, with one eye on the weather and another on the main chance—for it is an ill drought which a Balkan clergyman cannot turn to some advantage—told a deputation of women elders that prayers to Saint Mina would be more likely to irritate than appease:

" I can assure you, Mina is not prepared to help the peasants. Your fathers have made him angry, it is useless for me to ask favours on your behalf. Take your prayers to Vertopi "—naming a priest of the Bicaj diocese, against whom he had an old grudge.

For the pilgrimage the older women brought out the beautiful Mirdita costumes of the olden time—the embroidered moccasins, the white or purple balloon trousers, the silk-fringed woollen tunics in pink, white and green, the white fichus and yashmaks. The widow Nasta arranged the order—it was single file most of the way, down over the ribs of the mountain. She assumed authority not because of age or physical strength—she was short, fragile but wiry—but because of a sharp tongue and a sharp eye and a commanding manner. Her hooked nose and gipsyish features, beneath a magnificent mop of white hair, gave her the look of a slight but fearsome prophetess of the Age of Ignorance.

They roused the staggering goats and a donkey or two from the cellars beneath the fortress-cottages, draped red and green blankets over their backs and hung garlands of laurel and bouquets of drooping hollyhock round their necks. Two children, Gjada and Lena, the widow's niece and daughter, one pink and blonde as a Norse maiden and the other pinched and swarthy as a little Arab, combed out the he-goats' beards and tied small cravats of red ribbon on them.

Attended by musicians, who plucked a dreary tune from the strings of their *chiftelis*, the procession moved off to petition Vertopi. Women led it, women called the halts and the sessions of song and prayer, the little girls of the village followed, wrapped in frothy lace like miniature brides, and a few men and boys slunk after it, having nothing better to do, wearing the expression of hopeless resignation which settles most readily on the face of the mountain peasant.

They left on Sunday morning and came back on Tuesday afternoon. For ten days afterwards no cloud appeared in any part of the sky—and a watcher on the heights behind Kristoforica can survey the full hemisphere. Daily the sun broke from the eastern skyline white and angry-looking, glared over Kristoforica for ten caustic hours and descended in flames, as though into a furnace of molten orange metal, to be heated up for next day. You saw no one out of doors in that blinding light. Men lived in darkness in the gloom of their cottages, performing undemanding tasks or more often stretched out under the pale brittle leaves of the laurel plantation. The masonry of a Mirdita cottage-fortress tapers upward and provides no shade in a summer sun.

The women, the sowers and harvesters, were on the go before dawn and again after sunset, but it was a go to which they were chained by conditioning, a futile routine. No plough-blade could get a bite on the ground; the share bounced over it—as well plough limestone rock. The women drove their forks ferociously at the patches of barren soil, only to bend the tines. An aged villager died, and four men spent a whole day digging a grave two feet deep.

On those August days the village itself seemed to have died. All the customary sounds were stilled: the chatter of girls in the fields, the rustle of a dog sneaking through the vines, the scratching of hens on a dust-heap, the croaking of frogs. The frogs lay on the edge of the creeks which had opened up and split the marsh into bone-dry islands, and gasped for air.

Every night at the fountain the women gathered to mourn for themselves and to execrate, in their patient, desultory, dispassionate fashion, the saints and priests who accepted trinkets and corn-buns and gave nothing in return. Nasta put into words the feeling all had faintly apprehended, the premonition of which everyone had become aware but hardly knew how to speak:

" Sisters! Those prayers were never answered. The menfolk will do nothing. We must set up the *dordolec*." She crossed herself, and so did the rest. In the darkness, huddled together beside the dripping fountain, they looked like a group of nuns at their evening devotions.

The lottery was soon organised. Nasta sat with the box of ancient, knotted black pine on her knees. The women formed a half-circle round her, their gnarled fingers on the shoulders of the children, to whom the *dordolec* was a new and important game. A few men hung about, half in and half out of earshot, watching with all their apathy and resignation. Little Mara's father mumbled a joke of some kind and, catching his wife's eye, drew himself up and stood looking serious and frightened. A frog croaked from the marsh.

When Nasta shook the box a dozen pieces of wood rattled inside it. She beckoned and, one by one, the little girls came forward to draw. " Don't look at it. Lena, Cila, don't look at your tickets until everyone has drawn." Clutching their slips of wood, the children retired to their mothers. Gjada, plump, blonde, twelve years old, handed hers to her mother, who closed the child's fingers round it. " No, keep it. It's yours. Don't look yet." Mara giggled as she felt round the box for the last piece. " I hope it's not me. I hope it's not Gjada either."

The box was empty. Nasta shook it violently, tossing her white head, and turned it upside down. Mothers pushed their children forward to show her the slips of wood. There were eleven blanks and on Gjada's a black cross. Nasta grinned and kissed her. " You are the lucky one! Gjada is our *dordolec*."

On Sunday morning Gjada's friends came early to waken her and escort her to church. All the women were there, and some of the older men. From above the ceiling, where the priest had locked himself in his room, came the rap of stick against stonework and the sound of his cracked voice: " Pagans! I don't approve! You women! Come back and sweep out my church—don't forget, come back and clean everything up."

It might have been a harvest festival, or the travesty of one: the stalks of fruitless wheat, the grey vine leaves and grapes in tight knots, hard and sterile as acorns, the tendrils of spotted ivy, the wreaths of brittle laurel whose leaves already carpeted the floor. Everyone carried a candle; now and again a fistful of drooping cornstalks flared up and was flung away and stamped out. Up above, through a chink in the stonework, the priest breathed noisily and cursed the congregation.

Gjada's friends stripped her at the altar, washed her and covered her with wreaths of twisted leaves. She shivered, in spite of the heat of the morning and the claustrophobic airlessness of the building. Argument broke out among the elders over the positioning of her crown—a ludicrous helmet constructed from the branches of an ivy blanched with disease. There were objections to the manner in which the children wound the laurel sprays round her body, some holding that she should have freedom to move her arms. The ruff of spiked rosemary, others complained, was too tight for her neck; for a peasant's daughter she was a well-built little girl. While they were binding her legs with ferns and vine-tendrils, certain old wives cried out that the *dordolec* would not be able to walk with the correct gait.

Nasta overruled them all. Only the oldest of the old could remember more than one previous *dordolec*, and that one had been years earlier, when Nasta herself was little more than a child. While they argued, the children grew bored and began furtively dressing themselves like *dordoleci* in fallen leaves and twigs. Gjada, impressed with the solemnity of her office, stood still and said nothing.

The elders inspected her, satisfied themselves that she was chastely smothered and guided her by the shoulders to the door. She tottered out at the head of the procession, a gliding, rustling tree of variegated foliage.

Everyone else wore the Turkish-style costume, the faded, ill-fitting finery of the regional dress. There was music from *chiftelis* and clarinets, drums and a chant, waveringly led by Nasta and soon picked up by the young ones, which in the Munella highlands is a ritual hymn to the rain god. Gjada's maids of honour took their places ahead of her, carrying on their hips in the fashion approved by older women two jars filled at the fountain, and every few yards they turned and jerked water over her. The singing grew louder, the capering of the children wilder. A stranger, hearing the shouts, seeing first a cloud of dust approaching and then the parade taking shape in it, would have thought he had arrived at a village wedding.

Several men of Kristoforica strolled after the *dordolec*, pretending to be there by accident. All the small boys joined in, to dance with the music, take sly tugs at the girls' ribbons and tickle each other with the twigs which Gjada shed.

Two wrinkled, stooping figures waited at the door of the first cottage. The old woman had put on the festive weeds of long ago, black and white, perhaps her wedding dress. They diffused the odour of the tomb. Her husband wore the white fez which is not often seen these days in rural Albania. It was his only concession to ceremony. Below it he went collarless, with open corduroy waistcoat and labourer's patched trousers, tied at the knee with string.

He dropped a flat cake of corn-bread into the sack with which Mara and Cila danced up to him. By his wife's side stood a huge water-jar. She grasped it in two black, sinewy hands and with a sudden brisk movement upended it over the *dordolec*. Gjada's muffled squeal penetrated the screen of leaves. She shook herself like a dog clambering out of a pool. The party shouted and beat its drums and some of the little girls, under the direction of their mothers and grandmothers, went into a slow dance, a kind of saraband, waving their laurel branches above their heads, plucking the leaves and letting them fall like raindrops. Gjada stood still. She might have been a tree-stump, covered with parasitic foliage, green, brown and white, from which the water dripped in a ring of puddles.

The procession moved along an apparently aimless route, but one which actually conformed to an old complicated protocol. It visited cottage after cottage, some of them twice, in an order of precedence for which no one, not even Nasta, could explain the original reason. Before each house, where the passage was broad enough to permit it, a dance and a discordant tune brought the villagers to a halt. In between, among the boulders, blindly tottering along paths so narrow that no one could support her, Gjada was having a difficult time. Once she fell and to Lena who helped her up she whispered, " I don't feel well."

" I can't hear you through the leaves," Lena said.

By noon she had recovered, while many had dropped out. Only the older women plodded in front and behind, their garments stained and darkened with sweat, their heads bowed. A choir of ragged voices, faithful to Nasta's hoarse lead, raised the monotone chant: " Rain, rain, pour on Kristoforica." The musicians marched in silence, and the way they carried their instruments suggested they had disowned them. The wedding gaiety had vanished; the *dordolec's* retinue might have been a funeral cortège.

Twelve-year-olds, carrying five-year-olds, took short cuts to different points at which they expected the procession to reappear. Older children, arriving at a strip of shadow under a wall, sat in the dust and idly tormented a panting dog. The men had given up the procession altogether and retired to the shelter of their poor shrubs. And then the *dordolec* began to dance.

Each fresh jug of water on her head seemed to intoxicate Gjada. Her shouts and antics brought the children running. On a small square of almost level ground—they were skirting the marsh—she began to whirl round in the manner of the old wandering dervishes who infested those parts of Albania a hundred years ago. Nasta grinned, the women stamped their feet with delight, the musicians remembered their instruments and the children, yelling, ran close to catch on their faces the spray which flew from the *dordolec's* ivy-crowned head and laurel skirts.

A frog croaked as the procession moved on. The girl Cila darted away, rummaged among dried fern and brought him out.

" This is the devil that drank all the water! "

The peasants screamed with laughter. Cila swung the frog by one skinny leg and tossed him to Mara, who gripped him until his eyes bulged out of their sockets, then quickly threw him at Lena.

" Kill him, kill him ! " Nasta screeched. " It won't rain while that devil is alive." She was fussing over the *dordolec*. Instead of standing patiently, Gjada had started tossing her head-dress, trying to shake the leaves out of her eyes, and fumbling to free her arms from the branches. She sank to the ground again, floating gracefully down like a curtseying wood-nymph in some classical ballet.

" Nasta, I don't like it. I want to come out. Is it much farther? "

Nasta set her on her feet. Streams of water dripped from the laurels. The old woman muttered to her, and others clustered round, vigorously shaking their grey heads as they rearranged the foliage and pinioned the girl's arms more tightly to her sides. They were speaking—every young girl knew it intuitively—of *dordoleci* who had failed to come through the ordeal and were disgraced; whose families and even neighbours were disgraced, talked about to the present day. They confirmed beliefs that every twelve-year-old child must at least dimly acknowledge: that only the *dordolec's* purity makes it strong, that a *dordolec* without the power to withstand the fatigue of a day-long procession in midsummer heat is plainly impure. To fall, to faint, not to return to the church door—it is an admission that virtue has been surrendered. Such a *dordolec* is no maiden. How will she ever find a husband? How can she hope to bring rain?

Gjada, a cylinder of bedraggled leaves, stumbled on, scattering fragments of fern and laurel behind her. Her playmates found a pile of stones and reduced the frog to a green smear in the dust, at which a dog sniffed and bared its teeth.

Down the ribs and up again, over the serpentine paths it had followed all day, the parade completed a second circuit of Kristoforica. The sun was going down and the accumulated heat of the day rose in almost visible undulations from the rocks. The procession grew longer. Smaller children, mere infants, who had watched it with serious expressions from their mothers' knees, scrambled after it. Boys who had scarcely learned to walk toddled into Gjada's path with cupped handfuls of water and sprinkled her again and again. Bolder children pushed close to her, grasping her branches, trying to pull them down to see if the *dordolec* really was Gjada. She shook off the waterdrops and danced at them, growling, a wet, shaggy green monster, and they ran away screaming.

By the ruined house, close to the Place of Tears, the girl collapsed. Fern and foliage settled into a heap, a soft bonfire of leaves, and the crown of diseased ivy slipped to the ground. Gjada did not move or speak when a woman tried to fit it to her blonde head. One after another they pleaded with her, urged her on, threatened her with trembling fists. It was only a few steps to the churchyard, not more than fifty yards and all downhill—down calcined masses of rock, so steep a descent that she could almost have jumped into church, in through the priest's little barred window.

Nasta tore the crown away and dashed a full jug of water on her pale stained face. Gjada shivered, murmured something and closed her lips. One bare foot spasmodically twitched. The spiked rosemary necklace, when Nasta wrenched it off, left blood stains on her throat. Over her body a mother—not Gjada's, whom shame had already driven to the back of the crowd—argued with Nasta.

" Don't stand looking, get some wine."

" Wine? Who has wine? It's too late for wine, move away, let her breathe."

" She's a child, a baby."

" She's the *dordolec*."

An old man shuffled by, talking to himself. " A farce, you mean. All nonsense, don't you know that, you women? "

The *dordolec* was done for. All the women wept. One

of them raised the ritual wailing cry that is meant to pierce the stone walls of the farthest house in a Mirdita village. The children wept too, looking up through their fingers to weeping parents to assure themselves that the imitation was proper.

Breathlessly keening, two or three old women knelt to disturb the half-clothed body, to arrange the plump small limbs in a foolish attitude and bind the contaminated ivy round hair as yellow as the faded vine-leaves. It was like dressing a limp-jointed, prostrate doll.

" Leave it, leave it," said Nasta. " It will be dark soon. We've done our best."

The sun had disappeared behind Munella's fez of snow. An evening breeze, no cooler than its glare, stirred the stifling blanket of air which had lain all day over Kristoforica. The puddles and trickles of water, even those which traced the *dordolec's* last footsteps, were quite dried up.

The child had fallen at a convenient spot. Just behind the ruined house there were smooth round stones for all. Small boys hurried to pick out the big ones and erect private heaps of boulders they could hardly lift, much less throw. " That's foolish," said Nasta sharply. " Here, Mara, Lena, choose small pebbles, like these."

The villagers formed a half-circle round the *dordolec*, between house wall and cliff edge, on an earth pavement as hard as stone. Nasta threw, and the rest joined in. It was all done seriously and silently, with the absorption of adults imparting, and children mastering, a difficult game, while the frogs croaked again from the marsh.

[March 1968